State Transportation Statistics
2015

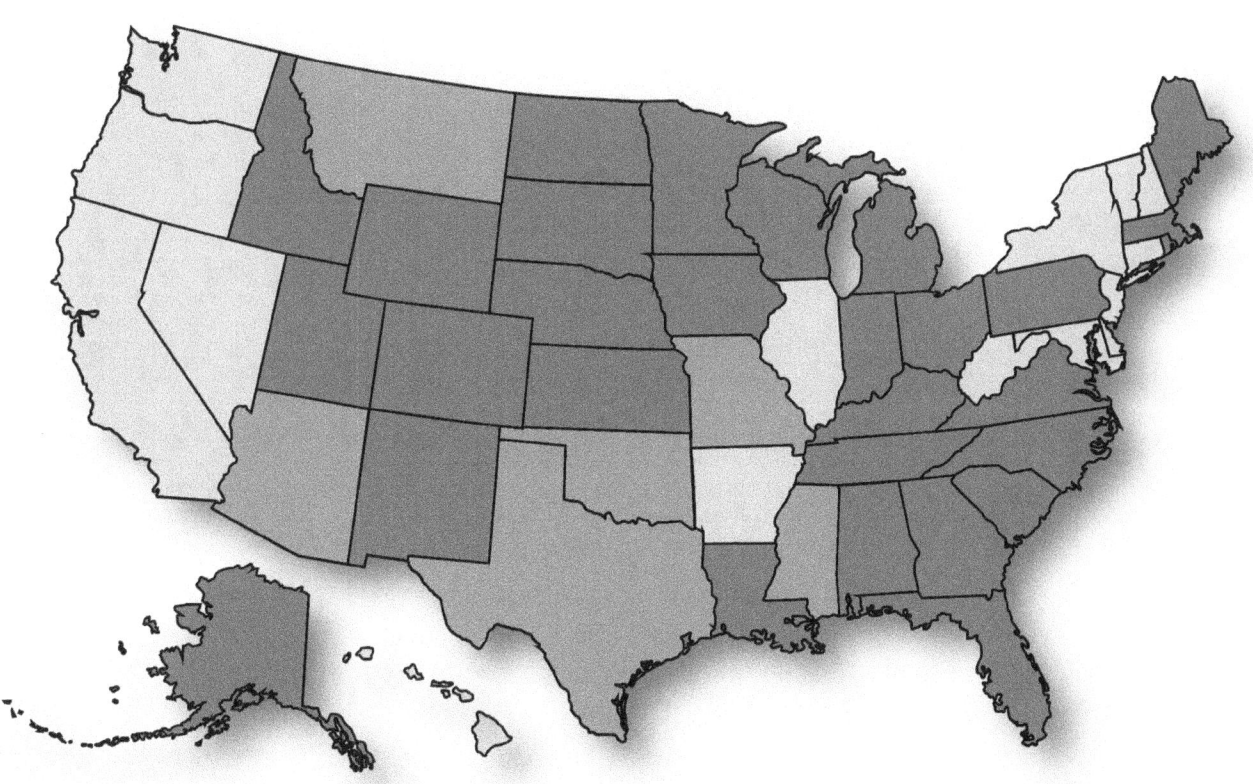

U.S. Department of Transportation

Bureau of Transportation Statistics

Acknowledgements

U.S. Department of Transportation

Anthony Foxx
Secretary of Transportation

Victor Mendez
Deputy Secretary of Transportation

Gregory Winfree
*Assistant Secretary for
Research and Technology*

Bureau of Transportation Statistics

Patricia Hu
Director

Rolf Schmitt
Deputy Director

Michael Sprung
*Director, Office of
Transportation Analysis*

Project Managers
Mindy Liu
Long X. Nguyen

Contributors
Ant-quanique Dancy
William Moore
Alpha Wingfield

To obtain *State Transportation Statistics 2015* and other BTS publications:

Internet: www.bts.gov
Mail: U.S. Department of Transportation
            Bureau of Transportation Statistics
            ATTN: Product Orders
            1200 New Jersey Avenue, SE
            Washington, DC 20590

Your comments on *State Transportation Statistics* reports are welcome.

BTS Information Service
E-mail: answers@bts.gov
Phone: 202-366-DATA (3282)

Photo credits by chapter:
1. iStockphoto.com
2. BTS stock photo
3. BTS stock photo
4. William Moore
5. BTS stock photo
6. BTS stock photo
7. BTS stock photo

About *State Transportation Statistics 2015*

The Bureau of Transportation Statistics (BTS) presents *State Transportation Statistics 2015*, a statistical profile of transportation in the 50 States and the District of Columbia. This is the 13th annual edition of *State Transportation Statistics*, a companion document to *National Transportation Statistics (NTS)*, which is updated quarterly on the BTS website.

Like the previous editions, this document presents transportation information from BTS and other Federal Government agencies and national sources. A picture of each State's transportation infrastructure, freight movement and passenger travel, system safety, vehicles, transportation-related economy and finance, energy usage, and the environment is presented in table form. Tables have been updated with the most recently available data.

Included in this *State Transportation Statistics 2015* report is a brief description of the data sources used and a glossary of terms. Also contained in this publication is a summary table that displays the approximate timing of future data releases and contact information for each State's department of transportation.

This report is available free of charge and can be downloaded from our website at www.bts.gov. A State Transportation Facts and Figures application also featured on the BTS website uses selected data from this report to present State-by-State comparisons and rankings.

Quality Assurance Statement

The Bureau of Transportation Statistics (BTS) provides high quality information to serve government, industry, and the public in a manner that promotes public understanding. Standards and policies are used to ensure and maximize the quality, objectivity, utility and integrity of its information. BTS reviews quality issues on a regular basis and adjusts its programs and processes to ensure continuous quality improvement.

Notice

This document is disseminated under the sponsorship of the Department of Transportation in the interest of information exchange. The United States Government assumes no liability for its contents or use thereof.

Table of Contents

Chapter 3 Freight Transportation

Chapter 4 Passenger Travel

Chapter 5   Registered Vehicles and Vehicle-Miles Traveled

Chapter 6   Economy and Finance

Chapter 7   Energy and Environment

Appendices

Chapter 1
Infrastructure

Table 1-1: Public Road Length, Miles by Functional System: 2013

State	Interstate	Other principal and minor arterials[1]	Major and minor collectors	Local	Total
Alabama	1,002	9,716	22,386	68,733	101,837
Alaska	1,081	1,571	3,300	9,727	15,680
Arizona	1,168	6,021	8,072	51,178	66,441
Arkansas	656	7,441	21,061	72,499	101,656
California	2,451	30,002	32,223	110,313	174,989
Colorado	952	9,259	16,245	62,109	88,565
Connecticut	346	3,004	3,206	14,918	21,474
Delaware	41	680	1,039	4,633	6,393
District of Columbia	12	286	157	1,047	1,501
Florida	1,495	13,590	14,560	92,442	122,088
Georgia	1,247	14,329	23,037	90,006	128,620
Hawaii	55	824	752	2,800	4,430
Idaho	612	4,249	10,611	32,611	48,082
Illinois	2,185	14,771	22,169	106,583	145,708
Indiana	1,188	8,758	22,523	65,084	97,553
Iowa	782	9,778	31,629	72,240	114,429
Kansas	874	9,688	33,698	96,427	140,687
Kentucky	801	6,169	16,562	56,066	79,598
Louisiana	926	5,685	9,972	44,844	61,427
Maine	367	2,199	5,914	14,401	22,882
Maryland	481	4,110	5,059	22,772	32,422
Massachusetts	575	6,768	4,550	24,478	36,370
Michigan	1,244	15,008	24,458	81,431	122,141
Minnesota	914	13,686	30,408	93,759	138,767
Mississippi	700	7,740	15,892	50,784	75,116
Missouri	1,379	10,487	25,109	94,925	131,900
Montana	1,192	6,088	16,245	51,408	74,933
Nebraska	482	8,144	20,772	64,371	93,770
Nevada	596	3,471	5,612	30,460	40,139
New Hampshire	225	1,745	2,642	11,485	16,098
New Jersey	431	6,391	4,437	28,034	39,293
New Mexico	1,000	4,963	9,188	55,620	70,772
New York	1,724	14,601	20,737	77,666	114,728
North Carolina	1,255	10,018	17,351	77,579	106,202
North Dakota	571	5,941	11,929	68,637	87,078
Ohio	1,574	11,253	22,869	87,602	123,297
Oklahoma	933	8,417	25,490	78,100	112,940
Oregon	730	7,112	18,589	44,798	71,228
Pennsylvania	1,857	13,762	19,847	84,470	119,936
Rhode Island	70	914	887	4,235	6,106
South Carolina	851	7,233	15,089	43,059	66,232
South Dakota	679	6,430	19,004	56,446	82,558
Tennessee	1,104	9,305	17,994	67,132	95,536
Texas	3,415	33,280	65,154	211,378	313,228
Utah	937	3,772	8,162	33,384	46,254
Vermont	320	1,320	3,119	9,506	14,266
Virginia	1,119	8,764	14,394	50,472	74,748
Washington	764	8,412	17,292	55,980	82,448
West Virginia	555	3,498	8,635	26,063	38,750
Wisconsin	743	12,910	23,501	77,990	115,145
Wyoming	914	3,671	10,279	14,161	29,024
United States, total	47,575	417,232	803,807	2,846,848	4,115,462
U.S. total (incl. Puerto Rico)[2]	47,857	418,966	805,541	2,859,789	4,132,153

[1]Includes other freeways and expressways.
[2]Data for Puerto Rico are for 2010.

NOTE: The difference in total miles between tables 1-1 and 1-2 results from the Federal Highway Administration's expansion of sample data to derive estimates of road length by different variables. FHWA considers the length totals in this table to be the control totals should a single value be required.

SOURCE: U.S. Department of Transportation, Federal Highway Administration, *Highway Statistics*, HM-20, available at www.fhwa.dot.gov/policyinformation/statistics.cfm as of June 2015.

Table 1-2: Public Road Length, Miles by Ownership: 2013

State	State highway agency	County	Town, township, municipal	Other jurisdiction[1]	Federal agency[2]	Total
Alabama	10,902	62,519	26,777	169	1,471	101,837
Alaska	5,591	3,626	1,802	2,349	2,311	15,680
Arizona	6,800	17,864	22,657	4,620	14,500	66,441
Arkansas	16,411	65,931	16,673	0	2,642	101,656
California	15,104	65,306	76,129	3,432	15,018	174,989
Colorado	9,061	55,995	16,110	851	6,548	88,565
Connecticut	3,720	0	17,339	359	56	21,474
Delaware	5,386	0	806	78	122	6,393
District of Columbia	1,374	0	0	28	99	1,501
Florida	12,099	70,095	37,579	87	2,228	122,088
Georgia	17,926	87,542	19,359	166	3,626	128,620
Hawaii	948	3,285	0	68	130	4,430
Idaho	4,982	15,600	6,235	13,782	7,483	48,082
Illinois	15,986	16,488	112,238	751	245	145,708
Indiana	11,175	66,097	19,006	0	1,275	97,553
Iowa	8,883	89,823	14,965	621	138	114,429
Kansas	10,298	113,346	15,866	238	938	140,687
Kentucky	27,620	39,841	10,637	547	952	79,598
Louisiana	16,689	32,708	11,330	35	665	61,427
Maine	8,378	364	13,682	320	138	22,882
Maryland	5,158	21,346	4,794	290	833	32,422
Massachusetts	3,018	0	32,587	640	101	36,370
Michigan	9,664	89,444	21,198	61	1,773	122,141
Minnesota	11,811	46,532	76,181	1,715	2,529	138,767
Mississippi	10,899	51,891	11,258	649	420	75,116
Missouri	33,887	73,383	23,166	5	1,459	131,900
Montana	11,006	42,562	4,807	4,239	12,320	74,933
Nebraska	9,948	61,186	22,283	120	232	93,770
Nevada	5,318	26,355	4,820	373	3,272	40,139
New Hampshire	3,921	0	11,964	104	108	16,098
New Jersey	2,341	6,650	28,733	1,011	558	39,293
New Mexico	12,034	39,348	6,269	189	12,932	70,772
New York	15,034	20,233	77,299	1,458	705	114,728
North Carolina	79,546	0	22,435	906	3,315	106,202
North Dakota	7,378	10,156	67,979	19	1,546	87,078
Ohio	19,226	29,102	73,064	1,136	770	123,297
Oklahoma	12,265	78,411	21,147	1,105	13	112,940
Oregon	7,661	32,949	10,922	677	19,019	71,228
Pennsylvania	39,787	293	77,694	1,341	821	119,936
Rhode Island	1,103	0	4,874	35	93	6,106
South Carolina	41,396	20,329	2,366	191	1,950	66,232
South Dakota	7,767	35,266	35,469	1,626	2,431	82,558
Tennessee	13,899	57,906	22,195	344	1,192	95,536
Texas	80,323	146,826	84,707	167	1,205	313,228
Utah	5,869	24,238	11,098	516	4,534	46,254
Vermont	2,628	0	11,463	50	125	14,266
Virginia	58,411	1,721	11,752	63	2,801	74,748
Washington	7,054	39,232	18,672	8,743	8,747	82,448
West Virginia	34,407	0	3,227	282	834	38,750
Wisconsin	11,766	20,764	81,771	136	709	115,145
Wyoming	6,751	14,620	2,431	1,036	4,185	29,024
United States, total	780,609	1,797,172	1,327,813	57,727	152,115	4,115,462
U.S. total (incl. Puerto Rico)[3]	785,191	1,797,172	1,339,879	57,728	152,145	4,132,153

[1]Includes state park, state toll, other state agency, other local agency and other roadways not identified by ownership.
[2]Roadways in Federal parks, forests, and reservations that are not part of the state and local highway systems.
[3]Data for Puerto Rico are for 2009.

NOTE: The difference in total miles between tables 1-1 and 1-2 results from the Federal Highway Administration's (FHWA) expansion of sample data to derive estimates of road length by different variables. FHWA considers the length totals in table 1-1 to be the control totals should a single value be required.

SOURCE: U.S. Department of Transportation, Federal Highway Administration, *Highway Statistics*, HM-10, available at www.fhwa.dot.gov/policyinformation/statistics.cfm as of June 2015.

Table 1-3: Toll Roads, Toll Bridges and Tunnels, and Toll Ferry Routes: 2012

State	Toll road mileage[1]	Number of toll bridges[2]	Number of toll tunnels[2]	Number of toll ferry routes[2,3]
Alabama	3.1	3	0	2
Alaska	0.0	0	1	16
Arizona	0.0	0	0	0
Arkansas	0.0	0	0	0
California	134.8	8	0	1
Colorado	84.0	0	0	0
Connecticut	0.0	0	0	6
Delaware	46.7	1	0	1
District of Columbia	0.0	0	0	0
Florida	427.9	14	0	0
Georgia	6.2	0	0	0
Hawaii	0.0	0	0	0
Idaho	0.0	0	0	0
Illinois	374.5	4	0	5
Indiana	157.0	2	0	0
Iowa	0.0	5	0	1
Kansas	236.0	0	0	0
Kentucky	0.0	0	0	3
Louisiana	1.5	4	0	0
Maine	108.2	0	0	15
Maryland	27.6	5	2	2
Massachusetts	138.2	1	2	2
Michigan	0.0	7	1	12
Minnesota	27.0	1	0	0
Mississippi	0.0	0	0	0
Missouri	0.0	1	0	7
Montana	0.0	0	0	0
Nebraska	0.0	4	0	0
Nevada	6.4	0	0	0
New Hampshire	127.0	0	0	0
New Jersey	335.0	26	2	1
New Mexico	0.0	0	0	0
New York	511.4	28	4	10
North Carolina	9.2	0	0	4
North Dakota	0.0	1	0	0
Ohio	241.2	2	0	6
Oklahoma	595.1	0	0	0
Oregon	0.0	2	0	5
Pennsylvania	596.7	15	0	2
Rhode Island	0.0	1	0	3
South Carolina	23.5	0	0	0
South Dakota	0.0	0	0	0
Tennessee	0.0	0	0	3
Texas	497.8	27	1	1
Utah	1.0	0	0	1
Vermont	11.9	0	0	4
Virginia	57.1	5	2	1
Washington	14.5	4	0	19
West Virginia	86.8	2	0	1
Wisconsin	0.0	0	0	4
Wyoming	0.0	0	0	0
United States, total	4,887.2	140	13	115
U.S. total (incl. Puerto Rico)	5,433.8	141	13	120

[1]Length includes approaches and connecting links which were financed as an integral part of the toll project. The length of toll bridges includes approach sections which may be used toll free by local residents.

[2]Multiple structures at a single facility are counted as one bridge or tunnel. Does not include bridges or tunnels that are part of roadway segments reported under Toll road mileage.

[3]Excludes ferries providing exclusive service for passengers or freight as opposed to vehicles.

NOTE: Totals reflect crossings between states as one facility or ferry route, including 33 bridges, 2 tunnels, and 28 ferry routes. Data as of January 1, 2013.

SOURCE: U.S. Department of Transportation, Federal Highway Administration, Office of Highway Policy Information, *Toll Facilities in the United States*, table T-1, available at www.fhwa.dot.gov/policyinformation/tollpage as of June 2014.

Table 1-4: Road Condition: 2013
(Miles)

State	Not Reported	International Roughness Index (IRI)					Present Serviceability Rating (PSR)				
		<60	60-94	95-170	171-220	>220	>3.9	3.5-3.9	2.6-3.4	2.1-2.5	<=2.0
Alabama	0	4,376	9,227	8,024	1,361	1,110	1	4	55	63	67
Alaska	74	361	1,003	1,290	419	487	0	0	0	0	0
Arizona	1,045	2,213	2,463	2,305	396	240	562	0	447	0	226
Arkansas	233	968	4,381	7,718	2,292	1,009	6	26	3,869	0	0
California	1,999	965	6,624	21,086	9,798	9,374	751	790	1,893	421	392
Colorado	271	1,125	4,542	7,002	1,876	1,556	52	23	11	2	0
Connecticut	0	196	806	2,532	1,117	1,474	0	0	0	0	0
Delaware	0	92	637	532	135	113	0	0	0	0	0
District of Columbia	1	0	1	22	32	395	0	0	2	0	1
Florida	628	3,967	5,683	2,612	498	346	822	1,015	2,769	241	186
Georgia	233	4,103	12,111	9,608	1,691	1,871	0	0	0	0	0
Hawaii	3	60	147	646	285	363	0	0	0	0	0
Idaho	212	804	1,773	1,253	149	126	1,206	896	1,923	858	596
Illinois	0	2,634	9,636	12,304	3,226	3,141	0	0	0	0	0
Indiana	261	4,306	6,470	7,411	1,849	1,973	0	0	0	0	0
Iowa	3,174	1,283	1,853	1,858	427	412	0	0	0	0	0
Kansas	0	4,449	6,806	3,181	799	713	125	2,048	4,986	598	563
Kentucky	128	1,858	3,857	5,678	717	410	0	0	0	0	0
Louisiana	150	1,030	3,868	4,683	1,516	1,658	0	1	6	0	7
Maine	0	368	1,229	3,011	1,083	625	4	0	0	0	0
Maryland	10	773	1,652	1,961	600	804	0	0	0	0	0
Massachusetts	27	423	874	1,979	720	686	0	0	6,278	0	0
Michigan	74	3,373	3,755	2,599	637	574	3,761	2,214	6,366	5,107	5,962
Minnesota	225	5,460	6,929	6,689	1,244	943	0	0	0	0	0
Mississippi	6	2,365	4,893	8,790	2,857	2,467	0	0	0	0	0
Missouri	769	2,504	6,190	11,478	3,638	1,462	0	0	0	0	0
Montana	6	1,822	4,860	4,361	699	401	0	0	0	0	0
Nebraska	115	2,799	3,254	4,282	428	84	0	0	0	0	0
Nevada	370	1,383	1,278	1,328	82	68	0	19	58	2	2
New Hampshire	4	720	867	938	366	534	0	0	17	0	0
New Jersey	52	433	847	2,766	1,573	2,272	678	283	1,512	92	25
New Mexico	501	1,975	1,798	2,998	1,176	1,121	0	0	0	0	0
New York	57	905	6,565	11,990	3,382	4,294	4	7	32	13	2
North Carolina	426	1,941	7,587	7,853	1,297	835	155	5	11	6	0
North Dakota	0	1,745	2,495	1,287	171	134	1,246	3,993	1,176	1,040	115
Ohio	12	1,826	7,459	7,384	1,521	1,075	0	0	0	0	0
Oklahoma	35	1,837	6,338	12,014	3,694	5,028	0	0	0	0	0
Oregon	139	1,312	3,071	3,093	575	316	2,633	2,307	3,002	385	203
Pennsylvania	229	1,337	5,825	11,483	3,131	2,372	0	0	0	0	0
Rhode Island	4	39	99	560	216	249	113	86	163	119	67
South Carolina	0	2,006	5,649	10,765	1,789	746	0	0	0	0	0
South Dakota	26	1,639	4,152	3,514	347	73	377	75	3,701	216	727
Tennessee	69	4,200	4,536	4,178	567	373	0	0	0	0	0
Texas	737	4,832	10,761	9,795	1,256	1,104	1,943	1,961	6,803	1,830	1,782
Utah	68	664	1,936	3,873	1,023	424	0	51	457	8	3
Vermont	7	485	916	1,172	403	426	0	0	0	0	0
Virginia	43	796	4,726	9,211	2,279	1,575	525	450	919	154	92
Washington	0	879	3,289	8,977	3,576	2,885	0	0	0	0	0
West Virginia	63	88	1,600	5,402	1,291	1,649	19	24	127	120	11
Wisconsin	0	3,863	5,986	8,956	3,301	3,168	0	0	0	0	0
Wyoming	39	1,216	3,031	2,274	360	233	0	0	0	0	0
United States, total	12,527	90,793	206,333	276,698	73,890	65,776	14,986	16,276	46,580	11,272	11,033
U.S. total (incl. Puerto Rico)	12,558	90,793	206,369	277,266	74,625	66,850	15,206	16,509	47,078	11,326	11,033

NOTES: Data may not sum to totals. Road condition ratings are reported using the International Roughness Index (IRI) and the Present Serviceability Rating (PSR). States are required to report to the Federal Highway Administration (FHWA) IRI data for the Interstates, other principal arterials, rural minor arterials, and the National Highway System regardless of functional system. The IRI is also recommended by FHWA for measuring all other functional classifications because the IRI uses a more standardized and objective measurement methodology. Some States elect to report PSR for some sections of rural major collectors, urban minor arterials, and urban collectors. Pavement rating data are not reported for local or rural minor collector functional systems.

According to the pavement condition criteria used in the Highway Performance Monitoring System, an IRI rating less than 95 or a PSR rating greater than or equal to 3.5 indicates "good" ride quality. An IRI rating of less than or equal to 170 or a PSR rating for greater than or equal to 2.5 indicates "acceptable" ride quality. For further information, refer to the U.S. Department of Tansportation, Federal Highway Administration, 2013 Status of the Nation's Highways, Bridges, and Transit: Conditions and Performance Report, Exhibit 3-1, available at www.fhwa.dot.gov/policy/2013cpr as of June 2015.

SOURCE: U.S. Department of Transportation, Federal Highway Administration, *Highway Statistics*, HM-63 and HM-64, available at www.fhwa.dot.gov/policyinformation/statistics.cfm as of June 2015.

Table 1-5: Number of Road Bridges by Functional System: 2014

State	Urban					Rural			
	Interstate	Other freeways and expressways	Other arterials	Collector	Local	Interstate	Other arterials	Collector	Local
Alabama	558	86	926	291	1,013	690	2,633	5,517	4,374
Alaska	41	0	106	43	50	146	170	298	690
Arizona	313	377	1,344	426	573	1,240	1,660	1,438	664
Arkansas	352	163	761	157	463	467	2,372	5,020	3,051
California	2,612	3,071	4,979	1,354	1,773	1,203	2,860	3,376	4,178
Colorado	562	401	974	343	511	553	1,295	1,773	2,256
Connecticut	740	560	808	434	534	83	225	327	507
Delaware	91	28	189	81	65	0	102	114	195
District of Columbia	68	26	95	16	46	0	1	1	0
Florida	1,225	1,178	2,329	1,035	1,191	616	1,675	1,379	1,509
Georgia	575	212	2,053	613	1,347	422	2,346	3,818	3,409
Hawaii	184	89	137	70	103	27	258	159	110
Idaho	113	0	339	106	98	279	544	998	1,954
Illinois	1,417	178	2,756	1,070	1,339	875	2,314	4,475	12,164
Indiana	723	262	1,337	582	827	892	1,600	5,135	7,661
Iowa	340	0	1,164	349	508	371	2,272	7,342	11,954
Kansas	490	454	1,012	416	556	549	2,633	8,280	10,695
Kentucky	416	133	646	271	405	373	1,647	4,432	5,871
Louisiana	868	157	1,102	313	900	551	2,043	2,824	4,224
Maine	113	19	139	102	81	173	325	719	748
Maryland	701	424	782	296	699	185	373	837	1,008
Massachusetts	897	454	1,645	525	565	90	190	335	440
Michigan	827	316	1,508	470	576	387	1,222	2,623	3,143
Minnesota	420	225	935	284	360	291	1,683	3,193	5,570
Mississippi	298	109	611	287	393	482	2,789	4,734	7,388
Missouri	899	1,077	816	655	1,107	463	2,321	5,037	12,010
Montana	84	0	98	32	66	747	1,003	1,079	2,142
Nebraska	119	52	365	90	147	212	2,177	3,576	8,636
Nevada	219	90	300	220	277	319	151	173	149
New Hampshire	141	55	250	104	179	223	271	425	819
New Jersey	983	774	2,057	652	973	77	189	299	605
New Mexico	279	1	440	143	116	600	1,014	844	514
New York	1,658	1,123	2,619	1,087	1,384	651	1,428	3,258	4,248
North Carolina	741	540	1,569	600	1,565	448	1,639	3,562	7,453
North Dakota	59	0	141	21	33	147	607	893	2,528
Ohio	1,356	776	1,985	993	1,377	854	2,302	6,809	10,534
Oklahoma	502	420	1,043	568	665	604	2,587	7,198	9,560
Oregon	307	69	761	351	195	361	1,206	2,289	2,513
Pennsylvania	1,365	826	3,018	1,302	1,487	1,074	2,514	4,067	7,038
Rhode Island	132	117	270	84	53	11	24	45	30
South Carolina	353	80	813	534	557	376	1,264	2,675	2,686
South Dakota	117	6	160	51	66	338	972	1,319	2,843
Tennessee	719	317	1,871	436	969	706	2,786	5,353	6,920
Texas	3,223	4,068	6,343	2,533	4,778	2,273	8,249	11,214	10,256
Utah	411	41	345	94	275	436	348	463	601
Vermont	57	2	92	42	32	256	374	696	1,194
Virginia	1,007	435	1,540	518	879	671	1,544	2,654	4,552
Washington	649	481	965	236	285	294	899	2,059	2,252
West Virginia	252	71	342	133	278	403	766	1,989	2,953
Wisconsin	515	360	1,238	204	546	610	2,262	2,546	5,828
Wyoming	160	6	119	48	45	765	514	533	937
United States, total	31,251	20,709	58,237	21,665	33,310	24,864	74,643	140,202	203,564
U.S. total (incl. Puerto Rico)	31,496	20,821	58,612	21,834	33,529	25,057	74,870	140,535	203,995

NOTE: Some discrepancies exist between the total number of bridges reported in tables 1-5, 1-6, and 1-7 because of bridges not identified in one or more of the categories and other anomalies.

SOURCE: U.S. Department of Transportation, Federal Highway Administration, Office of Bridge Technology, National Bridge Inventory, Functional Classification of Bridges by Highway System, available at www.fhwa.dot.gov/bridge/nbi.cfm as of July 2015.

Table 1-6: Number of Road Bridges by Owner: 2014

State	Federal	State highway agency	State toll authority	Other state agency	Local highway agency	Local toll authority	Other local agency	Private (including railroad)	Total
Alabama	167	5,734	0	9	10,115	0	2	30	16,057
Alaska	560	809	0	4	149	0	3	1	1,526
Arizona	438	4,741	0	19	2,826	0	1	6	8,031
Arkansas	186	7,271	0	41	5,305	0	0	2	12,805
California	816	12,347	0	79	11,998	5	54	16	25,315
Colorado	294	3,444	0	0	4,787	121	6	14	8,666
Connecticut	7	2,814	0	0	1,246	0	0	4	4,071
Delaware	5	831	0	0	11	16	0	0	863
District of Columbia	36	213	0	1	2	0	1	0	253
Florida	150	5,480	1,149	44	5,069	9	46	65	12,012
Georgia	175	6,652	0	1	7,902	0	1	46	14,777
Hawaii	36	729	0	1	369	0	0	2	1,137
Idaho	717	1,325	0	13	1,716	0	655	1	4,427
Illinois	41	7,766	454	2	18,171	0	8	93	26,535
Indiana	64	5,484	332	61	13,044	1	12	19	19,017
Iowa	34	4,103	0	17	20,136	1	0	2	24,293
Kansas	115	5,031	363	1	19,535	0	0	1	25,046
Kentucky	98	9,005	0	7	5,045	0	2	32	14,189
Louisiana	265	7,769	0	17	4,872	5	26	5	12,959
Maine	19	1,971	166	8	230	0	1	24	2,419
Maryland	93	2,553	313	36	2,289	0	1	4	5,289
Massachusetts	19	3,460	8	83	1,565	1	1	0	5,137
Michigan	89	4,441	4	27	6,480	0	20	3	11,064
Minnesota	88	3,616	0	7	9,136	0	3	34	12,884
Mississippi	462	5,775	0	1	10,833	0	0	17	17,088
Missouri	64	10,344	0	1	13,878	1	67	20	24,375
Montana	803	2,478	0	0	1,970	0	0	0	5,251
Nebraska	82	3,512	0	35	11,599	0	99	46	15,373
Nevada	40	1,069	0	2	728	0	47	10	1,896
New Hampshire	71	1,300	163	1	923	1	1	3	2,463
New Jersey	34	2,370	1,145	215	2,675	31	2	18	6,490
New Mexico	234	2,975	0	2	736	0	1	3	3,951
New York	49	7,487	774	94	8,542	172	109	105	17,332
North Carolina	394	16,861	22	3	815	0	0	2	18,097
North Dakota	80	1,129	0	2	3,199	0	4	10	4,424
Ohio	11	10,361	462	0	16,075	0	4	59	26,972
Oklahoma	128	6,791	766	10	15,431	0	4	2	23,132
Oregon	1,186	2,718	0	18	4,033	2	48	6	8,011
Pennsylvania	67	15,153	777	9	6,147	46	6	225	22,430
Rhode Island	2	586	14	3	146	0	1	1	753
South Carolina	69	8,467	0	1	780	0	0	19	9,336
South Dakota	122	1,797	0	20	3,933	0	0	0	5,872
Tennessee	353	8,265	0	6	11,406	0	2	3	20,035
Texas	179	34,002	298	19	17,755	524	85	36	52,898
Utah	177	1,808	0	2	1,027	0	0	0	3,014
Vermont	26	1,087	0	0	1,626	0	0	6	2,745
Virginia	357	11,911	12	5	1,404	62	0	49	13,800
Washington	779	3,277	1	4	4,032	3	8	3	8,107
West Virginia	49	6,890	99	3	103	0	10	9	7,163
Wisconsin	117	5,200	0	0	8,776	0	0	16	14,109
Wyoming	319	1,955	0	3	844	0	0	3	3,124
United States, total	10,766	283,157	7,322	937	301,414	1,001	1,341	1,075	607,013
U.S. total (incl. Puerto Rico)	12,385	283,176	7,322	1,278	301,414	1,002	1,341	1,075	607,014

NOTES: Some discrepancies exist between the total number of bridges reported in tables 1-5, 1-6, and 1-7 because of bridges not identified in one or more of the categories and other anomalies. Other state agency includes state parks, forests, reservations, and other state agencies. Local highway agency includes county, town or township, and city or municipal highway agencies. Other local agency includes local parks, forests, reservations, and other local agencies. Private includes highway bridges owned by railroads and other private entities. Details for each state may not add to totals because totals include bridges for which ownership is unknown.

SOURCE: U.S. Department of Transportation, Federal Highway Administration, Office of Bridge Technology, National Bridge Inventory, Highway Bridge by Owner, available at www.fhwa.dot.gov/bridge/nbi.cfm as of June 2015.

Table 1-7: Road Bridge Condition: 2014

State	All bridges	Structurally deficient	Functionally obsolete	Percent of all bridges Structurally deficient	Percent of all bridges Functionally obsolete
Alabama	16,057	1,388	2,144	8.6	13.4
Alaska	1,526	153	198	10.0	13.0
Arizona	8,031	256	684	3.2	8.5
Arkansas	12,805	861	1,994	6.7	15.6
California	25,315	2,501	4,306	9.9	17.0
Colorado	8,666	529	859	6.1	9.9
Connecticut	4,071	373	975	9.2	23.9
Delaware	863	48	123	5.6	14.3
District of Columbia	253	14	164	5.5	64.8
Florida	12,012	243	1,760	2.0	14.7
Georgia	14,777	785	1,623	5.3	11.0
Hawaii	1,137	61	422	5.4	37.1
Idaho	4,427	405	471	9.1	10.6
Illinois	26,535	2,216	1,971	8.4	7.4
Indiana	19,017	1,902	2,201	10.0	11.6
Iowa	24,293	5,022	1,183	20.7	4.9
Kansas	25,046	2,416	1,813	9.6	7.2
Kentucky	14,189	1,191	3,253	8.4	22.9
Louisiana	12,959	1,837	1,944	14.2	15.0
Maine	2,419	364	432	15.0	17.9
Maryland	5,289	317	1,104	6.0	20.9
Massachusetts	5,137	459	2,224	8.9	43.3
Michigan	11,064	1,295	1,754	11.7	15.9
Minnesota	12,884	830	363	6.4	2.8
Mississippi	17,088	2,275	1,290	13.3	7.5
Missouri	24,375	3,310	3,145	13.6	12.9
Montana	5,251	400	514	7.6	9.8
Nebraska	15,373	2,653	986	17.3	6.4
Nevada	1,896	34	215	1.8	11.3
New Hampshire	2,463	324	451	13.2	18.3
New Jersey	6,490	595	1,673	9.2	25.8
New Mexico	3,951	284	359	7.2	9.1
New York	17,332	2,012	4,733	11.6	27.3
North Carolina	18,097	2,199	3,135	12.2	17.3
North Dakota	4,424	701	243	15.8	5.5
Ohio	26,972	2,080	4,452	7.7	16.5
Oklahoma	23,132	4,216	1,575	18.2	6.8
Oregon	8,011	439	1,419	5.5	17.7
Pennsylvania	22,430	5,049	4,388	22.5	19.6
Rhode Island	753	174	255	23.1	33.9
South Carolina	9,336	1,031	891	11.0	9.5
South Dakota	5,872	1,174	238	20.0	4.1
Tennessee	20,035	1,083	2,863	5.4	14.3
Texas	52,898	1,127	8,867	2.1	16.8
Utah	3,014	102	317	3.4	10.5
Vermont	2,745	206	676	7.5	24.6
Virginia	13,800	1,120	2,454	8.1	17.8
Washington	8,107	382	1,711	4.7	21.1
West Virginia	7,163	960	1,541	13.4	21.5
Wisconsin	14,109	1,212	759	8.6	5.4
Wyoming	3,124	422	284	13.5	9.1
United States, total	607,013	61,030	83,399	10.1	13.7
U.S. total (incl. Puerto Rico)	607,014	61,331	83,483	10.1	13.8

NOTES: Some discrepancies exist between the total number of bridges reported in tables 1-5, 1-6, and 1-7 because of bridges not identified in one or more of the categories and other anomalies. Definitions of the terms Structurally Deficient and Functionally Obsolete can be found in the Federal Highway Administration 2013 *Conditions and Performance Report* at http://www.fhwa.dot.gov/policy/2013cpr/.

SOURCE: U.S. Department of Transportation, Federal Highway Administration, Office of Bridge Technology, National Bridge Inventory, Functional Classification of Bridges by Highway System, available at www.fhwa.dot.gov/bridge/nbi.cfm as of June 2015.

Table 1-8: Motor Bus Transit Route Mileage: 2013

State	Directional route-miles		
	Exclusive right-of-way	Controlled right-of-way	Mixed right-of-way
Alabama	0.0	0.0	1,446.9
Alaska	0.0	0.0	247.1
Arizona	0.0	329.6	4,799.6
Arkansas	0.0	0.0	541.1
California	508.1	722.6	39,070.4
Colorado	43.6	9.8	4,694.7
Connecticut	52.4	0.0	3,843.6
Delaware	0.0	0.0	1,470.3
District of Columbia	10.4	56.6	2,559.2
Florida	42.6	79.2	14,991.7
Georgia	183.7	0.0	4,122.1
Hawaii	1.2	34.7	1,702.7
Idaho	0.0	0.0	284.2
Illinois	3.7	0.0	8,287.5
Indiana	0.0	0.0	2,713.9
Iowa	0.0	0.0	35,836.6
Kansas	0.0	0.0	897.3
Kentucky	0.0	0.0	2,048.4
Louisiana	14.0	0.0	1,739.9
Maine	0.0	0.0	144.0
Maryland	14.8	16.2	5,948.1
Massachusetts	6.2	22.6	6,295.5
Michigan	0.0	0.0	9,091.7
Minnesota	15.5	385.3	4,699.7
Mississippi	0.0	0.0	494.7
Missouri	0.8	14.1	3,211.0
Montana	0.0	0.0	463.0
Nebraska	0.0	0.0	881.0
Nevada	47.2	35.4	1,666.8
New Hampshire	0.0	0.0	180.0
New Jersey	1.0	59.0	12,943.9
New Mexico	0.0	0.0	1,484.4
New York	45.6	167.9	14,737.3
North Carolina	22.0	0.0	4,457.1
North Dakota	0.0	0.0	240.7
Ohio	9.8	134.3	8,061.3
Oklahoma	0.0	0.0	1,520.7
Oregon	13.4	10.1	2,672.6
Pennsylvania	76.9	46.9	12,536.6
Rhode Island	0.8	0.0	1,198.5
South Carolina	0.0	0.0	3,036.9
South Dakota	0.0	0.0	191.1
Tennessee	0.0	0.0	2,836.1
Texas	117.0	539.7	13,067.1
Utah	14.8	0.0	3,900.1
Vermont	0.0	0.0	445.6
Virginia	0.0	436.6	5,277.6
Washington	469.9	335.6	7,230.4
West Virginia	0.0	0.0	1,171.0
Wisconsin	23.2	0.0	4,015.1
Wyoming	0.0	0.0	0.0
United States, total	1,738.5	3,436.1	265,396.8
U.S. total (incl. Puerto Rico)	1,766.7	3,436.1	265,962.3

NOTES: Motor bus includes commuter bus, bus, bus rapid transit, and trolleybus. Directional route-miles is the mileage in each direction over which public transportation vehicles travel while in revenue service. Directional route-miles are a measure of the facility or roadway, not the service carried on the facility, such as the number of routes or vehicle-miles. Directional route-miles are computed with regard to direction of service, but without regard to the number of traffic lanes or rail tracks existing in the right-of-way. Exclusive right-of-way refers to lanes reserved at all times for transit use and other high occupancy vehicles (HOVs). Controlled right-of-way refers to lanes restricted for at least a portion of the day for use by transit vehicles and other HOVs. Mixed right-of-way refers to lanes used for general automobile traffic. Route-miles are assigned to the state of the transit agency's headquarters.

SOURCE: U.S. Department of Transportation, Federal Transit Adminstration, National Transit Database, table 24, available at www.ntdprogram.gov as of June 2015.

Table 1-9: Characteristics of Rail Transit by Transit Authority: 2013

Rail transit mode/transit agency	Primary city served	States served	Directional route-miles	Number of crossings	Number of stations[1]	Number of ADA accessible stations[2]
Heavy rail, total	11	17	1,601.4	27	1028	534
Metropolitan Atlanta Rapid Transit Authority	Atlanta	GA	96.1	0	38	38
Maryland Transit Administration	Baltimore	MD	29.4	0	14	14
Massachusetts Bay Transportation Authority	Boston	MA, NH, RI	76.3	0	53	49
Chicago Transit Authority	Chicago	IL, IN	207.8	25	145	97
The Greater Cleveland Regional Transit Authority	Cleveland	OH	38.1	0	18	15
Los Angeles County Metropolitan Transportation Authority	Los Angeles	CA	31.9	0	16	16
Miami-Dade Transit	Miami	FL	49.8	0	23	23
MTA New York City Transit	New York	NY, NJ, CT	487.5	0	468	96
Port Authority Trans-Hudson Corporation	New York	NY, NJ, CT	28.6	2	13	7
Staten Island Rapid Transit Operating Authority	New York	NY, NJ, CT	28.6	0	22	4
Port Authority Transit Corporation	Philadelphia	PA, NJ, DE, MD	31.5	0	13	7
Southeastern Pennsylvania Transportation Authority	Philadelphia	PA	74.9	0	75	38
San Francisco Bay Area Rapid Transit District	San Francisco	CA	209.0	0	44	44
Washington Metropolitan Area Transit Authority	Washington	DC, MD, VA	211.8	0	86	86
Light rail, total	29	25	1,789.4	3,628	925	825
Capital Metropolitan Transportation Authority	Austin	TX	64.2	79	9	9
Maryland Transit Administration	Baltimore	MD	57.6	52	33	33
Massachusetts Bay Transportation Authority	Boston	MA, NH, RI	51.0	65	74	36
Niagara Frontier Transportation Authority	Buffalo	NY	12.4	8	14	14
Charlotte Area Transit System	Charlotte	NC	18.6	19	19	19
The Greater Cleveland Regional Transit Authority	Cleveland	OH	30.4	22	34	10
Dallas Area Rapid Transit	Dallas	TX	171.4	162	61	61
Denver Regional Transportation District	Denver	CO	94.2	57	46	46
Metropolitan Transit Authority of Harris County	Houston	TX	14.8	68	16	16
Kenosha Transit	Kenosha	WI	1.9	19	2	1
Central Arkansas Transit Authority	Little Rock	AR	3.8	24	0	0
Los Angeles County Metropolitan Transportation Authority	Los Angeles	CA	136.3	152	66	66
Memphis Area Transit Authority	Memphis	TN, MS, AR	10.0	62	7	7
Metro Transit	Minneapolis	MN	24.7	50	19	19
New Orleans Regional Transit Authority	New Orleans	LA	26.9	247	10	10
New Jersey Transit Corporation	Newark	NJ	116.2	120	55	61
Hampton Roads Transit	Norfolk	VA	14.8	22	11	11
Southeastern Pennsylvania Transportation Authority	Philadelphia	PA	82.9	695	45	2
Valley Metro Rail, Inc.	Phoenix	AZ	39.2	140	33	33
Port Authority of Allegheny County	Pittsburgh	PA	49.6	44	26	26
City of Portland	Portland	OR	14.78	191	2	2
Tri-County Metropolitan Transportation District of Oregon	Portland	OR, WA	133.5	214	37	37
Sacramento Regional Transit District	Sacramento	CA	76.1	133	38	38
Utah Transit Authority	Salt Lake City	UT	93.9	144	56	56
North County Transit District	San Diego	CA	44.0	41	15	15
San Diego Metropolitan Transit System	San Diego	CA	108.4	96	53	53
San Francisco Municipal Railway	San Francisco	CA	83.1	417	9	9
Santa Clara Valley Transportation Authority	San Jose	CA	81.0	168	65	65
Central Puget Sound Regional Transit Authority	Seattle	WA	34.4	51	13	13
King County Department of Transportation	Seattle	WA	2.7	18	11	11
Bi-State Development Agency	St. Louis	MO, IL	91.1	25	37	37
Hillsborough Area Regional Transit Authority	Tampa	FL	5.4	23	9	9
Commuter rail, total[3]	19	23	8,733.9	3,450	1,247	841
Rio Metro Regional Transit District	Albuquerque	NM	193.1	86	13	13
Alaska Railroad Corporation	Anchorage	AK	959.9	133	10	10
Maryland Transit Administration	Baltimore	MD	400.4	40	42	24
Massachusetts Bay Transportation Authority	Boston	MA, NH, RI	776.1	258	137	100
Northern New England Passenger Rail Authority	Boston	MA, ME, NH	287.6	103	12	12
Northeast Illinois Regional Commuter Railroad Corporation	Chicago	IL, WI	975.4	571	241	173
Northern Indiana Commuter Transportation District	Chicago	IL, IN	179.8	117	20	13
Dallas Area Rapid Transit	Dallas	TX	72.3	44	10	10
Denton County Transportation Authority	Dallas	TX	42.6	43	5	5
Connecticut Department of Transportation	Hartford	CT	101.2	3	9	8
Southern California Regional Rail Authority	Los Angeles	CA	777.8	423	55	55
South Florida Regional Transportation Authority	Miami	FL	142.2	73	18	18
Metro Transit	Minneapolis	MN	77.9	36	7	7
Regional Transportation Authority	Nashville	TN	62.8	35	6	6
Metro-North Commuter Railroad Company	New York	NY, NJ, CT	545.7	158	112	46
MTA Long Island Rail Road	New York	NY, NJ, CT	638.2	343	124	103
New Jersey Transit Corporation	New York	NY, NJ, CT	1,001.8	330	164	77
Pennsylvania Department of Transportation	Philadelphia	PA	144.4	4	12	5
Southeastern Pennsylvania Transportation Authority	Philadelphia	PA	446.9	283	154	66
Utah Transit Authority	Salt Lake City	UT	174.5	65	16	16
North County Transit District	San Diego	CA	82.2	34	8	8
Peninsula Corridor Joint Powers Board	San Francisco	CA	153.7	55	32	26
Altamont Commuter Express	San Jose	CA	172.0	127	10	10
Central Puget Sound Regional Transit Authority	Seattle	WA	163.8	66	12	12
Virginia Railway Express	Washington	DC, VA, MD	161.5	20	18	18
United States, total	38	34	12,124.7	7,105	3,200	2,200

[1]Many light rail lines have numerous stops in the street that do not meet the definition of a station.

[2]Additional stations may be wheelchair accessible but do not comply with other provisions of the Americans with Disabilities Act.

[3]Excludes commuter-type services operated independently by Amtrak or another intercity rail provider.

KEY: U = data are unavailable, ADA = Americans with Disabilities Act of 1990, MTA = Metropolitan Transportation Authority.

NOTES: Beginning in 2012, National Transit Database data are reported according to revised modal classifications. Light rail includes systems classified as light rail, hybrid rail, and street car rail. This table does not include other transit rail systems such as cable car, inclined plane, and monorail/automated guideway. For definition of Directional route-miles see table 1-8. Heavy rail, light rail, and commuter rail are defined in the glossary. For more information on individual transit agencies, see Annual National Transit Profiles available at www.ntdprogram.gov/ntdprogram/data. htm. For more information on footnotes, see the National Transit Database Glossary available at www.ntdprogram.gov/ntdprogram/Glossary.htm.

SOURCE: U.S. Department of Transportation, Federal Transit Adminstration, National Transit Database, table 21 and 23, available at www.ntdprogram.gov as of July 2015.

Table 1-10: Public and Private Airports, Heliports, and Seaplane Bases: 2013

State	Airports	Heliports	Seaplane bases	Total
Alabama	180	87	7	274
Alaska	554	43	139	736
Arizona	189	108	0	297
Arkansas	215	80	0	295
California	522	411	9	942
Colorado	265	179	0	444
Connecticut	51	68	4	123
Delaware	31	10	0	41
District of Columbia	3	13	0	16
Florida	501	292	46	839
Georgia	336	114	2	452
Hawaii	32	16	0	48
Idaho	227	50	5	282
Illinois	478	248	6	732
Indiana	405	128	17	550
Iowa	199	86	0	285
Kansas	333	33	0	366
Kentucky	150	95	0	245
Louisiana	229	212	11	452
Maine	115	19	46	180
Maryland	149	66	4	219
Massachusetts	75	133	15	223
Michigan	355	94	6	455
Minnesota	327	64	57	448
Mississippi	186	43	0	229
Missouri	363	116	3	482
Montana	231	36	2	269
Nebraska	198	34	1	233
Nevada	97	27	0	124
New Hampshire	54	78	8	140
New Jersey	100	207	7	314
New Mexico	135	31	1	167
New York	388	183	17	588
North Carolina	338	107	1	446
North Dakota	256	15	0	271
Ohio	450	215	3	668
Oklahoma	294	85	1	380
Oregon	325	94	2	421
Pennsylvania	432	345	8	785
Rhode Island	9	14	1	24
South Carolina	158	33	2	193
South Dakota	143	33	0	176
Tennessee	212	113	1	326
Texas	1,466	553	0	2,019
Utah	91	55	0	146
Vermont	61	16	6	83
Virginia	291	134	3	428
Washington	370	168	17	555
West Virginia	75	39	10	124
Wisconsin	435	98	17	550
Wyoming	95	26	0	121

SOURCE: U.S. Department of Transportation, Federal Aviation Administration, Administrator's Factbook 2013, personal communication as of August 2015.

Table 1-11: Top 50 Commercial Service Airport Enplanements by Air Carrier Category: 2013

(For airports with scheduled service and 2,500 or more passengers enplaned)

Airport	Rank	Large certificated air carriers	Commuter and small certificated air carriers	Foreign air carriers	Total enplanements
Atlanta, GA: Hartsfield-Jackson Atlanta International	1	44,637,041	33,550	632,736	45,303,327
Los Angeles, CA: Los Angeles International	2	25,847,206	12,263	6,580,509	32,439,978
Chicago, IL: Chicago O'Hare International	3	29,503,162	486,465	2,332,500	32,322,127
Dallas/Fort Worth, TX: Dallas/Fort Worth International	4	28,488,499	185	546,871	29,035,555
Denver, CO: Denver International	5	24,994,870	189,374	311,796	25,496,040
New York, NY: John F. Kennedy International	6	17,035,122	2,998	8,024,920	25,063,040
San Francisco, CA: San Francisco International	7	18,853,016	102	2,848,334	21,701,452
Charlotte, NC: Charlotte Douglas International	8	20,512,874	728,234	100,306	21,341,414
Las Vegas, NV: McCarran International	9	18,469,206	10,245	1,429,067	19,908,518
Phoenix, AZ: Phoenix Sky Harbor International	10	19,145,992	10,430	367,438	19,523,860
Miami, FL: Miami International	11	15,298,878	142,853	4,013,136	19,454,867
Houston, TX: George Bush Intercontinental/Houston	12	17,783,534	161,200	1,011,744	18,956,478
Newark, NJ: Newark Liberty International	13	15,544,481	333,982	1,672,379	17,550,842
Orlando, FL: Orlando International	14	15,223,612	54,679	1,657,823	16,936,114
Seattle, WA: Seattle/Tacoma International	15	15,944,363	0	710,751	16,655,114
Minneapolis, MN: Minneapolis-St Paul International	16	16,169,638	28,655	78,846	16,277,139
Detroit, MI: Detroit Metro Wayne County	17	15,506,511	1,183	176,339	15,684,033
Boston, MA: Logan International	18	13,105,579	151,754	1,517,139	14,774,472
Philadelphia, PA: Philadelphia International	19	13,657,147	851,608	217,006	14,725,761
New York, NY: LaGuardia	20	12,798,018	22,762	550,372	13,371,152
Fort Lauderdale, FL: Fort Lauderdale-Hollywood International	21	10,570,528	123,363	813,372	11,507,263
Baltimore, MD: Baltimore/Washington International Thurgood Marshall	22	10,901,703	60,770	90,262	11,052,735
Washington, DC: Washington Dulles International	23	8,188,462	551,554	1,832,273	10,572,289
Chicago, IL: Chicago Midway International	24	9,726,146	397	180,255	9,906,798
Washington, DC: Ronald Reagan Washington National	25	9,700,202	47,911	89,431	9,837,544
Salt Lake City, UT: Salt Lake City International	26	9,663,086	2,695	0	9,665,781
Honolulu, HI: Honolulu International	27	8,094,186	41,387	1,360,751	9,496,324
San Diego, CA: San Diego International	28	8,647,344	14,597	211,844	8,873,785
Tampa, FL: Tampa International	29	7,913,976	122,274	230,465	8,266,715
Portland, OR: Portland International	30	7,392,879	7,985	50,926	7,451,790
St. Louis, MO: Lambert-St. Louis International	31	5,890,929	302,096	18,180	6,211,205
Houston, TX: William P Hobby	32	5,371,409	411	57	5,371,877
Nashville, TN: Nashville International	33	5,015,741	6,859	25,940	5,048,540
Austin, TX: Austin - Bergstrom International	34	4,896,963	1,683	223	4,898,869
Kansas City, MO: Kansas City International	35	4,811,901	8,394	14,916	4,835,211
Oakland, CA: Metropolitan Oakland International	36	4,680,383	12,561	77,863	4,770,807
New Orleans, LA: Louis Armstrong New Orleans International	37	4,552,542	1,043	21,444	4,575,029
Santa Ana, CA: John Wayne Airport-Orange County	38	4,424,669	3	113,722	4,538,394
Raleigh/Durham, NC: Raleigh-Durham International	39	4,414,850	33,000	31,246	4,479,096
Cleveland, OH: Cleveland-Hopkins International	40	3,971,751	383,840	19,048	4,374,639
San Jose, CA: Norman Y. Mineta San Jose International	41	4,233,840	398	74,430	4,308,668
Sacramento, CA: Sacramento International	42	4,202,283	40	52,228	4,254,551
San Juan, PR: Luis Munoz Marin International	43	3,826,532	172,982	116,988	4,116,502
Dallas, TX: Dallas Love Field	44	4,012,459	6,935	1,048	4,020,442
San Antonio, TX: San Antonio International	45	3,816,978	7,979	179,448	4,004,405
Pittsburgh, PA: Pittsburgh International	46	3,671,268	114,994	24,964	3,811,226
Fort Myers, FL: Southwest Florida International	47	3,619,737	18,192	150,298	3,788,227
Indianapolis, IN: Indianapolis International	48	3,494,238	10,145	17,309	3,521,692
Milwaukee, WI: General Mitchell International	49	3,201,178	1,636	10,904	3,213,718
Columbus, OH: Port Columbus International	50	3,018,378	24,663	19,009	3,062,050
Top 50 Airports, total		574,445,290	5,303,309	40,608,856	620,357,455
United States, total (including U.S. territories)		684,668,326	11,698,417	42,148,518	738,515,261

NOTES: Ranked by total enplaned passengers on air carriers of all types, including foreign air carriers. In previous years, the source of the data for this table was the FAA which includes information on Air Taxi operators. The current table uses data from the Office of Airline Information, which does not collect data on Air Taxi operators. Air carrier enplanements may not add to total enplanements because totals include enplanements for which carrier type is unknown.

SOURCE: U.S. Department of Transportation, Bureau of Transportation Statistics, TranStats Database, T-100 Market (All Carriers), available at www.transtats.bts.gov as of July 2015.

Table 1-12: Airport Enplanements by State and Air Carrier Category: 2013

State	Large certificated air carriers	Commuter and small certificated air carriers	Foreign air carriers	Total enplanements
Alabama	2,333,955	2,625	5	2,336,585
Alaska	3,032,642	1,414,218	39,413	4,486,273
Arizona	21,683,896	222,665	367,485	22,274,046
Arkansas	1,727,416	17,927	0	1,745,343
California	78,820,748	67,014	10,177,638	89,065,400
Colorado	26,626,656	215,686	311,968	27,154,310
Connecticut	2,560,335	137,993	20,170	2,718,498
Delaware	52,570	182	0	52,752
District of Columbia[1]	0	0	0	0
Florida	62,744,528	666,285	7,120,541	70,531,354
Georgia	45,822,965	67,850	632,783	46,523,598
Hawaii	14,166,182	206,408	1,561,056	15,933,646
Idaho	1,623,264	160	40	1,623,464
Illinois	40,363,316	545,233	2,512,780	43,421,329
Indiana	4,288,325	13,464	17,309	4,319,098
Iowa	1,669,377	19,810	0	1,689,187
Kansas	828,926	24,579	0	853,505
Kentucky	4,964,237	42,328	14,061	5,020,626
Louisiana	5,788,011	32,841	21,444	5,842,296
Maine	1,067,404	45,114	570	1,113,088
Maryland	10,914,012	124,333	90,380	11,128,725
Massachusetts	13,180,375	437,312	1,517,188	15,134,875
Michigan	17,777,179	85,030	179,541	18,041,750
Minnesota	16,514,874	30,844	78,887	16,624,605
Mississippi	1,039,695	20,645	0	1,060,340
Missouri	11,239,567	366,102	33,932	11,639,601
Montana	1,622,920	31,781	23	1,654,724
Nebraska	2,168,564	37,608	27	2,206,199
Nevada	20,197,639	114,554	1,429,082	21,741,275
New Hampshire	1,184,018	18,600	31	1,202,649
New Jersey	16,222,447	347,485	1,672,878	18,242,810
New Mexico	2,582,109	30,976	0	2,613,085
New York	37,360,154	653,399	8,589,400	46,602,953
North Carolina	26,915,046	977,898	131,562	28,024,506
North Dakota	1,121,226	23,754	0	1,144,980
Ohio	9,145,558	499,464	38,195	9,683,217
Oklahoma	3,106,473	57,985	59	3,164,517
Oregon	8,393,973	16,597	51,032	8,461,602
Pennsylvania	18,418,987	1,456,718	246,555	20,122,260
Rhode Island	1,863,274	41,591	418	1,905,283
South Carolina	3,544,246	227,946	7,849	3,780,041
South Dakota	762,129	20,085	0	782,214
Tennessee	8,528,051	146,603	25,940	8,700,594
Texas	68,851,777	255,760	1,743,988	70,851,525
Utah	9,828,852	20,197	5	9,849,054
Vermont	590,570	18,531	1,929	611,030
Virginia	21,478,785	1,065,180	1,923,759	24,467,724
Washington	18,464,910	27,373	711,077	19,203,360
West Virginia	260,899	127,946	9	388,854
Wisconsin	4,815,440	1,964	10,911	4,828,315
Wyoming	490,880	41,294	25	532,199
United States, total (excl. U.S. territories)	678,749,382	11,067,937	41,281,945	731,099,264
United States, total (incl. U.S. territories)	684,668,326	11,698,417	42,148,518	738,515,261

[1]Reagan National is legally and geographically a part of Virginia.

NOTE: Enplanements consist of all persons boarding a flight other than crew and passengers who boarded at an earlier stop. In previous years the source of the data for this table was the FAA, which provides information on Air Taxi operators. The current table uses data from the Office of Airline Information, which does not collect data on Air Taxi operators. General aviation passengers are also excluded from the data. Air carrier enplanements may not add to total enplanements because totals include enplanements for which carrier type is unknown.

SOURCE: U.S. Department of Transportation, Bureau of Transportation Statistics, TranStats Database, T-100 Market (All Carriers), available at www.transtats.bts.gov as of July 2015.

Table 1-13: Number of Freight Railroads by Class: 2012

State	Class I	Regional	Local Linehaul	Local Switching and terminal	Canadian[1]	Total
Alabama	5	1	17	3	0	26
Alaska	0	1	0	0	0	1
Arizona	2	0	4	3	0	9
Arkansas	3	0	16	5	0	24
California	2	0	14	8	0	24
Colorado	2	3	6	3	0	14
Connecticut	1	3	4	0	0	8
Delaware	2	0	2	3	0	7
District of Columbia	2	0	0	1	0	3
Florida	2	2	9	1	0	14
Georgia	2	0	21	1	0	24
Hawaii	0	0	0	0	0	0
Idaho	2	1	7	2	0	12
Illinois	7	3	13	17	0	40
Indiana	5	1	22	13	0	41
Iowa	5	1	5	3	0	14
Kansas	4	3	4	2	0	13
Kentucky	5	1	7	0	0	13
Louisiana	6	0	9	3	0	18
Maine	0	2	5	1	0	8
Maryland	2	1	4	2	0	9
Massachusetts	1	3	5	3	0	12
Michigan	4	0	13	9	1	27
Minnesota	4	1	9	3	1	18
Mississippi	5	1	18	3	0	27
Missouri	6	0	4	7	0	17
Montana	2	2	4	0	0	8
Nebraska	3	1	5	3	0	12
Nevada	2	0	0	0	0	2
New Hampshire	0	2	7	0	0	9
New Jersey	3	1	7	6	0	17
New Mexico	2	0	3	1	0	6
New York	3	4	23	8	1	39
North Carolina	2	0	14	7	0	23
North Dakota	2	2	4	0	0	8
Ohio	4	1	14	15	0	34
Oklahoma	3	0	12	4	0	19
Oregon	2	1	11	4	0	18
Pennsylvania	4	3	29	21	0	57
Rhode Island	0	1	0	0	0	1
South Carolina	2	0	9	4	0	15
South Dakota	2	1	4	2	0	9
Tennessee	6	0	14	5	0	25
Texas	3	0	25	21	0	49
Utah	2	0	2	3	0	7
Vermont	0	3	5	0	0	8
Virginia	2	0	6	1	0	9
Washington	2	1	15	6	0	24
West Virginia	2	0	5	1	0	8
Wisconsin	4	1	3	0	0	8
Wyoming	3	0	0	1	0	4
United States, total	7	21	356	190	1	575

[1]Refers to non-Class I, Canadian-owned lines.

NOTES: According to the Association of American Railroads, a Class I railroad in 2012 is a railroad with operating revenues of at least $$452.7 million. A Regional railroad is a non-Class I, line-haul, freight railroad operating 350 or more miles of road or with revenues of at least $40 million or both. A Local railroad is a railroad which is neither a Class I nor a Regional railroad, and is engaged primarily in line-haul service. A Switching and terminal railroad is a non-Class I railroad engaged primarily in switching and/or terminal services for other railroads. States do not sum to totals; totals count railroads that operate in multiple states only once.

SOURCE: Association of American Railroads, *Railroad Ten-Year Trends*, available at www.aar.org/StatisticsAndPublications as of August 2015.

Table 1-14: Miles of Freight Railroad Operated by Class of Railroad: 2012[1]

State	Class I	Regional	Local Linehaul	Local Switching and terminal	Canadian[2]	Total[3]
Alabama	2,255	236	635	68	0	3,194
Alaska	0	506	0	0	0	506
Arizona	1,235	0	259	149	0	1,643
Arkansas	1,677	0	895	126	0	2,698
California	3,919	0	999	377	0	5,295
Colorado	2,018	198	368	78	0	2,662
Connecticut	6	210	148	0	0	364
Delaware	183	0	47	20	0	250
District of Columbia	15	0	0	5	0	20
Florida	1,693	431	774	2	0	2,900
Georgia	3,251	0	1,384	18	0	4,653
Hawaii	0	0	0	0	0	0
Idaho	962	33	481	147	0	1,623
Illinois	5,851	148	649	338	0	6,986
Indiana	2,510	304	1,076	185	0	4,075
Iowa	3,189	364	271	45	0	3,869
Kansas	2,816	1,429	367	243	0	4,855
Kentucky	2,117	270	221	0	0	2,608
Louisiana	2,354	0	515	58	0	2,927
Maine	0	621	493	2	0	1,116
Maryland	557	0	172	29	0	758
Massachusetts	261	529	159	24	0	973
Michigan	1,557	0	1,751	233	1	3,542
Minnesota	3,625	3	651	127	44	4,450
Mississippi	1,614	8	716	114	0	2,452
Missouri	3,399	0	419	139	0	3,957
Montana	2,061	865	274	0	0	3,200
Nebraska	2,567	324	469	15	0	3,375
Nevada	1,192	0	0	0	0	1,192
New Hampshire	0	174	170	0	0	344
New Jersey	189	91	176	525	0	981
New Mexico	1,431	0	96	310	0	1,837
New York	1,758	328	1,231	128	2	3,447
North Carolina	2,335	0	709	214	0	3,258
North Dakota	2,182	766	382	0	0	3,330
Ohio	3,240	433	1,265	350	0	5,288
Oklahoma	2,009	0	968	296	0	3,273
Oregon	1,103	321	843	129	0	2,396
Pennsylvania	2,428	772	1,374	577	0	5,151
Rhode Island	0	19	0	0	0	19
South Carolina	1,948	0	266	97	0	2,311
South Dakota	1,494	74	98	87	0	1,753
Tennessee	1,836	0	751	62	0	2,649
Texas	8,369	0	1,236	864	0	10,469
Utah	1,249	0	59	35	0	1,343
Vermont	0	224	366	0	0	590
Virginia	2,773	0	438	4	0	3,215
Washington	1,735	0	1,272	185	0	3,192
West Virginia	1,855	0	365	6	0	2,226
Wisconsin	2,595	674	180	0	0	3,449
Wyoming	1,851	0	0	9	0	1,860
United States, total	95,264	10,355	26,438	6,420	47	138,524

[1]Miles operated under trackage rights provided by another (owning) railroad are excluded. Miles of railroad operated is synonymous with route-miles (so that a mile of single track is counted the same as a mile of double track). Sidings, turnouts, yard switching mileage, and mileage not operated are excluded. Year-to-year changes in miles operated are due to both changes in track mileage and changes in the number of railroads with rights for the same track.
[2]Refers to non-Class I, Canadian-owned lines.
[3]Excludes 656 miles of track owned by Amtrak.

NOTES: According to the Association of American Railroads, a Class I railroad in 2012 is a railroad with operating revenues of at least $452.7 million. A Regional railroad is a non-Class I, line-haul, freight railroad operating 350 or more miles of road or with revenues of at least $40 million or both. A Local railroad is a railroad which is neither a Class I nor a Regional railroad, and is engaged primarily in line-haul service. A Switching and terminal railroad is a non-Class I railroad engaged primarily in switching and/or terminal services for other railroads. This table is not comparable to past versions of this table.

SOURCE: Association of American Railroads, *Railroad Ten-Year Trends*, available at www.aar.org/StatisticsAndPublications as of July 2015.

Table 1-15: Top 50 Water Ports by Tonnage: 2012 and 2013

Port	2012				2013			
	Rank	Millions of short tons			Rank	Millions of short tons		
		Total	Foreign	Domestic		Total	Foreign	Domestic
South Louisiana, LA, Port of	1	252.1	119.3	132.7	1	238.6	111.7	126.9
Houston, TX	2	238.2	162.4	75.7	2	229.2	159.6	69.7
New York, NY and NJ	3	132.0	87.0	45.1	3	123.3	76.6	46.7
Beaumont, TX	5	78.5	49.7	28.8	4	94.4	61.0	33.4
Long Beach, CA	6	77.4	65.8	11.6	5	84.5	73.7	10.8
New Orleans, LA	4	79.3	36.5	42.9	6	77.2	34.0	43.2
Corpus Christi, TX	7	69.0	45.7	23.3	7	76.2	44.2	31.9
Baton Rouge, LA	9	60.0	23.3	36.7	8	63.9	25.1	38.7
Los Angeles, CA	8	61.8	54.9	7.0	9	57.9	52.0	5.9
Plaquemines, LA, Port of	10	58.3	24.6	33.6	10	56.9	23.1	33.8
Lake Charles, LA	13	54.4	31.3	23.1	11	56.6	31.1	25.5
Mobile, AL	12	54.9	29.8	25.1	12	54.0	30.7	23.3
Texas City, TX	11	56.7	36.0	20.8	13	49.7	30.4	19.3
Norfolk Harbor, VA	15	46.2	40.5	5.8	14	48.9	42.3	6.6
Huntington - Tristate	14	52.9	0.0	52.9	15	46.8	0.0	46.8
Baltimore, MD	16	42.1	36.8	5.3	16	36.6	30.0	6.6
Duluth-Superior, MN and WI	19	34.7	7.8	26.9	17	36.5	7.7	28.7
Port Arthur, TX	23	30.6	19.9	10.7	18	34.7	25.2	9.5
St. Louis, MO and IL	18	35.0	0.0	35.0	19	33.6	0.0	33.6
Pittsburgh, PA	17	35.2	0.0	35.2	20	32.7	0.0	32.7
Pascagoula, MS	21	33.8	24.8	9.0	21	32.4	24.1	8.3
Tampa, FL	22	31.7	10.1	21.6	22	32.4	10.7	21.7
Savannah, GA	20	34.1	31.9	2.2	23	32.0	30.2	1.8
Newport News, VA	24	30.5	29.2	1.3	24	29.8	29.0	0.8
Valdez, AK	26	27.9	0.0	27.9	25	28.2	0.0	28.2
Philadelphia, PA	25	28.5	16.5	12.0	26	26.0	14.9	11.2
Richmond, CA	30	22.6	12.7	9.9	27	23.5	14.1	9.4
Portland, OR	27	25.5	17.2	8.3	28	23.4	15.0	8.4
Tacoma, WA	28	24.9	19.0	5.9	29	22.9	18.4	4.5
Port Everglades, FL	32	21.1	11.1	10.0	30	21.7	11.8	9.9
Seattle, WA	29	23.7	18.4	5.3	31	20.6	14.8	5.7
Freeport, TX	31	22.1	16.5	5.6	32	19.7	12.5	7.2
Oakland, CA	34	18.7	16.4	2.3	33	19.3	16.5	2.8
Paulsboro, NJ	35	17.4	11.5	5.8	34	19.1	12.0	7.1
Charleston, SC	33	19.1	17.0	2.1	35	18.5	16.5	2.0
Boston, MA	37	16.3	11.6	4.7	36	17.1	11.4	5.7
Two Harbors, MN	38	16.2	0.8	15.4	37	16.7	0.1	16.6
Jacksonville, FL	39	15.4	9.2	6.2	38	16.5	9.7	6.7
Chicago, IL	36	17.1	1.5	15.6	39	15.4	1.6	13.9
Honolulu, HI	40	14.3	1.0	13.4	40	14.3	1.4	12.9
Memphis, TN	41	13.6	0.0	13.6	41	14.2	0.0	14.2
Longview, WA	45	12.2	10.5	1.7	42	13.7	11.2	2.5
Detroit, MI	43	12.9	2.6	10.3	43	13.0	2.3	10.7
Indiana Harbor, IN	42	13.2	0.3	12.9	44	12.4	0.3	12.1
Portland, ME	44	12.8	11.8	1.0	45	12.0	11.1	0.9
Marcus Hook, PA	79	4.3	1.6	2.7	46	11.9	5.6	6.3
Cincinnati, OH	51	11.1	0.0	11.1	47	11.7	0.0	11.7
Cleveland, OH	50	11.3	1.4	9.9	48	11.5	1.5	9.9
Galveston, TX	47	11.6	4.8	6.9	49	11.4	4.3	7.1
Albany, NY	60	7.5	0.8	6.7	50	11.0	1.0	10.0
United States, total water ports		2,465.3	1,317.9	1,147.5		2,462.7	1,291.1	1,171.6

NOTE: Top 50 water ports are not additive due to shared tonnage between ports.

SOURCE: U.S. Army Corps of Engineers, Navigation Data Center, Waterborne Commerce Statistics Center, Principal Ports of the United States, available at www.navigationdatacenter.us/data/datappor.htm as of June 2015.

Table 1-16: Inland Waterway Mileage: 2013
(Includes only the 39 states and the District of Columbia with inland waterways)

State	Miles[1]
Alabama	1,270
Alaska	5,500
Arkansas	1,860
California	290
Connecticut	120
Delaware	100
District of Columbia	10
Florida	1,540
Georgia	720
Idaho	110
Illinois	1,100
Indiana	350
Iowa	490
Kansas	120
Kentucky	1,590
Louisiana	2,820
Maine	70
Maryland	530
Massachusetts	90
Minnesota	260
Mississippi	870
Missouri	1,030
Nebraska	320
New Hampshire	10
New Jersey	360
New York	390
North Carolina	1,150
Ohio	440
Oklahoma	150
Oregon	680
Pennsylvania	260
Rhode Island	40
South Carolina	480
South Dakota	80
Tennessee	950
Texas	830
Virginia	670
Washington	1,060
West Virginia	680
Wisconsin	230
United States, total[2]	25,000

[1]Mileages are rounded to the nearest 10 miles.
[2]States do not add to total due to waterways on state boundaries.

NOTES: The waterway mileages were determined by the following methodology: Length of channels included were those channels (Corps projects and nonprojects) with a controlling draft of 9 feet or greater, and had commercial cargo traffic reported for CY98 of CY99, and were not offshore (i.e., channels in coastal areas included only the miles from the entrance channel inward). Channels within major bays are included (e.g., Chesapeake Bay, San Francisco Bay, Puget Sound, Long Island Sound, major sounds and straits in southeastern Alaska). Channels in the Great Lakes are not included, but waterways connecting lakes and the St. Lawrence Seaway inside the United States are included.

SOURCE: U.S. Army Corps of Engineers, Waterborne Commerce Statistics Center, National Waterway Network, personal communication as of July 2015.

Table 1-17: Number of Metropolitan Planning Organizations: 2015

State	Total	Multi-state	Intra-state
Alabama	14	2	12
Alaska	2	0	2
Arizona	8	1	7
Arkansas	8	2	6
California	19	2	17
Colorado	5	0	5
Connecticut	8	0	8
Delaware	3	2	1
District of Columbia	2	2	0
Florida	27	1	26
Georgia	16	3	13
Hawaii	2	0	2
Idaho	5	1	4
Illinois	15	4	11
Indiana	14	3	11
Iowa	9	4	5
Kansas	5	1	4
Kentucky	9	4	5
Louisiana	9	0	9
Maine	4	0	4
Maryland	7	5	2
Massachusetts	10	0	10
Michigan	13	0	13
Minnesota	8	4	4
Mississippi	4	1	3
Missouri	8	2	6
Montana	3	0	3
Nebraska	4	2	2
Nevada	4	1	3
New Hampshire	4	0	4
New Jersey	3	1	2
New Mexico	5	1	4
New York	14	0	14
North Carolina	18	0	18
North Dakota	3	2	1
Ohio	17	5	12
Oklahoma	4	1	3
Oregon	9	1	8
Pennsylvania	20	2	18
Rhode Island	1	0	1
South Carolina	11	1	10
South Dakota	3	1	2
Tennessee	11	5	6
Texas	25	2	23
Utah	4	0	4
Vermont	1	0	1
Virginia	15	3	12
Washington	12	2	10
West Virginia	8	5	3
Wisconsin	14	4	10
Wyoming	2	0	2
United States, total	405	39	366
U.S. total (incl. Puerto Rico)	408	39	369

NOTES: The boundaries of multi-state metropolitan planning organizations (MPOs) cross state lines.

SOURCE: U.S. Department of Transportation, Federal Highway Administration and Federal Transit Administration, Transportation Planning Capacity Building, Metropolitan Planning Organization Database, available at www.planning. dot.gov/mpo.asp as of October 2015.

Chapter 2

Safety

Table 2-1: Highway Traffic Fatalities and Fatality Rates: 2013

State	Traffic fatalities[1]	Licensed drivers (thousands)	Registered vehicles[2] (thousands)	Vehicle-miles traveled (millions)	Population (thousands)	Fatality rate per 100,000 Population
Alabama	852	3,859	4,787	65,046	4,834	17.6
Alaska	51	529	786	4,848	737	6.9
Arizona	849	4,791	5,381	60,586	6,635	12.8
Arkansas[2]	483	2,097	2,418	33,493	2,959	16.3
California	3,000	24,390	28,075	329,534	38,431	7.8
Colorado	481	3,837	4,683	46,968	5,272	9.1
Connecticut	276	2,534	2,856	30,941	3,599	7.7
Delaware	99	724	947	9,308	925	10.7
District of Columbia	20	406	333	3,527	649	3.1
Florida	2,407	13,670	15,132	192,702	19,600	12.3
Georgia[2]	1,179	6,607	7,780	109,355	9,995	11.8
Hawaii	102	915	1,335	10,099	1,409	7.2
Idaho	214	1,111	1,692	15,980	1,613	13.3
Illinois[2]	991	8,262	10,193	105,297	12,891	7.7
Indiana	783	4,500	5,574	78,311	6,571	11.9
Iowa[2]	317	2,144	3,541	31,641	3,092	10.3
Kansas	350	2,018	2,628	30,208	2,896	12.1
Kentucky[2]	638	3,019	4,032	46,996	4,400	14.5
Louisiana[2]	703	3,278	3,957	47,758	4,629	15.2
Maine[2]	145	1,011	1,199	14,129	1,329	10.9
Maryland	465	4,140	3,834	56,688	5,939	7.8
Massachusetts[3]	326	4,766	4,985	56,311	6,709	4.9
Michigan	947	6,987	8,192	95,132	9,898	9.6
Minnesota[2]	387	3,331	5,219	56,974	5,422	7.1
Mississippi[2]	613	1,969	2,074	38,758	2,992	20.5
Missouri	757	4,280	5,821	69,458	6,045	12.5
Montana	229	767	1,540	12,033	1,015	22.6
Nebraska	211	1,375	1,891	19,322	1,869	11.3
Nevada[2]	262	1,756	2,203	24,649	2,791	9.4
New Hampshire[4,5]	135	1,061	1,409	12,903	1,323	10.2
New Jersey	542	6,081	7,061	74,530	8,912	6.1
New Mexico	310	1,457	1,882	25,086	2,087	14.9
New York[4,5]	1,199	11,211	10,674	129,737	19,696	6.1
North Carolina[6]	1,289	6,823	7,814	105,213	9,849	13.1
North Dakota	148	514	845	10,100	724	20.4
Ohio	989	8,030	10,360	112,767	11,572	8.5
Oklahoma[2]	678	2,418	3,460	47,999	3,853	17.6
Oregon	313	2,773	3,604	33,706	3,928	8.0
Pennsylvania	1,208	8,897	10,461	98,628	12,781	9.5
Rhode Island[3]	65	749	853	7,775	1,053	6.2
South Carolina	767	3,536	3,987	48,986	4,772	16.1
South Dakota[2]	135	604	1,015	9,122	846	16.0
Tennessee[2]	995	4,605	5,452	71,067	6,497	15.3
Texas[2]	3,382	15,447	20,171	244,525	26,506	12.8
Utah	220	1,661	2,061	27,005	2,903	7.6
Vermont	69	543	612	7,116	627	11.0
Virginia	740	5,603	7,051	80,767	8,270	8.9
Washington[2]	436	5,302	6,393	57,211	6,974	6.3
West Virginia	332	1,177	1,453	19,232	1,854	17.9
Wisconsin[2]	543	4,171	5,339	59,486	5,743	9.5
Wyoming[2]	87	421	831	9,309	583	14.9
United States, total	32,719	212,160	255,877	2,988,323	316,498	11.4

[1]Total fatalities includes nonoccupants of motor vehicles.
[2]State did not report active registrations and registers vehicles annually. Annual transaction data shown.
[3]State did not report active registrations and offers multi-year registrations. Data estimated from current and previously published data.
[4]State did not provide current data, licensed drivers estimated by FHWA.
[5]State did not report current year data. Previous year data used for private vehicles.
[6]State data estimated from North Carolina Department of Transportation published data and other data sources.

SOURCES: Fatalities: U.S. Department of Transportation, National Highway Traffic Safety Administration, Fatality Analysis Reporting System Encyclopedia, available at www-fars.nhtsa.dot.gov as of July 2015. Drivers, vehicles, and VMT: U.S. Department of Transportation, Federal Highway Administration, Highway Statistics, DL-22, MV-1, and VM-2, available at www.fhwa.dot.gov/policyinformation/statistics. cfm as of July 2015. Population: U.S. Department of Commerce, U.S. Census Bureau, Population Estimates, available at www.census.gov/popest as of July 2015.

Table 2-2: Passenger Car and Light Truck Occupants Killed and Restraint Use: 2013

State	Restraint used		No restraint used		Restraint use unknown		Total occupants
	Fatalities	Percent	Fatalities	Percent	Fatalities	Percent	
Alabama	271	41.0	369	55.0	25	4.0	665
Alaska	13	48.0	12	44.0	2	7.0	27
Arizona	175	39.0	227	50.0	49	11.0	451
Arkansas	135	40.0	174	51.0	31	9.0	340
California	986	61.0	500	31.0	125	8.0	1,611
Colorado	124	39.0	177	56.0	16	5.0	317
Connecticut	80	44.0	75	41.0	27	15.0	182
Delaware	26	52.0	23	46.0	1	2.0	50
District of Columbia	6	100.0	0	0.0	0	0.0	6
Florida	601	49.0	553	45.0	64	5.0	1,218
Georgia	350	43.0	376	46.0	85	10.0	811
Hawaii	15	36.0	23	55.0	4	10.0	42
Idaho	54	34.0	98	62.0	7	4.0	159
Illinois	292	45.0	276	42.0	82	13.0	650
Indiana	279	51.0	201	37.0	64	12.0	544
Iowa	108	46.0	102	43.0	27	11.0	237
Kansas	103	39.0	146	55.0	16	6.0	265
Kentucky	220	47.0	245	53.0	0	0.0	465
Louisiana	197	41.0	248	52.0	31	7.0	476
Maine	55	49.0	56	50.0	1	1.0	112
Maryland	153	55.0	108	39.0	18	6.0	279
Massachusetts	59	29.0	96	47.0	51	25.0	206
Michigan	329	55.0	183	30.0	89	15.0	601
Minnesota	149	58.0	80	31.0	30	12.0	259
Mississippi	201	41.0	284	58.0	4	1.0	489
Missouri	192	34.0	325	58.0	42	8.0	559
Montana	50	31.0	108	67.0	3	2.0	161
Nebraska	44	26.0	105	62.0	20	12.0	169
Nevada	56	46.0	57	46.0	10	8.0	123
New Hampshire	35	38.0	56	62.0	0	0.0	91
New Jersey	174	53.0	141	43.0	14	4.0	329
New Mexico	72	38.0	96	51.0	20	11.0	188
New York	337	55.0	186	30.0	91	15.0	614
North Carolina	453	52.0	355	41.0	63	7.0	871
North Dakota	28	25.0	66	59.0	18	16.0	112
Ohio	288	41.0	352	50.0	59	8.0	699
Oklahoma	200	42.0	248	52.0	26	5.0	474
Oregon	138	64.0	54	25.0	24	11.0	216
Pennsylvania	282	35.0	419	52.0	98	12.0	799
Rhode Island	17	46.0	19	51.0	1	3.0	37
South Carolina	214	44.0	242	50.0	32	7.0	488
South Dakota	32	32.0	61	61.0	7	7.0	100
Tennessee	294	41.0	351	49.0	74	10.0	719
Texas	1,107	50.0	900	41.0	198	9.0	2,205
Utah	70	50.0	57	41.0	13	9.0	140
Vermont	28	55.0	21	41.0	2	4.0	51
Virginia	248	45.0	300	55.0	1	0.0	549
Washington	164	57.0	89	31.0	34	12.0	287
West Virginia	95	38.0	113	46.0	39	16.0	247
Wisconsin	158	42.0	186	49.0	32	9.0	376
Wyoming	20	30.0	41	62.0	5	8.0	66
United States, total	9,777	46.0	9,580	45.0	1,775	8.0	21,132

NOTES: Fatalities in this table include passenger car and light truck occupants only. Occupants of other vehicle types - heavy trucks, motorcycles, and buses - are excluded, as are other types of highway-related fatalities such as pedestrian fatalities. Hence, the fatalities represented here are lower than those in table 2-1. Percentages may not add to totals due to rounding.

SOURCE: U.S. Department of Transportation, National Highway Traffic Safety Administration, Fatality Analysis Reporting System Encyclopedia, available at www-fars.nhtsa.dot.gov as of June 2015.

Table 2-3: Large Truck Involvement in Fatal Crashes: 2013

State	Total occupant fatalities in all motor vehicle crashes	Total vehicles involved in all fatal motor vehicle crashes	Large trucks			
			Occupant fatalities		Involved in fatal crashes	
			Number	Percent of state total	Number	Percent of state total
Alabama	785	1,116	25	3.2	107	2.7
Alaska	44	67	2	4.5	4	0.1
Arizona	659	1,173	11	1.7	69	1.8
Arkansas	430	638	16	3.7	86	2.2
California	2,121	4,125	33	1.6	249	6.4
Colorado	417	630	11	2.6	51	1.3
Connecticut	237	375	2	0.8	19	0.5
Delaware	73	150	2	2.7	10	0.3
District of Columbia	10	31	1	10.0	3	0.1
Florida	1,755	3,358	25	1.4	187	4.8
Georgia	970	1,636	26	2.7	157	4.0
Hawaii	75	123	3	4.0	7	0.2
Idaho	197	277	6	3.0	32	0.8
Illinois	833	1,353	17	2.0	136	3.5
Indiana	687	1,093	16	2.3	115	2.9
Iowa	294	434	10	3.4	59	1.5
Kansas	318	473	12	3.8	66	1.7
Kentucky	577	880	10	1.7	71	1.8
Louisiana	590	969	13	2.2	74	1.9
Maine	130	189	0	0.0	16	0.4
Maryland	348	648	5	1.4	61	1.6
Massachusetts	250	417	4	1.6	29	0.7
Michigan	769	1,363	7	0.9	88	2.3
Minnesota	346	563	10	2.9	74	1.9
Mississippi	554	781	17	3.1	57	1.5
Missouri	677	1,002	19	2.8	77	2.0
Montana	204	266	2	1.0	19	0.5
Nebraska	197	279	6	3.0	27	0.7
Nevada	186	372	4	2.2	24	0.6
New Hampshire	118	168	1	0.8	11	0.3
New Jersey	396	750	9	2.3	64	1.6
New Mexico	255	389	16	6.3	55	1.4
New York	816	1,579	16	2.0	114	2.9
North Carolina	1,093	1,756	16	1.5	125	3.2
North Dakota	145	215	20	13.8	64	1.6
Ohio	876	1,485	27	3.1	151	3.9
Oklahoma	604	972	29	4.8	116	3.0
Oregon	258	421	5	1.9	34	0.9
Pennsylvania	1,040	1,694	31	3.0	170	4.4
Rhode Island	48	83	0	0.0	5	0.1
South Carolina	651	1,030	10	1.5	67	1.7
South Dakota	126	184	2	1.6	18	0.5
Tennessee	901	1,400	19	2.1	121	3.1
Texas	2,837	4,651	111	3.9	493	12.6
Utah	183	289	5	2.7	21	0.5
Vermont	64	89	1	1.6	7	0.2
Virginia	654	1,001	24	3.7	100	2.6
Washington	374	593	5	1.3	38	1.0
West Virginia	302	431	9	3.0	48	1.2
Wisconsin	494	801	13	2.6	85	2.2
Wyoming	83	106	7	8.4	25	0.6
United States, total	27,051	44,868	691	2.6	3,906	8.7

SOURCE: U.S. Department of Transportation, National Highway Traffic Safety Administration, Fatality Analysis Reporting System Encyclopedia, available at www-fars.nhtsa.dot.gov as of July 2015.

Table 2-4: Key Provisions of Safety Belt Use Laws: 2012

State	Effective[1] Enforcement[2]	Base fine[3]	Seat belt required Seats[4]	Ages[5]	Exemptions
Alabama	7/18/1991 Primary	Not more than $25	Front	All	Medical reasons, model year <1965, rural mail carriers/ newspaper delivery vehicles, vehicles operating in reverse.
Alaska	9/12/1990 Primary	Not more than $15	All	16 years and older	School buses, emergency vehicles, mail or newspaper delivery vehicles, non-highway vehicles (generally, off-road or snowmobiles).
Arizona	1/1/1991 Secondary	Not more than $10	All	5-15 years	Designed for >10 passengers, model year <1972, rural mail carriers, medical reasons.
			Front	5 years and older	
Arkansas	7/15/1991 Primary	Not more than $25	Front	All	Model year < 1972. Not required when an emergency exists that threatens the life of a child or person operating a motor vehicle. Any child who is physically unable because of a medical condition (as certified by a physician) is exempted.
California	1/1/1986 Primary	Not more than $20	All	16 years and older	Medical reasons, emergency vehicles, rural postal service vehicles, newspaper delivery vehicles, recycling vehicles, taxis.
Colorado	7/1/1987 Secondary	$65	Front	All	Ambulence crew, peace officer, medical reasons, passenger buses, school buses, postal service vehicles, delivery and pickup service vehicles.
Connecticut	1/1/1986 Primary	$50[4]	Front	All	Medical reasons, emergency vehicles other than fire-fighting apparatus, postal service vehicles, newspaper delivery vehicles.
Delaware	1/1/1992 Primary	$25	All	16 years and older	Medical reasons, postal service vehicles, tractors, off-highway vehicles, electric personal assistive mobility devices.
District of Columbia	12/12/1985 Primary	$50	All	16 years and older	Vehicles manufactured before July 1, 1966; medical reasons; all seat belts occupied; seating for >8 people, taxis (6pm-6am).
Florida	7/1/1986 Primary	$30	All	6-17 years	Medical reasons; newspaper delivery vehicles; solid waste/ recyclable collection service vehicles working designated routes; persons traveling in the living quarters of a recreational vehicle or a space within a truck body primarily intended for merchandise or property; school buses; buses that transport for compensation; farm tractors or implements of husbandry; trucks >26,000 lb.
			Front	6 years and older	
Georgia	9/1/1988 Primary	Not more than $15	All	8-17 years	Pickups, vehicles designed for >10 passengers, off-road vehicles, vehicles used for frequent stops (all seats), rural postal vehicles, newspaper delivery vehicles, emergency vehicles, driver in reverse, taxis, public transit vehicles.
			Front	18 years and older	
Hawaii	12/16/1985 Primary	$45	All	8-17 years	Bus or school bus >10,000 lb, emergency vehicles, taxicabs. DOT may establish additional exemptions.
			Front	15 years and older	
Idaho	7/1/1986 Secondary	$10	All	7 years and older	Vehicles >8,000 lb, mail carriers, implements of husbandry, motorcycles.
Illinois	1/1/1988 Primary	Not more than $25	All	18 years and under if driver is under 19 years	Motorcycles, vehicles that stop frequently for medical reasons, rural letter carriers, model year <1965.
			Front	16 years and older	
Indiana	7/1/1987 Primary	Not more than $25	All	All	Medical reasons, vehicles that stop frequently, farm vehicles, RVs, postal vehicles, non-drivers in parades, public utility vehicles, towing recovery vehicles, occupant other than operator of vehicle used by a public utility in an emergency.
Iowa	7/1/1986 Primary	$50	All	17 years and under	Delivery vehicles that do not exceed 25 mph between stops, bus passengers, medical reasons, model year <1965, emergency vehicles, motorcycles, rural letter carriers.
			Front	18 years and older	
Kansas	7/1/1986 Primary[7]	$10[6]	All	14-17 years	Designed for >10 people, truck >12,000 lb, off-road vehicles, postal vehicles, vehicles delivering newspapers.
			Front	18 years and older	
Kentucky	7/15/1994 Primary	Not more than $25	All	All	Designed for >10 people, farm trucks registered for agricultural use only and with gross weight 2,000 lb or greater, motorcycles.
Louisiana	7/1/1986 Primary	$25	All	13 years and older	Vehicles with gross weight >10,000 lb, utility vehicles traveling <20 mph, model year <1981, postal vehicles, farm vehicles, persons delivering newspapers.
Maine	12/26/1995 Primary	$50	All	All	Medical reasons, rural mail carriers, persons delivering newspapers, postal vehicles, passengers riding in taxi or limousine for hire.
Maryland	7/1/1986 Primary	Not more than $26	All	15 years and under	"Historical" vehicles, for-hire vehicles, motorcycles, trucks, buses, vehicles delivering mail, vehicles built before June 1, 1964.
			Front	16 years and older	
Massachusetts	2/1/1994 Secondary	$25[8]	All	All	Buses, trucks 18,000 lb or more, taxis, utility vehicles, model year <1966, postal vehicles, farm vehicles, authorized emergency vehicles, side-facing seat in car owned for antique collecting.

Table 2-4: Key Provisions of Safety Belt Use Laws: 2012 (continued)

State	Effective[1]	Enforcement[2]	Base fine[3]	Seat belt required		Exemptions
				Seats[4]	Ages[5]	
Michigan	7/1/1985	Primary	$25	Front	All	Medical reasons, taxis, buses, school buses, postal service vehicles, model year <1965, commercial vehicles making frequent stops.
Minnesota	8/1/1986	Primary	$25	All	All	Farm pickup trucks, postal vehicles, commercial vehicles making frequent stops and going <25 mph between stops, vehicles driving in reverse, persons riding in a vehicle in which all the seating positions equipped with seat belts are occupied by other persons in seat belts, model year <1965, medical reasons.
Mississippi	7/1/1994	Primary	$25	Front	All	Vehicles driving in reverse, farm vehicles, medical reasons, buses, postal vehicles, utility meter readers' vehicles, all-terrain vehicles, vehicles designed to carry >15 persons, trailers.
Missouri	9/28/1985	Secondary (primary for <16 years old)	Not more than $10[10]	Front	All	Vehicles designed for >10 people, trucks >12,000 lb, postal service vehicles, vehicles requiring frequent entry or exit, agricultural vehicles.
Montana	10/1/1987	Secondary	$20	All	All	Medical reasons, motorcycles, taxis, vehicles making frequent stops, occupants of motor vehicle in which all seat belts are being used by other occupants.
Nebraska	1/1/1993	Secondary	$25	All	16 years and under	Taxis, mopeds, motorcycles, emergency vehicles, model year <1973, parade vehicles.
				Front	18 years and older	
Nevada	7/1/1987	Secondary	Not more than $25	All	All	Medical reasons, public transportation vehicles, postal service vehicles, emergency vehicles, delivery vehicles not exceeding 15 mph. Any vehicle or seating position if the State determines compliance is impractical.
New Hampshire	n/a	No law for persons 18 years or older (primary for <18 years old)	$50 for persons <18 years old	All	17 years and younger	n/a
New Jersey	3/1/1985	Primary (secondary for rear seat occupants)	$20	All	All	Vehicles manufactured before 1966, medical reasons, rural letter carriers, fewer belts than seats.
New Mexico	1/1/1986	Primary	$25	All	All	Vehicles >10,000 lb, medical reasons, rural letter carriers.
New York	12/1/1984	Primary	Not more than $50	All	15 years and under	Buses, school buses, taxis, liveries, emergency, rural letter carriers.
				Front	All	
North Carolina	10/1/1985	Primary (secondary for rear seat occupants)	$25.50 ($10 ofr rear seat)	All	All	Medical reasons, farm vehicles, postal vehicles, designated commercial vehicles, delivery vehicles traveling <20 mph, trash/recycling trucks.
North Dakota	7/14/1994	Secondary	Not more than $20	All	17 years and under	Designed for >10 people, farm vehicles, rural mail carriers, medical reasons, all front seat belts in use by other occupants.
				Front	All	
Ohio	5/6/1986	Secondary	$30 driver/$20 passenger	All	8-14 years	Postal service vehicles, medical reasons, vehicles delivering newspapers.
				Front	15 years and older	
Oklahoma	2/1/1987	Primary	$20	All	All	Farm vehicles, RVs, motorcycles, motorized bicycles, postal service vehicles, school buses, taxicabs, emergency vehicles.
				Front	12 years and older	
Oregon	12/7/1990	Primary	No more than $250	All	16 years and older	Vehicles in interstate commerce, designed for >15 passengers, newspaper and mail vehicles, meter and transit vehicles, for-hire vehicles, trash trucks, emergency vehicles, taxicab operators.
Pennsylvania	11/23/1987	Secondary	$10	All	8-17 years	Vehicles manufactured before 1966, medical reasons, trucks >7,000 lb, rural letter carriers, delivery vehicles, vehicles traveling <15 mph.
				Front	18 years and older	
Rhode Island	6/18/1991	Primary[12]	$85	All	18 years and older	Vehicles manufactured before 1966, medical reasons, postal service vehicles.
South Carolina	7/1/1989	Primary	Not more than $25	All	All	Medical reasons, emergency vehicles, postal service vehicles, delivery vehicles, parade vehicles; school, church, or day care buses; vehicles except taxis, vehicles in which all seating positions with seat belts are already occupied, persons occupying vehicles not originally equipped with seat belts.
South Dakota	1/1/1995	Secondary	$25	All	17 years and under	Motorcycles, motorized bicycles, vehicles manufactured before 1973, medical reasons, passenger buses, school buses, farm vehicles, rural mail carriers, newspaper or periodical delivery vehicles.
				Front	18 years and older	
Tennessee	4/21/1986	Primary	Not more than $50[13]	All	All	Vehicles >8,500 lb, rural letter carriers, utility workers, newspaper delivery vehicles, automobile salespersons who drive <50 miles per day on average, parade vehicles, hayrides crossing a highway from one field to another if operated at <15 mph.
Texas	9/1/1985	Primary	$50	All	All	Farm vehicles <48,000 lb, postal service vehicles, newspaper delivery, meter readers.

Table 2-4: Key Provisions of Safety Belt Use Laws: 2012 (continued)

State	Effective[1]	Enforcement[2]	Base fine[3]	Seat belt required Seats[4]	Ages[5]	Exemptions
Utah	4/28/1986	Secondary (primary for drivers and occupants 18 years and younger)	Not more than $45	All	All	Vehicles manufactured before 1966, medical reasons, all seats occupied or person is riding in a seating position not equipped with seat belts.
Vermont	1/1/1994	Secondary (primary for drivers and occupants 17 years and younger)	$25	All	All	Buses, taxis, rural mail carriers, delivery vehicles traveling <15 mph, emergency vehicles, farm tractors, vehicles ordered by emergency personnel to evacuate persons from stricken area.
Virginia	1/1/1988	Secondary (primary for passengers 17 years and younger in all seats)	$25	All / Front	17 years and under / 18 years and older	Medical reasons, trucks >10,000 lb, school buses, motor homes, taxis, police vehicles enforcing parking or transporting prisoners, law enforcement officers when seat belts are impractical, rural mail carriers, newspaper delivery vehicles, utility meter readers, commercial vehicles making frequent stops.
Washington	6/11/1986	Primary	$124	All	All	Medical reasons, vehicles designed for >10 people; when all designated seating positions are occupied; vehicles exempted by State regulation, including farm construction or commercial vehicles making frequent stops.
West Virginia	9/1/1993	Secondary	Not more than $25	All / Front	8-17 years / All	Motorcycles, vehicles designed for >10 people, vehicles manufactured before 1967, medical reasons, rural mail carriers, trailers. All seat belts in use and vehicle contains more passengers than total number of seat belts or other safety devices installed in compliance with Federal motor vehicle safety standards.
Wisconsin	12/1/1987	Primary	$10	All	All	Emergency vehicles in which compliance could endanger passngers; taxis, farm trucks engaged in farming, rural mail carriers, land surveyors.
Wyoming	6/8/1989	Secondary	Not more than $25[16]	All	All	Medical reasons, postal vehicles; excess passengers exempted if all seats occupied.

[1]Effective date of first belt law in the state.

[2]Primary enforcement enables police officers to stop vehicles and write citations whenever they observe a violation of the seat belt law. Secondary enforcement allows police officers to write a citation for seat belt infractions only after stopping a vehicle for some other traffic infraction.

[3]Additional processing and surcharge fees are likely to apply.

[4]The word "All" used in this category means everyone must be restrained. For children, that may be in a CR

[5]May include rear-facing CRs, forward-facing CRs, and booster seats.

[6]If a driver under 18 years old commits a violation, he/she is subject to a higher fine of $75.

[7]Secondary enforcement for other seating positions.

[8]The fine is $60 for violators 14-17 years old.

[9]Louisiana HB 197 was signed by the Governor on May 29, 2012, to expand the seat belt requirement for all seating positions to include SUVs.

[10]Drivers in Massachusetts may be fined $25 for violating the belt law themselves and $25 for each unrestrained passenger 12-16 years old.

[11]The fine is $50 for violators 8-15 years old.

[12]Rhode Island's primary seat belt law includes a sunset provision that will revert the law to secondary enforcement on June 30, 2013.

[13]In lieu of a court appearance, a first offender may pay a fine of $10; for a second or subsequent offense, the fine is $20.

[14]Upgraded to primary enforcement on May 23, 2013, effective July 9, 2013.

[15]Penalty not less than $30 or more than $75 for a violation involving children <4 years old and not less than $10 or more than $25 for children 4–8 years old.

[16]Not less than $10 for passenger or more than $25 for driver.

KEY: n/a = not applicable

NOTES: For the most current provisions of state seat belt laws, see the Insurance Institute for Highway Safety's Safety Belt Use Laws, available at /iihs.org/laws/SafetyBeltUse.aspx. For more information on child restraint laws, see Traffic Safety Facts Annual Report, available at www-nrd.nhtsa.dot.gov/Cats.

SOURCES: Effective Dates: Insurance Institute for Highway Safety, Highway Loss Data Institute, Safety Belt Use Laws, available at www.iihs.org/iihs/topics/t/safety-belts/topicoverview as of June 2015. Enforcement, Base fine, Seat belt required and Exemptions: U.S. Department of Transportation, National Highway Traffic Safety Administration, Traffic Safety Facts 2012, table 8, available at www-nrd.nhtsa.dot.gov/Cats as of June 2015.

Table 2-5: Helmet Use Laws: 2015

State	Motorcycle riders covered by helmet law	Bicycle riders covered by helmet law
Alabama	all riders	15 and younger
Alaska	17 and younger[1]	no law
Arizona	17 and younger	no law
Arkansas	20 and younger	no law
California	all riders	17 and younger
Colorado	17 and younger and passengers 17 and younger	no law
Connecticut	17 and younger	15 and younger
Delaware	18 and younger[2]	17 and younger
District of Columbia	all riders	15 and younger
Florida	20 and younger[3]	15 and younger
Georgia	all riders	15 and younger
Hawaii	17 and younger	15 and younger
Idaho	17 and younger	no law
Illinois	no law	no law
Indiana	17 and younger	no law
Iowa	no law	no law
Kansas	17 and younger	no law
Kentucky	20 and younger[4]	no law
Louisiana	all riders	11 and younger
Maine	17 and younger[5]	15 and younger
Maryland	all riders	15 and younger
Massachusetts	all riders	1-16 (riding with children younger than 1 prohibited)
Michigan	20 and younger[6]	no law
Minnesota	17 and younger[7]	no law
Mississippi	all riders	no law
Missouri	all riders	no law
Montana	17 and younger	no law
Nebraska	all riders	no law
Nevada	all riders	no law
New Hampshire	no law	15 and younger
New Jersey	all riders	16 and younger
New Mexico	17 and younger	17 and younger
New York	all riders	1-13 (riding with children younger than 1 prohibited)
North Carolina	all riders	15 and younger
North Dakota	17 and younger[8]	no law
Ohio	17 and younger[9]	no law
Oklahoma	17 and younger	no law
Oregon	all riders	15 and younger
Pennsylvania	20 and younger[10]	11 and younger
Rhode Island	20 and younger[11]	15 and younger
South Carolina	20 and younger	no law
South Dakota	17 and younger	no law
Tennessee	all riders	15 and younger
Texas	20 and younger[12]	no law
Utah	17 and younger	no law
Vermont	all riders	no law
Virginia	all riders	no law
Washington	all riders	no law
West Virginia	all riders	14 and younger
Wisconsin	17 and younger[13]	no law
Wyoming	17 and younger	no law

[1]Alaska's motorcycle helmet use law covers passengers of all ages, operators younger than 18, and operators with instructional permits.

[2]In Delaware, every motorcycle operator or rider age 19 and older must carry an approved helmet.

[3]In Florida, the law requires that all riders younger than 21 years wear helmets, without exception. Those 21 years and older may ride without helmets only if they can show proof that they are covered by a medical insurance policy.

[4]In Kentucky, the law requires that all riders younger than 21 years wear helmets, without exception. Those 21 and older may ride without helmets only if they can show proof that they are covered by a medical insurance policy. Motorcycle helmet laws in Kentucky also cover operators with instructional/learner's permits.

[5]Motorcycle helmet laws in Maine cover operators with instructional/learner's permits and operators in their first year of licensure. Maine's motorcycle helmet use law also covers passengers 17 and younger and passengers riding with operators who are required to wear a helmet.

[6]In Michigan, the law requires that all riders younger than 21 wear helmets, without exception. Those 21 and older may ride without helmets only if they carry additional insurance and have passed a motorcycle safety course or have had their motorcycle endorsement for at least two years. Motorcycle passengers who want to exercise this option also must be 21 or older and carry additional insurance.

[7]Motorcycle helmet laws in Minnesota cover operators with instructional/learner's permits.

[8]North Dakota's motorcycle helmet use law covers all passengers traveling with operators who are covered by the law.

[9]Ohio's motorcycle helmet use law covers all operators during the first year of licensure and all passengers of operators who are covered by the law.

[10]Pennsylvania's motorcycle helmet use law covers all operators during the first two years of licensure unless the operator has completed the safety course approved by PennDOT or the Motorcycle Safety Foundation.

[11]Rhode Island's motorcycle helmet use law covers all passengers (regardless of age) and all operators during the first year of licensure (regardless of age).

[12]Texas exempts riders 21 or older if they can either show proof of successfully completing a motorcycle operator training and safety course or can show proof of having a medical insurance policy. A peace officer may not stop or detain a person who is the operator of or a passenger on a motorcycle for the sole purpose of determining whether the person has successfully completed the motorcycle operator training and safety course or is covered by a health insurance plan.

[13]Motorcycle helmet laws in Wisconsin cover operators with instructional/learner's permits.

SOURCE: Insurance Institute for Highway Safety, Highway Loss Data Institute, Motorcycle and bicycle helmet use laws, available at www.iihs.org/iihs/topics#statelaws as of June 2015.

Table 2-6: Safety Belt Use: 2000, 2005, 2010, 2013, 2014
(Percentage of drivers and passengers in the front right seat using safety belts)

State	2000	2005	2010	2013	2014
Alabama	70.6	81.8	91.4	97.3	95.7
Alaska	61.0	78.4	86.8	86.1	88.4
Arizona	75.2	94.2	81.8	84.7	87.2
Arkansas	52.4	68.3	78.3	76.7	74.4
California	88.9	92.5	96.2	97.4	97.1
Colorado	65.1	79.2	82.9	82.1	82.4
Connecticut	76.3	81.6	88.2	86.6	85.1
Delaware	66.1	83.8	90.7	92.2	91.9
District of Columbia	82.6	88.8	92.3	95.2	92.4
Florida	64.8	73.9	87.4	87.2	88.8
Georgia	73.6	89.9	89.6	95.5	97.3
Hawaii	80.4	95.3	97.6	94.0	93.5
Idaho	58.6	76.0	77.9	81.6	80.2
Illinois	70.2	86.0	92.6	93.7	94.1
Indiana	62.1	81.2	92.4	91.6	90.2
Iowa	78.0	87.1	93.1	91.9	92.8
Kansas	61.6	69.0	81.8	80.7	85.7
Kentucky	60.0	66.7	80.3	85.0	86.1
Louisiana	68.2	77.7	75.9	82.5	84.1
Maine	U	75.8	82.0	83.0	85.0
Maryland	85.0	91.1	94.7	90.7	92.1
Massachusetts	50.0	64.8	73.7	74.8	76.6
Michigan	83.5	92.9	95.2	93.0	93.3
Minnesota	73.4	83.9	92.3	94.8	94.7
Mississippi	50.4	60.8	81.0	74.4	78.3
Missouri	67.7	77.4	76.0	80.1	78.8
Montana	75.6	80.0	78.9	74.0	74.0
Nebraska	70.5	79.2	84.1	79.1	79.0
Nevada	78.5	94.8	93.2	94.8	94.0
New Hampshire	U	U	72.2	68.6	73.0
New Jersey	74.2	86.0	93.7	88.3	91.0
New Mexico	86.6	89.5	89.8	91.4	92.0
New York	77.3	85.0	89.8	90.4	91.1
North Carolina	80.5	86.7	89.7	87.5	88.6
North Dakota	47.7	76.3	74.8	80.9	77.7
Ohio	65.3	78.7	83.8	84.5	85.0
Oklahoma	67.5	83.1	85.9	83.6	86.3
Oregon	83.6	93.3	97.0	98.2	97.8
Pennsylvania	70.7	83.3	86.0	84.0	83.6
Rhode Island	64.4	74.7	78.0	77.5	85.6
South Carolina	73.9	69.7	85.4	90.5	91.7
South Dakota	53.4	68.8	74.5	66.5	68.7
Tennessee	59.0	74.4	87.1	84.8	87.7
Texas	76.6	89.9	93.8	90.3	90.7
Utah	75.7	86.9	89.0	82.4	83.4
Vermont	61.6	84.7	85.2	84.9	84.1
Virginia	69.9	80.4	80.5	79.7	77.3
Washington	81.6	95.2	97.6	94.5	94.5
West Virginia	49.8	84.9	82.1	84.0	82.2
Wisconsin	65.4	73.3	79.2	82.4	84.7
Wyoming	66.8	U	78.9	81.9	79.2
Nationwide	71.0	82.0	85.0	87.0	87.0

KEY: U = unavailable
SOURCE: U.S. Department of Transportation, *National Highway Traffic Safety Administration*, Seat Belt Use in 2014—Use Rates in the States and Territories, available at www-nrd.nhtsa.dot.gov/Cats as of June 2015.

Table 2-7: Pedestrian Fatalities Involving Motor Vehicles: 2013

State	Total traffic fatalities	Pedestrians killed	Pedestrian fatalities as percent of total	Population (thousands)	Pedestrian fatality rate per 100,000 population
Alabama	852	59	6.9	4,834	1.2
Alaska	51	6	11.8	737	0.8
Arizona	849	151	17.8	6,635	2.3
Arkansas	483	45	9.3	2,959	1.5
California	3,000	701	23.4	38,431	1.8
Colorado	481	50	10.4	5,272	0.9
Connecticut	276	36	13.0	3,599	1.0
Delaware	99	25	25.3	925	2.7
District of Columbia	20	9	45.0	649	1.4
Florida	2,407	501	20.8	19,600	2.6
Georgia	1,179	176	14.9	9,995	1.8
Hawaii	102	23	22.5	1,409	1.6
Idaho	214	14	6.5	1,613	0.9
Illinois	991	125	12.6	12,891	1.0
Indiana	783	77	9.8	6,571	1.2
Iowa	317	20	6.3	3,092	0.6
Kansas	350	25	7.1	2,896	0.9
Kentucky	638	55	8.6	4,400	1.3
Louisiana	703	97	13.8	4,629	2.1
Maine	145	11	7.6	1,329	0.8
Maryland	465	108	23.2	5,939	1.8
Massachusetts	326	68	20.9	6,709	1.0
Michigan	947	148	15.6	9,898	1.5
Minnesota	387	32	8.3	5,422	0.6
Mississippi	613	53	8.6	2,992	1.8
Missouri	757	73	9.6	6,045	1.2
Montana	229	24	10.5	1,015	2.4
Nebraska	211	12	5.7	1,869	0.6
Nevada	262	65	24.8	2,791	2.3
New Hampshire	135	12	8.9	1,323	0.9
New Jersey	542	129	23.8	8,912	1.4
New Mexico	310	49	15.8	2,087	2.3
New York	1,199	335	27.9	19,696	1.7
North Carolina	1,289	173	13.4	9,849	1.8
North Dakota	148	1	0.7	724	0.1
Ohio	989	85	8.6	11,572	0.7
Oklahoma	678	58	8.6	3,853	1.5
Oregon	313	48	15.3	3,928	1.2
Pennsylvania	1,208	147	12.2	12,781	1.2
Rhode Island	65	14	21.5	1,053	1.3
South Carolina	767	100	13.0	4,772	2.1
South Dakota	135	9	6.7	846	1.1
Tennessee	995	80	8.0	6,497	1.2
Texas	3,382	480	14.2	26,506	1.8
Utah	220	28	12.7	2,903	1.0
Vermont	69	5	7.2	627	0.8
Virginia	740	75	10.1	8,270	0.9
Washington	436	49	11.2	6,974	0.7
West Virginia	332	28	8.4	1,854	1.5
Wisconsin	543	37	6.8	5,743	0.6
Wyoming	87	4	4.6	583	0.7
United States, total	32,719	4,735	14.5	316,498	1.5

NOTE: Details may not add to totals due to rounding.

SOURCE: Fatalities: U.S. Department of Transportation, National Highway Traffic Safety Administration, Fatality Analysis Reporting System Encyclopedia, available at www-fars.nhtsa.dot.gov as of June 2015. Population: U.S. Department of Commerce, U.S. Census Bureau, Population Estimates, available at www.census.gov/popest as of June 2015.

Table 2-8: Fatalities in Motor Vehicle Crashes Involving High Blood Alcohol Concentration: 2012 and 2013

(BAC ≥ 0.08 grams per deciliter)

State	2012			2013		
	Total fatalities	Fatalities involving high blood alcohol	Percent	Total fatalities	Fatalities involving high blood alcohol	Percent
Alabama	865	257	29.7	852	260	31.0
Alaska	59	15	25.4	51	15	30.0
Arizona	825	227	27.5	849	219	26.0
Arkansas	552	143	25.9	483	123	25.0
California	2,857	802	28.1	3,000	867	29.0
Colorado	472	133	28.2	481	142	30.0
Connecticut	236	85	36.0	276	114	41.0
Delaware	114	34	29.8	99	38	39.0
District of Columbia	15	4	26.7	20	6	31.0
Florida	2,424	697	28.8	2,407	676	28.0
Georgia	1,192	301	25.3	1,179	297	25.0
Hawaii	126	51	40.5	102	33	33.0
Idaho	184	54	29.3	214	58	27.0
Illinois	956	321	33.6	991	322	32.0
Indiana	779	228	29.3	783	198	25.0
Iowa	365	92	25.2	317	103	32.0
Kansas	405	98	24.2	350	102	29.0
Kentucky	746	168	22.5	638	167	26.0
Louisiana	722	241	33.4	703	234	33.0
Maine	164	49	29.9	145	42	29.0
Maryland	505	160	31.7	465	141	30.0
Massachusetts	349	123	35.2	326	118	36.0
Michigan	938	259	27.6	947	255	27.0
Minnesota	395	114	28.9	387	95	25.0
Mississippi	582	179	30.8	613	210	34.0
Missouri	826	280	33.9	757	248	33.0
Montana	205	89	43.4	229	92	40.0
Nebraska	212	74	34.9	211	60	28.0
Nevada	258	82	31.8	262	79	30.0
New Hampshire	108	32	29.6	135	46	34.0
New Jersey	589	164	27.8	542	146	27.0
New Mexico	365	97	26.6	310	93	30.0
New York	1,168	344	29.5	1,199	364	30.0
North Carolina	1,292	402	31.1	1,289	371	29.0
North Dakota	170	72	42.4	148	62	42.0
Ohio	1,123	385	34.3	989	271	27.0
Oklahoma	708	205	29.0	678	170	25.0
Oregon	336	86	25.6	313	105	33.0
Pennsylvania	1,310	408	31.1	1,208	368	30.0
Rhode Island	64	24	37.5	65	24	38.0
South Carolina	863	358	41.5	767	335	44.0
South Dakota	133	45	33.8	135	41	31.0
Tennessee	1,014	295	29.1	995	277	28.0
Texas	3,398	1,296	38.1	3,382	1,337	40.0
Utah	217	34	15.7	220	38	17.0
Vermont	77	23	29.9	69	18	27.0
Virginia	777	211	27.2	740	254	34.0
Washington	444	145	32.7	436	149	34.0
West Virginia	339	95	28.0	332	91	27.0
Wisconsin	615	200	32.5	543	178	33.0
Wyoming	123	40	32.5	87	25	29.0
United States, total	33,561	10,322	30.8	32,719	10,076	31.0

NOTE: National Highway Traffic Safety Administration estimates the proportion of fatalities with a high Blood Alcohol Concentration for cases in which alcohol test results are unknown. The sum of individual state fatalities with a high BAC may therefore not add to the U.S. total due to rounding of these estimates.

SOURCE: U.S. Department of Transportation, National Highway Traffic Safety Administration, *Traffic Safety Fact Sheet, Alcohol-Impaired Driving*, available at www-nrd.nhtsa.dot.gov/Cats as of June 2015.

Table 2-9: Maximum Posted Speed Limits by Type of Road: 2015
(Speed limit in miles per hour)

State	Interstate		Other limited-access roads	Other roads
	Rural	Urban		
Alabama	70	65	65	65
Alaska	65	55	65	55
Arizona	75	65	65	65; trucks: 65
Arkansas	70; trucks: 65	65[1]	65[1]	65[1]
California	70; trucks: 55	65; trucks: 55	70; trucks: 55	65; trucks: 55
Colorado	75	65	65	65
Connecticut	65	55	65	55
Delaware	65	55	65	55
District of Columbia	n/a	55	n/a	25
Florida	70	65	70	65
Georgia	70	70	65	65
Hawaii	60[2]	60[2]	55[2]	45[2]
Idaho	75; 80 on specified segments of road[3]; trucks: 70	75; 80 on specified segments of road[3]; trucks: 65	70	70
Illinois	70[4]	55	65	55
Indiana	70; trucks: 65	55	60	55
Iowa	70	55	70	65
Kansas	75	75	75	65
Kentucky	65; 70 on specified segments of road[5]	65	65	55
Louisiana	75	70	70	65
Maine	75	75	75	60
Maryland	70 (effective, October 1, 2015)	70 (effective, October 1, 2015)	70 (effective, October 1, 2015	55
Massachusetts	65	65	65	55
Michigan	70 (trucks 60); <70 (trucks 55)	65	70	55
Minnesota	70	65	65	60
Mississippi	70	70	70	65
Missouri	70	60	70	65
Montana	80 (effective, October 1, 2015); trucks: 65	65	day: 70; night: 65	day: 70; night: 65
Nebraska	75	65	65	60
Nevada	80 (effective, October 1, 2015)	65	70	70
New Hampshire	65; 70 on specified segments of road[6]	65	55	55
New Jersey	65	55	65	55
New Mexico	75	75	65	55
New York	65	65	65	55
North Carolina	70	70	70	55
North Dakota	75	75	70	65
Ohio	70	65	70	55
Oklahoma	75	70	70	70
Oregon	65; trucks: 55	55	55	55
Pennsylvania	70	70	70	55
Rhode Island	65	55	55	55
South Carolina	70	70	60	55
South Dakota	80	80[7]	70	70
Tennessee	70	70	70	65
Texas	75; 80 or 85 on specified segment of road[8]	75	75	75
Utah	75; 80 on specified segments of road[9]	65	75	65
Vermont	65	55	50	50
Virginia	70	70	65	55
Washington	70; 75 on specified segments of road[10] (effective August 2015); trucks: 60	60	60	60
West Virginia	70	55	65	55
Wisconsin	70	70	70	55
Wyoming	75; 80 on specified segments of road[11]	75; 80 on specified segments of road[11]	70	70

[1]In Arkansas, the speed limit may be raised on particular two-lane or four-lane highways to 65 mph if based on traffic and engineering studies.
[2]In Hawaii, the maximum speed limit is established by county ordinance or by the director of transportation.
[3]In Idaho, the speed limit may be increased to 80 mph on specific segments of highway on the basis of an engineering and traffic investigation.
[4]The Illinois law allows Cook, DuPage, Kane, Lake, Madison, McHenry, St. Clair and Will Counties to opt-out by adopting an ordinance that sets a lower maximum speed limit, empowering counties to make adjustments based on their own local needs. These counties have a maximum large truck speed limit of 60 mph outside of urban districts and 55 mph inside urban districts.
[5]In Kentucky, the speed limit may be increased to 70 mph on specific segments of highway on the basis of an engineering and traffic investigation.
[6]2013 New Hampshire House Bill 146 raised the speed limit from 65 to 70 mph on the portion of I-93 from mile marker 45 to the Vermont border.
[7]The Transportation Commission may establish a maximum speed limit of less than 80 upon any highway or portion of highway under the jurisdiction of the Department of Transportation, and any portion of highway under the jurisdiction of a state or federal agency.
[8]Sections of I-10 and I-20 in West Texas and sections of Highway 45 in Travis County have a speed limit for passenger cars and light trucks of 80 mph. Speed limits of up to 85 mph may be established if the highway is originally constructed and designed to accommodate the higher speed and it has been determined by an engineering study to be reasonable and safe. State Highway 130 (portions toll) has a posted limit of 85 mph.
[9]In Utah, the speed limit may be increased beyond 75 mph on any freeway or limited access highway on the basis of an engineering and traffic investigation. The highest posted limit in Utah is currently 80mph.
[10]In Washington State, maximum speed limits on highways or portions of highways may be posted as high as 75 mph if based on a traffic and engineering study, effective August 2015.
[11]In Wyoming, the speed limit may be increased to 80 mph on specific segments of highway on the basis of an engineering and traffic investigation.

NOTES:Interstates are divided into urban and rural sections based primarily on population size and population density. Many roads, particularly urban interstates, often have a lower posted speed limit than the maximum allowable shown in this table.

SOURCE: Insurance Institute for Highway Safety, Highway Loss Data Institute, Maximum posted speed limits, available at www.iihs.org/iihs/topics/t/speed/topicoverview as of June 2015.

Table 2-10: Rail Accidents/Incidents: 2013
(Includes freight railroad, Amtrak, and commuter rail operations)

State	Accidents/Incidents	Fatalities	Injuries
Alabama	202	18	109
Alaska	41	0	39
Arizona	104	7	69
Arkansas	139	10	82
California	806	108	585
Colorado	113	7	77
Connecticut	128	4	247
Delaware	62	0	53
District of Columbia	136	0	135
Florida	318	34	221
Georgia	276	28	201
Hawaii	0	0	0
Idaho	66	6	29
Illinois	984	35	727
Indiana	301	31	185
Iowa	163	13	96
Kansas	197	8	110
Kentucky	134	14	74
Louisiana	248	13	145
Maine	33	1	19
Maryland	147	10	124
Massachusetts	204	7	177
Michigan	189	9	116
Minnesota	237	11	158
Mississippi	105	9	82
Missouri	221	9	158
Montana	104	2	70
Nebraska	202	3	127
Nevada	37	3	23
New Hampshire	4	0	3
New Jersey	779	21	739
New Mexico	96	17	48
New York	1,293	30	1310
North Carolina	215	25	151
North Dakota	110	5	83
Ohio	284	31	157
Oklahoma	167	15	79
Oregon	126	7	89
Pennsylvania	635	23	527
Rhode Island	34	0	32
South Carolina	112	15	97
South Dakota	37	1	20
Tennessee	198	7	108
Texas	777	52	449
Utah	79	8	45
Vermont	26	2	21
Virginia	216	10	160
Washington	188	15	137
West Virginia	105	13	89
Wisconsin	166	6	111
Wyoming	54	1	27
United States, total	11,598	704	8,720

NOTE: Data are preliminary. Accidents/Incidents includes all events reportable to the U.S. Department of Transportation, Federal Railroad Administration under applicable regulations. These include: train accidents, reported on Form F 6180.54, comprised of collisions, derailments, and other events involving the operation of on-track equipment and causing reportable damage above an established threshold ($9,200 for 2010, per 49 CFR 225.19); highway-rail grade crossing incidents, reported on Form F 6180.57, involving impact between railroad on-track equipment and highway users at crossings; and other incidents, reported on Form F 6180.55a, involving all other reportable incidents or exposures that cause a fatality or injury to any person, or an occupational illness to a railroad employee.

SOURCE: U.S. Department of Transportation, Federal Railroad Administration, Office of Safety Analysis, available at safetydata.fra.dot. gov/OfficeofSafety as of July 2015.

Table 2-11: Highway-Rail Grade Crossing Incidents: 2013
(Includes freight railroad, Amtrak, and commuter rail operations)

State	Number of grade crossings	Incidents	Fatalities	Injuries
Alabama	4,550	85	5	45
Alaska	282	0	0	0
Arizona	1,157	23	0	8
Arkansas	3,983	37	5	18
California	9,297	146	37	76
Colorado	2,781	15	3	5
Connecticut	635	2	0	1
Delaware	393	7	0	1
District of Columbia	36	0	0	0
Florida	5,065	65	8	19
Georgia	7,549	96	13	65
Hawaii	8	0	0	0
Idaho	2,359	25	4	7
Illinois	11,955	126	13	40
Indiana	7,634	93	15	36
Iowa	6,910	49	5	25
Kansas	7,873	46	3	12
Kentucky	4,649	49	6	22
Louisiana	5,015	72	6	31
Maine	1,668	3	0	1
Maryland	1,278	11	2	14
Massachusetts	1,434	16	1	7
Michigan	7,149	61	3	26
Minnesota	6,801	53	6	34
Mississippi	4,306	43	3	34
Missouri	5,735	53	2	31
Montana	3,109	13	1	6
Nebraska	4,976	41	2	23
Nevada	542	4	1	1
New Hampshire	584	0	0	0
New Jersey	2,133	41	6	38
New Mexico	1,236	12	4	4
New York	5,368	35	7	11
North Carolina	7,125	56	7	29
North Dakota	4,723	27	3	18
Ohio	8,533	71	8	25
Oklahoma	5,036	42	8	13
Oregon	3,953	15	2	3
Pennsylvania	6,118	60	3	22
Rhode Island	144	0	0	0
South Carolina	3,928	44	5	21
South Dakota	2,927	13	1	5
Tennessee	4,619	62	2	25
Texas	13,857	225	19	95
Utah	1,257	17	4	5
Vermont	881	4	0	2
Virginia	4,451	33	1	9
Washington	4,801	24	3	7
West Virginia	3,356	19	2	28
Wisconsin	6,387	60	2	22
Wyoming	1,085	4	1	2
United States, total	211,631	2,098	232	972

NOTES: Data are preliminary. Any impact, regardless of severity, between railroad on-track equipment and any user of a public or private crossing site must be reported to the U.S. Department of Transportation, Federal Railroad Administration on Form F 6180.57. The crossing site includes sidewalks and pathways at, or associated with, the crossing. Counts of Fatalities and Injuries include motor vehicle occupants, people not in vehicles or the trains, as well as people on the train or railroad equipment.

SOURCE: U.S. Department of Transportation, Federal Railroad Administration, Office of Safety Analysis, available at safetydata.fra.dot.gov/OfficeofSafety as of July 2015.

Table 2-12: Highway-Rail Grade Crossings by Type: 2013
(Includes freight railroad, Amtrak, and commuter rail operations)

State	Total (number)	Percent of total Public, motor vehicle	Percent of total Private, motor vehicle	Percent of total Pedestrian
Alabama	4,550	61.3	38.0	0.7
Alaska	282	63.5	34.4	2.1
Arizona	1,157	63.1	36.6	0.3
Arkansas	3,983	67.9	31.9	0.2
California	9,297	63.0	35.1	1.9
Colorado	2,781	61.0	37.7	1.3
Connecticut	635	57.0	41.6	1.4
Delaware	393	68.7	30.8	0.5
District of Columbia	36	13.9	58.3	27.8
Florida	5,065	74.5	24.4	1.1
Georgia	7,549	68.2	31.1	0.7
Hawaii	8	100.0	0.0	0.0
Idaho	2,359	54.0	45.6	0.4
Illinois	11,955	65.0	32.0	3.0
Indiana	7,634	74.6	24.5	0.9
Iowa	6,910	62.7	36.7	0.6
Kansas	7,873	65.5	34.2	0.3
Kentucky	4,649	48.8	50.1	1.1
Louisiana	5,015	54.2	45.1	0.7
Maine	1,668	49.4	49.9	0.7
Maryland	1,278	49.1	49.1	1.7
Massachusetts	1,434	58.0	39.7	2.3
Michigan	7,149	67.6	31.1	1.3
Minnesota	6,801	64.1	35.0	0.9
Mississippi	4,306	51.2	48.3	0.5
Missouri	5,735	60.1	39.1	0.9
Montana	3,109	44.6	55.0	0.4
Nebraska	4,976	60.5	39.2	0.2
Nevada	542	53.5	45.6	0.9
New Hampshire	584	55.5	40.8	3.8
New Jersey	2,133	70.6	26.1	3.3
New Mexico	1,236	58.3	39.8	1.9
New York	5,368	49.9	48.8	1.3
North Carolina	7,125	55.6	43.4	1.0
North Dakota	4,723	73.6	26.0	0.4
Ohio	8,533	66.8	32.4	0.8
Oklahoma	5,036	73.9	25.9	0.3
Oregon	3,953	45.1	53.6	1.2
Pennsylvania	6,118	56.7	41.7	1.5
Rhode Island	144	46.5	35.4	18.1
South Carolina	3,928	67.0	32.0	1.0
South Dakota	2,927	63.9	35.9	0.2
Tennessee	4,619	59.7	39.6	0.7
Texas	13,857	66.0	33.8	0.2
Utah	1,257	54.4	45.3	0.3
Vermont	881	42.2	55.5	2.3
Virginia	4,451	42.5	56.7	0.9
Washington	4,801	49.2	49.8	1.0
West Virginia	3,356	41.7	56.9	1.4
Wisconsin	6,387	62.9	35.7	1.5
Wyoming	1,085	35.0	65.0	0.0
United States, total	211,631	58.5	40.4	2.0

NOTE: Data are preliminary.

SOURCE: U.S. Department of Transportation, Federal Railroad Administration, *Railroad Safety Statistics Preliminary Annual Report*, table 9-2, available at safetydata.fra.dot.gov/OfficeofSafety/publicsite/Prelim.aspx as of July 2015.

Table 2-13: Warning Devices at Public Highway-Rail Grade Crossings: 2013

State	Total (number)	Cross bucks	Gates	Flashing lights	Stop signs	Unknown	Special warning	HWTS, WW, bells	Other
		Percent of total							
Alabama	2,791	25.9	29.2	18.0	23.6	1.5	0.4	1.0	0.3
Alaska	179	26.3	43.0	4.5	19.0	2.2	2.8	0.0	2.2
Arizona	730	10.4	2.1	57.7	1.4	1.0	0.4	6.6	20.5
Arkansas	2,705	53.3	16.6	13.9	8.0	3.7	1.6	2.8	0.0
California	5,853	27.0	52.1	12.1	3.3	1.6	0.4	2.7	0.2
Colorado	1,697	46.7	29.0	10.0	9.1	1.9	1.2	1.8	0.4
Connecticut	362	6.4	29.0	39.2	12.2	2.2	7.7	1.7	0.0
Delaware	270	8.1	26.7	57.0	0.4	0.7	5.9	0.4	0.4
District of Columbia	5	0.0	0.0	40.0	20.0	0.0	40.0	0.0	0.0
Florida	3,774	14.9	65.6	10.6	5.1	0.9	1.6	0.3	0.1
Georgia	5,149	21.2	40.1	4.8	22.3	1.9	2.2	6.6	0.3
Hawaii	8	75.0	0.0	0.0	12.5	0.0	0.0	0.0	12.5
Idaho	1,273	30.8	13.4	13.6	41.2	0.7	0.1	0.2	0.0
Illinois	7,768	28.8	43.4	22.0	1.0	1.1	0.8	1.4	0.1
Indiana	5,693	21.7	36.7	20.3	16.7	1.1	0.1	2.7	0.2
Iowa	4,331	47.1	23.2	18.3	9.8	0.5	0.4	0.4	0.0
Kansas	5,153	57.7	29.1	6.7	3.6	1.0	0.7	1.1	0.1
Kentucky	2,269	40.0	21.1	29.4	2.2	3.9	1.6	0.5	0.0
Louisiana	2,717	35.7	35.8	15.1	9.2	3.1	0.6	0.2	0.2
Maine	824	31.8	12.6	46.1	1.3	0.1	6.8	0.6	0.0
Maryland	628	29.6	21.2	33.3	5.6	4.1	3.5	2.2	0.5
Massachusetts	832	13.2	41.0	32.1	1.3	3.4	6.5	1.6	0.4
Michigan	4,831	19.5	23.4	24.5	28.4	1.6	1.1	1.4	0.1
Minnesota	4,362	34.5	28.2	7.7	27.9	0.6	0.3	0.1	0.2
Mississippi	2,206	33.4	22.4	18.4	18.3	2.4	1.1	1.2	2.5
Missouri	3,444	45.0	29.6	16.9	3.2	2.7	1.4	1.0	0.1
Montana	1,388	57.3	22.2	11.6	5.3	1.3	0.4	0.1	1.7
Nebraska	3,012	61.0	22.8	5.9	7.7	2.0	0.3	0.2	0.0
Nevada	290	30.7	45.9	6.9	13.8	1.0	0.7	0.3	0.7
New Hampshire	324	27.8	10.2	33.6	15.4	3.4	6.2	0.3	0.3
New Jersey	1,505	15.1	33.0	38.4	1.2	3.8	6.6	1.3	0.0
New Mexico	720	41.0	39.6	9.2	4.3	1.4	0.0	0.0	0.1
New York	2,676	16.4	65.4	9.3	1.3	1.6	3.2	2.1	0.3
North Carolina	3,961	23.0	55.9	10.1	3.4	2.5	1.9	0.7	0.4
North Dakota	3,478	79.2	16.7	0.0	1.7	1.7	0.5	0.0	0.0
Ohio	5,703	31.5	50.1	13.6	2.1	0.4	0.5	1.5	0.0
Oklahoma	3,720	54.0	25.5	12.2	5.3	1.1	1.2	0.4	0.0
Oregon	1,784	28.9	41.6	3.4	20.9	1.7	1.5	0.6	0.8
Pennsylvania	3,470	28.2	27.9	29.1	4.8	1.7	4.8	2.2	0.4
Rhode Island	67	6.0	23.9	22.4	0.0	9.0	13.4	25.4	0.0
South Carolina	2,632	15.6	43.8	11.8	24.5	0.0	1.9	2.1	0.1
South Dakota	1,871	76.9	4.4	12.3	2.9	3.4	0.0	0.1	0.1
Tennessee	2,759	37.9	30.4	20.7	5.4	1.7	2.8	0.8	0.1
Texas	9,150	31.1	48.7	8.3	3.7	1.3	0.5	4.7	0.1
Utah	684	22.2	36.7	12.9	18.7	1.9	4.1	1.6	0.1
Vermont	372	27.7	12.1	44.4	6.2	0.5	7.8	0.3	0.0
Virginia	1,890	15.1	64.4	15.1	2.2	0.8	0.3	1.1	0.2
Washington	2,363	46.8	26.6	12.7	3.8	7.9	0.9	1.1	0.2
West Virginia	1,400	40.6	17.2	32.9	2.6	4.9	0.6	0.5	0.4
Wisconsin	4,016	34.4	22.5	22.9	18.0	0.8	0.3	0.7	0.2
Wyoming	380	27.9	54.7	12.4	2.4	0.5	0.3	0.8	0.0
United States, total	129,469	34.5	35.3	15.4	9.3	1.7	1.3	1.7	0.3

KEY: HWTS = highway traffic signals; WW = wigwags.

SOURCE: U.S. Department of Transportation, Federal Railroad Administration, *Railroad Safety Statistics Preliminary Annual Report*, table 9-4, available at safetydata.fra.dot.gov/OfficeofSafety/publicsite/Prelim.aspx as of July 2015.

Table 2-14: Train Accident/Incident Fatalities, Including at Highway-Rail Crossings, by Category of Person Killed: 2013
(Includes freight railroad, Amtrak, and commuter rail operations)

State	Worker on duty[1]	Passenger on train	Trespasser	Non-trespasser	Other
Alabama	0	0	12	3	0
Alaska	0	0	0	0	0
Arizona	0	0	6	1	0
Arkansas	0	0	4	4	1
California	0	0	99	6	0
Colorado	0	0	4	2	0
Connecticut	1	0	2	1	0
Delaware	0	0	0	0	0
District of Columbia	0	0	0	0	0
Florida	1	1	27	3	0
Georgia	0	0	19	5	0
Hawaii	0	0	0	0	0
Idaho	0	0	2	4	0
Illinois	1	0	28	6	0
Indiana	0	0	22	6	0
Iowa	0	1	6	4	0
Kansas	0	0	8	0	0
Kentucky	0	0	9	5	0
Louisiana	0	0	10	3	0
Maine	0	0	1	0	0
Maryland	0	0	8	0	0
Massachusetts	0	0	7	0	0
Michigan	0	0	8	1	0
Minnesota	0	0	7	4	0
Mississippi	0	0	7	2	0
Missouri	1	0	5	2	1
Montana	0	0	1	1	0
Nebraska	0	0	2	1	0
Nevada	0	0	2	1	0
New Hampshire	0	0	0	0	0
New Jersey	0	0	18	2	0
New Mexico	2	0	12	1	0
New York	1	1	21	2	1
North Carolina	1	0	23	1	0
North Dakota	0	0	2	3	0
Ohio	2	0	23	6	0
Oklahoma	0	0	9	4	0
Oregon	0	0	5	1	0
Pennsylvania	2	0	19	1	0
Rhode Island	0	0	0	0	0
South Carolina	0	0	12	2	0
South Dakota	0	0	0	1	0
Tennessee	0	0	5	2	0
Texas	1	0	33	16	0
Utah	0	0	5	2	1
Vermont	0	0	2	0	0
Virginia	0	0	10	1	0
Washington	0	0	15	0	0
West Virginia	0	0	10	2	1
Wisconsin	0	0	4	2	0
Wyoming	0	0	1	0	0
United States, total	13	3	535	114	5

[1] Includes railroad employees, contractors, and volunteers.

NOTE: As defined by the U.S. Department of Transportation, Federal Railroad Administration, a Trespasser is any person on a part of railroad property used in railroad operations whose presence is prohibited, forbidden, or unlawful. Employees who are trespassing on railroad property are reported as Trespassers. Nontrespassers are persons lawfully on that part of railroad property that is used in railroad operation (other than defined as employees, passengers, trespassers, volunteers, or contractor employees), and persons adjacent to railroad premises when they are injured as the result of the operation of a railroad. "Other" includes employees not on duty, nontrespassers off railroad property, and volunteers or contractors who are not engaged in either the operation of on-track equipment or any other safety-sensitive function for the railroad.

SOURCE: U.S. Department of Transportation, Federal Railroad Administration, Office of Safety Analysis, available at safetydata. fra.dot.gov/OfficeofSafety as of July 2015.

Table 2-15: Train Accident/Incident Injuries, Including at Highway-Rail Crossings, by Category of Person Injured: 2013

(Includes freight railroad, Amtrak, and commuter rail operations)

State	Worker on duty[1]	Passenger on train	Trespasser	Non-trespasser	Other
Alabama	49	4	19	26	2
Alaska	36	1	0	0	0
Arizona	32	12	12	7	1
Arkansas	49	3	4	8	2
California	206	137	67	72	19
Colorado	51	12	0	7	3
Connecticut	82	19	2	6	2
Delaware	40	5	1	4	1
District of Columbia	80	30	0	19	0
Florida	68	52	23	36	11
Georgia	76	8	33	28	13
Hawaii	0	0	0	0	0
Idaho	20	0	2	5	0
Illinois	351	129	46	101	44
Indiana	108	5	27	14	2
Iowa	50	6	4	18	5
Kansas	78	1	2	17	1
Kentucky	32	1	8	13	9
Louisiana	69	6	12	24	4
Maine	13	3	2	1	0
Maryland	57	28	7	17	1
Massachusetts	108	34	9	16	2
Michigan	62	17	6	25	0
Minnesota	95	7	7	19	3
Mississippi	22	19	5	8	0
Missouri	77	16	10	25	5
Montana	51	9	2	3	1
Nebraska	86	3	5	19	2
Nevada	8	6	6	2	0
New Hampshire	3	0	0	0	0
New Jersey	292	238	16	128	9
New Mexico	26	8	6	2	0
New York	549	265	24	333	22
North Carolina	53	35	18	23	7
North Dakota	48	7	4	12	2
Ohio	80	7	23	9	8
Oklahoma	43	1	18	9	2
Oregon	46	15	6	10	6
Pennsylvania	314	56	28	75	11
Rhode Island	18	9	0	3	0
South Carolina	20	15	13	17	2
South Dakota	14	0	0	5	0
Tennessee	52	2	17	18	3
Texas	194	29	63	62	19
Utah	18	6	5	2	1
Vermont	0	0	2	0	0
Virginia	66	47	12	10	6
Washington	76	20	10	8	6
West Virginia	39	3	9	3	2
Wisconsin	69	5	5	18	5
Wyoming	24	0	0	2	0
United States, total	4,100	1,341	600	1,289	244

[1]Includes railroad employee, contractor, and volunteer.

NOTES: As defined by the U.S. Department of Transportation, Federal Railroad Administration, a Trespasser is any person on a part of railroad property used in railroad operations whose presence is prohibited, forbidden, or unlawful. Employees who are trespassing on railroad property are reported as Trespassers. Nontrespassers are persons lawfully on that part of railroad property that is used in railroad operation (other than defined as employees, passengers, trespassers, volunteers, or contractor employees), and persons adjacent to railroad premises when they are injured as the result of the operation of a railroad. "Other" includes employees not on duty, nontrespassers off railroad property, and volunteers or contractors who are not engaged in either the operation of on-track equipment or any other safety-sensitive function for the railroad.

SOURCE: U.S. Department of Transportation, Federal Railroad Administration, Office of Safety Analysis, available at safetydata.fra.dot.gov/OfficeofSafety as of July 2015.

Table 2-16: Transit Incidents, Fatalities, Injuries, and Property Damage, All Transit Modes: 2012

State	Collision			Non-collision			Total property damage ($ thousands)
	Number of incidents	Fatalities	Injuries	Number of incidents	Fatalities	Injuries	
Alabama	7	0	9	11	0	13	107
Alaska	6	1	7	57	0	54	48
Arizona	56	1	75	83	2	82	668
Arkansas	5	0	10	10	0	11	34
California	498	36	842	2,190	24	2,195	6,064
Colorado	70	2	106	102	4	100	485
Connecticut	63	0	155	98	1	111	658
Delaware	35	0	92	52	0	52	407
District of Columbia	167	1	294	608	8	581	426
Florida	357	11	787	714	8	709	2,668
Georgia	117	1	260	380	2	352	566
Hawaii	23	4	28	104	0	104	265
Idaho	0	0	0	1	0	1	0
Illinois	365	11	762	1,360	19	1,277	3,555
Indiana	51	1	96	74	1	75	645
Iowa	10	0	15	10	0	6	164
Kansas	0	0	0	5	0	7	0
Kentucky	47	0	140	32	2	29	255
Louisiana	51	0	159	75	0	74	444
Maine	0	0	0	0	0	0	0
Maryland	183	3	401	283	1	285	1,265
Massachusetts	99	5	184	781	11	633	952
Michigan	75	1	146	146	1	139	768
Minnesota	55	1	74	110	0	115	419
Mississippi	3	0	20	12	0	12	120
Missouri	85	5	238	218	0	216	1,127
Montana	0	0	0	7	0	7	0
Nebraska	1	0	2	5	0	4	72
Nevada	50	4	100	96	0	95	609
New Hampshire	2	0	2	9	0	11	10
New Jersey	75	8	147	599	2	563	460,842
New Mexico	9	0	12	21	0	21	16
New York	548	50	958	7,564	42	6,685	423,554
North Carolina	83	1	245	106	0	143	1,472
North Dakota	0	0	0	1	0	1	15
Ohio	117	6	262	212	1	207	1,173
Oklahoma	6	0	16	9	1	7	116
Oregon	47	0	70	153	1	169	557
Pennsylvania	123	8	246	758	11	721	2,627
Rhode Island	21	0	35	33	0	30	477
South Carolina	18	0	71	11	0	9	149
South Dakota	1	0	7	0	0	0	6
Tennessee	29	0	62	60	0	55	257
Texas	317	16	588	542	8	517	3,482
Utah	49	3	56	34	4	24	2,160
Vermont	1	0	1	2	0	2	6
Virginia	60	0	137	67	2	66	566
Washington	100	3	124	247	0	239	908
West Virginia	11	0	17	3	0	5	317
Wisconsin	46	2	68	124	0	123	251
Wyoming	0	0	0	0	0	0	0
United States, total (excluding Puerto Rico)[1]	4,142	185	8,126	18,179	156	16,937	921,752
United States, total (including Puerto Rico)[1]	4,145	186	8,128	18,223	156	16,980	925,752

[1]Increase in property damage due to Hurricane Sandy.

NOTES: Collision includes at-grade crossings excluding suicides. Noncollision includes: 1) derailments; 2) personal casualties in parking facilities, inside vehicles, on right of way, boarding/alighting, and in station/bus stops; 3) evacuations for life safety; and 4) nonarson fires. For an incident to be reportable it must involve a transit vehicle or occur on transit property and either: 1) result in a fatality, injury or transit property damage greater than $25,000; 2) involve a nonarson fire; 3) involve a mainline derailment; or 4) involve an evacuation due to life safety 5) involve an act of God 6) involve a Hazardous Material Spill. Data are compiled from Federal Transit Administration's National Transit Database and Federal Railroad Administration's Rail Accident/Incident Reporting System.

SOURCE: U.S. Department of Transportation, Federal Transit Adminstration, personal communication as of August 2015.

Table 2-17: Recreational Boating Accidents: 2014

State	Number of accidents				Number of persons	
	Total	Fatal	Nonfatal injury	Property damage	Killed	Injured
Alabama	71	12	35	24	13	53
Alaska	18	10	3	5	11	4
Arizona	87	7	42	38	7	66
Arkansas	54	7	22	25	8	33
California	379	29	175	175	38	256
Colorado	57	12	30	15	12	37
Connecticut	40	5	17	18	5	27
Delaware	15	1	5	9	1	7
District of Columbia	2	0	1	1	0	1
Florida	581	62	202	317	70	327
Georgia	92	12	47	33	13	81
Hawaii	9	3	3	3	3	3
Idaho	43	10	15	18	10	17
Illinois	84	17	38	29	22	63
Indiana	40	9	14	17	9	25
Iowa	33	6	14	13	7	15
Kansas	17	6	7	4	6	12
Kentucky	46	8	24	14	9	38
Louisiana	113	18	60	35	18	114
Maine	35	5	14	16	5	14
Maryland	130	10	83	37	12	96
Massachusetts	82	5	31	46	6	56
Michigan	97	18	42	37	19	51
Minnesota	50	14	29	7	14	38
Mississippi	25	2	11	12	3	16
Missouri	142	13	79	50	14	101
Montana	14	3	9	2	3	15
Nebraska	26	1	18	7	1	20
Nevada	47	7	22	18	11	32
New Hampshire	44	1	19	24	1	27
New Jersey	111	3	41	67	3	77
New Mexico	13	0	11	2	0	13
New York	175	27	67	81	27	105
North Carolina	124	22	68	34	26	92
North Dakota	11	4	2	5	5	4
Ohio	100	15	33	52	22	43
Oklahoma	50	6	35	9	6	51
Oregon	61	7	17	37	7	27
Pennsylvania	66	20	23	23	21	39
Rhode Island	40	3	8	29	3	21
South Carolina	124	13	59	52	14	92
South Dakota	8	1	2	5	1	3
Tennessee	111	13	50	48	14	69
Texas	167	34	74	59	39	119
Utah	80	5	35	40	5	44
Vermont	5	1	4	0	1	9
Virginia	60	15	27	18	17	40
Washington	122	22	44	56	22	67
West Virginia	102	9	56	37	9	85
Wisconsin	24	3	8	13	3	13
Wyoming	11	4	4	3	4	8
United States, total (excluding territories)	4,038	540	1,779	1,719	600	2,666
United States, total (including territories)[1]	4,064	548	1,785	1,731	610	2,678

[1] Includes accidents in Guam, Puerto Rico, the Virgin Islands, American Samoa, Northern Mariana Islands, and those occurring offshore.

NOTES: An accident is listed under one category only, with Fatal being the highest priority, followed by Nonfatal injury, followed by Property damage. For example, if two vessels are in an accident resulting in a Fatality and a Nonfatal injury, the accident is counted as a fatal accident involving two vessels.
Data in this table do not include: 1) accidents involving only slight injury not requiring medical treatment beyond first-aid; 2) accidents involving property damage of less than $2,000; 3) accidents not caused or contributed to by a vessel, its equipment, or its appendages; 4) accidents where a person died or was injured from natural causes while aboard a vessel; 5) accidents in which the boat was used solely as a platform for other activities, such as swimming or skin diving. Such cases are not included because the victims freely left the safety of a boat. However, the data do include accidents involving people in the water who are struck by their boat or another boat; and 6) accidents involving damage, injury, or death on a docked or moored boat resulting from storms, unusual tidal, sea, or swell conditions, or when a vessel got underway in those conditions in an attempt to rescue persons put in peril.

SOURCE: U.S. Department of Homeland Security, U.S. Coast Guard, Boating Statistics 2014, table 30, available at www.uscgboating.org/statistics/accident_statistics.aspx as of June 2015.

Table 2-18: Alcohol Involvement in Recreational Boating Accidents: 2014

State	Total number of accidents	Accidents with alcohol as a contributing factor		
		Total number of accidents	Percent of state total	Persons killed
Alabama	71	7	9.9	5
Alaska	18	3	16.7	3
Arizona	87	7	8.0	1
Arkansas	54	7	13.0	2
California	379	14	3.7	5
Colorado	57	2	3.5	0
Connecticut	40	2	5.0	1
Delaware	15	2	13.3	0
District of Columbia	2	0	0.0	0
Florida	581	30	5.2	12
Georgia	92	7	7.6	2
Hawaii	9	0	0.0	0
Idaho	43	4	9.3	2
Illinois	84	17	20.2	8
Indiana	40	10	25.0	5
Iowa	33	6	18.2	2
Kansas	17	1	5.9	0
Kentucky	46	11	23.9	5
Louisiana	113	20	17.7	6
Maine	35	5	14.3	2
Maryland	130	7	5.4	1
Massachusetts	82	5	6.1	0
Michigan	97	8	8.2	4
Minnesota	50	8	16.0	4
Mississippi	25	2	8.0	2
Missouri	142	16	11.3	5
Montana	14	3	21.4	2
Nebraska	26	1	3.8	0
Nevada	47	6	12.8	2
New Hampshire	44	2	4.5	0
New Jersey	111	2	1.8	0
New Mexico	13	1	7.7	0
New York	175	13	7.4	7
North Carolina	124	13	10.5	5
North Dakota	11	5	45.5	3
Ohio	100	7	7.0	6
Oklahoma	50	5	10.0	2
Oregon	61	4	6.6	1
Pennsylvania	66	10	15.2	6
Rhode Island	40	2	5.0	1
South Carolina	124	7	5.6	3
South Dakota	8	3	37.5	1
Tennessee	111	6	5.4	2
Texas	167	17	10.2	5
Utah	80	2	2.5	1
Vermont	5	1	20.0	1
Virginia	60	6	10.0	3
Washington	122	9	7.4	4
West Virginia	102	5	4.9	1
Wisconsin	24	12	50.0	3
Wyoming	11	2	18.2	1
United States, total (excluding territories)	4,038	345	8.5	137
United States, total (including territories)[1]	4,064	345	8.5	137

[1]Includes accidents in Guam, Puerto Rico, the Virgin Islands, American Samoa, Northern Mariana Islands, and those occurring offshore.

NOTE: Data are based on alcohol use by a boat's occupants resulting directly or indirectly in an accident.

SOURCE: U.S. Department of Homeland Security, U.S. Coast Guard, *Boating Statistics 2014*, table 8 and 30, available at www.uscgboating. org/statistics/accident_statistics.aspx as of June 2015.

Table 2-19: Hazardous Materials Incidents: 2013 and 2014
(Not including pipelines or bulk, nonpackaged water incidents)

	2013						2014					
			Injuries			Damages			Injuries			Damages
State	Incidents	Deaths	Total	Major	Minor	($1,000)	Incidents	Deaths	Total	Major	Minor	($1,000)
Alabama	209	0	1	0	1	6,322	200	0	0	0	0	1,770
Alaska	168	0	0	0	0	150	175	0	0	0	0	30
Arizona	300	0	2	0	2	248	291	0	1	0	1	269
Arkansas	170	0	3	1	2	1,008	161	0	0	0	0	2,420
California	1,427	1	11	0	11	2,446	1,454	0	22	4	18	2,574
Colorado	341	0	1	0	1	2,666	371	0	10	0	10	3,153
Connecticut	165	0	1	0	1	423	215	0	2	0	2	178
Delaware	11	0	0	0	0		17	0	0	0	0	32
District of Columbia	2	0	0	0	0		1	0	1	0	1	
Florida	661	1	19	8	11	3,157	712	0	4	1	3	11,055
Georgia	580	4	6	1	5	1,343	611	0	6	0	6	1,186
Hawaii	9	0	0	0	0	113	11	0	0	0	0	2
Idaho	32	0	0	0	0	468	33	0	1	0	1	292
Illinois	1,281	1	4	0	4	1,502	1,336	0	5	0	5	1,693
Indiana	473	0	3	1	2	1,466	568	0	1	0	1	501
Iowa	163	0	1	0	1	1,098	162	0	4	1	3	349
Kansas	318	0	0	0	0	1,074	303	0	1	0	1	306
Kentucky	405	0	0	0	0	1,218	437	0	15	0	15	993
Louisiana	299	0	7	0	7	4,450	321	3	1	0	1	2,330
Maine	27	0	0	0	0	70	24	0	0	0	0	272
Maryland	222	0	0	0	0	11,044	260	0	0	0	0	129
Massachusetts	231	0	0	0	0	1,038	230	0	1	0	1	1,631
Michigan	315	0	2	0	2	323	395	0	5	0	5	1,710
Minnesota	249	1	9	2	7	2,079	253	0	1	1	0	722
Mississippi	101	0	4	0	4	391	140	0	0	0	0	3,464
Missouri	353	0	3	0	3	1,349	392	1	3	0	3	975
Montana	51	0	0	0	0	1,875	76	0	1	1	0	584
Nebraska	59	0	7	0	7	331	59	1	2	0	2	51
Nevada	115	0	5	0	5	108	123	0	0	0	0	45
New Hampshire	41	0	0	0	0	13	40	0	2	0	2	222
New Jersey	427	0	5	0	5	313	372	0	3	0	3	502
New Mexico	85	0	0	0	0	343	75	0	0	0	0	565
New York	507	0	13	3	10	1,316	491	1	8	0	8	2,704
North Carolina	366	0	2	1	1	1,647	386	0	4	0	4	1,284
North Dakota	54	0	0	0	0	3,706	71	0	1	1	0	754
Ohio	988	0	7	2	5	12,213	1,021	0	6	0	6	2,657
Oklahoma	183	0	2	0	2	1,666	256	1	2	1	1	1,707
Oregon	299	0	0	0	0	388	310	0	2	0	2	1,038
Pennsylvania	819	0	6	4	2	2,221	881	0	6	2	4	7,152
Rhode Island	29	0	0	0	0	43	47	0	0	0	0	13
South Carolina	121	0	1	1	0	988	194	0	4	0	4	589
South Dakota	15	0	0	0	0	76	19	0	1	0	1	84
Tennessee	756	0	0	0	0	1,217	831	0	2	0	2	2,363
Texas	1,475	1	32	5	27	6,822	1,806	1	18	1	17	8,612
Utah	291	0	5	0	5	927	260	0	1	0	1	532
Vermont	16	0	0	0	0	631	7	0	0	0	0	1,785
Virginia	201	2	2	1	1	1,655	225	0	8	0	8	2,812
Washington	194	0	4	2	2	700	217	0	0	0	0	2,981
West Virginia	55	0	0	0	0	2,016	58	0	0	0	0	732
Wisconsin	296	0	0	0	0	490	324	0	1	0	1	261
Wyoming	29	0	2	0	2	177	38	1	0	0	0	3,290
United States, total[1]	15,984	11	170	32	138	87,328	17,260	9	156	13	143	81,357

[1]Total excludes Incidents occurring in a U.S. territory or foreign country.

NOTES: Data for 2013 are revised. Hazardous material incident locations are often listed as the terminals or sorting centers where they are discovered. Therefore, states with this type of facility may show a disproportionate number of incidents. Hazardous materials transportation incidents required to be reported are defined in the Code of Federal Regulations (CFR), 49 CFR Part 171.15, 171.16 (Form F 5800.1). Incident means any of the following events: (1) a Fatality or Major injury caused by the release of a hazardous material; (2) the evacuation of 25 or more persons as a result of release of a hazardous material or exposure to fire; (3) a release or exposure to fire which results in the closure of a major transportation artery; (4) the alteration of an aircraft flight plan or operation; (5) the release of radioactive materials from Type B packaging; (6) the release of over 11.9 gallons or 88.2 pounds of a severe marine pollutant; or (7) the release of a bulk quantity (over 119 gallons or 882 pounds) of a hazardous material. Hazardous materials Deaths and Injuries are caused by the hazardous material in commerce. Hazardous materials incident data are subject to revision and correction by the Office of Hazardous Materials Safety.

SOURCE: U.S. Department of Transportation, Pipeline and Hazardous Materials Safety Administration, Office of Hazardous Materials Safety, Hazmat Intelligence Portal, Yearly Incident Summary Reports, available at www.phmsa.dot.gov/hazmat/library/data-stats/incidents as of June 2015.

Table 2-20: Hazardous Materials Incidents by Mode: 2013 and 2014
(Not including pipelines or bulk, nonpackaged water incidents)

State	2013 Mode Highway	Rail	Air	Water[2]	Total	2014 Mode Highway	Rail	Air	Water[2]	Total
Alabama	191	17	1	0	209	183	15	2	0	200
Alaska	3	0	143	22	168	2	16	156	17	191
Arizona	272	8	20	0	300	268	19	7	0	294
Arkansas	141	23	5	1	170	141	126	1	0	268
California	1,186	110	128	3	1,427	1,224	11	104	0	1,339
Colorado	317	10	14	0	340	351	0	9	0	360
Connecticut	157	0	8	0	165	210	0	5	0	215
Delaware	11	0	0	0	11	15	1	1	0	17
District of Columbia	2	0	0	0	2	1	0	0	0	1
Florida	581	10	52	18	660	630	12	51	19	712
Georgia	553	11	15	1	580	580	21	9	1	611
Hawaii	3	0	5	1	9	5	0	6	0	11
Idaho	28	0	4	0	32	24	2	7	0	33
Illinois	1,212	35	34	0	1,281	1,256	40	40	0	1,336
Indiana	423	15	35	0	472	510	15	43	0	568
Iowa	154	7	2	0	162	156	4	2	0	162
Kansas	292	15	11	0	318	289	6	8	0	303
Kentucky	212	9	185	0	406	263	8	166	0	437
Louisiana	252	41	5	1	299	291	28	2	0	321
Maine	25	0	2	0	27	22	1	1	0	24
Maryland	200	6	16	0	222	249	6	5	0	260
Massachusetts	203	3	25	0	231	209	1	20	0	230
Michigan	278	7	30	0	315	358	14	23	0	395
Minnesota	228	14	7	0	249	240	7	6	0	253
Mississippi	93	7	1	0	101	125	14	1	0	140
Missouri	326	14	13	0	353	367	11	14	0	392
Montana	41	6	4	0	51	66	8	2	0	76
Nebraska	55	4	0	0	59	50	6	3	0	59
Nevada	96	6	13	0	115	96	15	12	0	123
New Hampshire	38	0	3	0	41	35	0	5	0	40
New Jersey	359	11	51	6	427	328	9	34	1	372
New Mexico	70	14	1	0	85	69	4	2	0	75
New York	462	7	38	0	505	432	33	26	0	491
North Carolina	334	9	23	0	366	372	8	6	0	386
North Dakota	39	11	4	0	53	60	6	5	0	71
Ohio	939	20	29	0	988	973	22	26	0	1,021
Oklahoma	171	5	7	0	182	249	2	5	0	256
Oregon	258	18	23	0	299	268	30	12	0	310
Pennsylvania	760	38	20	1	816	812	34	34	0	880
Rhode Island	29	0	0	0	29	43	0	4	0	47
South Carolina	112	0	9	0	121	185	8	1	0	194
South Dakota	14	0	1	0	15	16	1	2	0	19
Tennessee	459	16	279	2	756	554	20	257	0	831
Texas	1,341	67	66	1	1,473	1,667	71	65	0	1,803
Utah	277	6	8	0	291	244	12	4	0	260
Vermont	15	0	1	0	16	7	0	0	0	7
Virginia	177	19	5	0	201	215	2	8	0	225
Washington	152	14	23	5	193	169	26	21	1	217
West Virginia	38	13	4	0	55	53	5	0	0	58
Wisconsin	278	12	6	0	296	310	7	7	0	324
Wyoming	21	7	1	0	29	33	5	0	0	38
United States, total[1]	13,878	665	1,380	62	15,971	15,275	712	1,230	39	17,256

[1] Total excludes Incidents occurring in a U.S. territory or foreign country.
[2] Includes only packaged shipments (i.e., nonbulk shipments).

NOTES: Data for 2013 are revised. Hazardous materials Incident data are subject to revision and correction by the Office of Hazardous Materials Safety. Hazardous materials transportation Incidents required to be reported are defined in the Code of Federal Regulations (CFR), 49 CFR Part 171.15, 171.16 (Form F 5800.1). Incident means any of the following events: (1) a fatality or major injury caused by the release of a hazardous material; (2) the evacuation of 25 or more persons as a result of release of a hazardous material or exposure to fire; (3) a release or exposure to fire which results in the closure of a major transportation artery; (4) the alteration of an aircraft flight plan or operation; (5) the release of radioactive materials from Type B packaging; (6) the release of over 11.9 gallons or 88.2 pounds of a severe marine pollutant; or (7) the release of a bulk quantity (over 119 gallons or 882 pounds) of a hazardous material.

SOURCE: U.S. Department of Transportation, Pipeline and Hazardous Materials Safety Administration, Office of Hazardous Materials Safety, Hazmat Intelligence Portal, *Yearly Incident Summary Reports*, available at www.phmsa.dot.gov/hazmat/library/data-stats/incidents as of June 2015.

Table 2-21: Natural Gas Distribution Pipeline Incidents: 2013 and 2014

State	2013 Number of incidents	Number of fatalities	Number of injuries	Damages ($1,000)	2014 Number of incidents	Number of fatalities	Number of injuries	Damages ($1,000)
Alabama	2	1	4	554	0	0	0	0
Alaska	0	0	0	0	1	0	0	301
Arizona	3	0	3	13	3	0	1	220
Arkansas	0	0	0	0	1	0	1	51
California	14	0	0	3,491	18	2	2	18,684
Colorado	3	0	3	969	1	0	0	133
Connecticut	2	0	0	938	0	0	0	0
Delaware	0	0	0	0	1	0	0	303
District of Columbia	0	0	0	0	0	0	0	0
Florida	1	0	0	128	1	0	0	3,021
Georgia	4	0	0	686	0	0	0	0
Hawaii	2	0	0	210	0	0	0	0
Idaho	0	0	0	0	0	0	0	0
Illinois	3	0	0	585	5	0	1	11,030
Indiana	2	0	0	110	5	1	1	463
Iowa	0	0	0	0	1	0	0	0
Kansas	2	0	0	353	2	0	1	53
Kentucky	2	1	1	391	2	0	0	5,101
Louisiana	1	0	0	75	2	1	1	7
Maine	0	0	0	0	0	0	0	0
Maryland	1	0	1	0	1	1	2	70
Massachusetts	4	0	0	955	2	0	0	81
Michigan	4	3	1	1,315	12	0	9	1,394
Minnesota	3	0	0	25	2	0	0	191
Mississippi	0	0	0	0	2	0	0	207
Missouri	1	1	4	0	5	0	0	1,663
Montana	0	0	0	0	2	0	2	281
Nebraska	3	0	1	192	1	0	0	44
Nevada	2	0	0	140	3	0	0	210
New Hampshire	0	0	0	0	0	0	0	0
New Jersey	2	0	0	1,072	2	1	10	21,379
New Mexico	0	0	0	0	1	0	0	55
New York	16	0	12	3,086	10	8	51	3,840
North Carolina	0	0	0	0	0	0	0	0
North Dakota	0	0	0	0	0	0	0	0
Ohio	4	0	1	148	4	0	0	1,725
Oklahoma	2	0	1	273	1	1	0	2
Oregon	0	0	0	0	0	0	0	0
Pennsylvania	4	0	0	522	4	1	1	1,017
Rhode Island	1	0	0	29	0	0	0	0
South Carolina	0	0	0	0	0	0	0	0
South Dakota	0	0	0	0	0	0	0	0
Tennessee	2	0	0	557	2	1	2	268
Texas	10	1	4	639	9	1	3	1,673
Utah	1	0	0	102	0	0	0	0
Vermont	0	0	0	0	0	0	0	0
Virginia	1	0	0	1	4	0	6	1,024
Washington	2	0	0	223	2	0	0	102
West Virginia	3	2	3	169	0	0	0	0
Wisconsin	0	0	0	0	1	0	0	141
Wyoming	0	0	0	0	0	0	0	0
United States, total	107	9	39	17,949	113	18	94	74,734

NOTES: Data for 2013 are revised. Incidents are reported on Form RSPA F 7100.1. Incident means any of the following events:
I. An event that involves a release of gas from a pipeline or a liquefied natural gas (LNG) facility and a) a death or personal injury necessitating in-patient hospitalization or b) estimated property damage, including cost of gas lost, of the operator or others, or both, of $50,000 or more.
II. An event that results in an emergency shutdown of an LNG facility.
III. An event that is significant, in the judgment of the operator, even though it did not meet the criteria of I or II.
Historical totals may change as the Office of Pipeline Safety receives supplemental information on incidents.

SOURCE: U.S. Department of Transportation, Pipeline and Hazardous Materials Safety Administration, Office of Pipeline Safety, Incident Statistics, available at www.phmsa.dot.gov/pipeline/library/data-stats as of July 2015.

Table 2-22: Natural Gas Transmission Pipeline Incidents: 2013 and 2014

State	2013				2014			
	Number of incidents	Number of fatalities	Number of injuries	Damages ($1,000)	Number of incidents	Number of fatalities	Number of injuries	Damages ($1,000)
Alabama	1	0	0	171	2	0	0	810
Alaska	0	0	0	0	0	0	0	0
Arizona	0	0	0	0	1	0	0	132
Arkansas	1	0	0	2	4	0	0	810
California	6	0	0	2,324	13	0	0	10,345
Colorado	3	0	0	234	0	0	0	0
Connecticut	0	0	0	0	0	0	0	0
Delaware	0	0	0	0	0	0	0	0
District of Columbia	0	0	0	0	0	0	0	0
Florida	1	0	0	147	1	0	0	1,494
Georgia	2	0	0	123	3	0	0	101
Hawaii	0	0	0	0	0	0	0	0
Idaho	0	0	0	0	1	0	0	559
Illinois	1	0	0	59	1	0	0	46
Indiana	0	0	0	0	3	0	0	171
Iowa	3	0	0	770	4	0	0	650
Kansas	3	0	0	2,123	3	0	0	1,209
Kentucky	0	0	0	0	5	0	1	3,317
Louisiana	20	0	2	15,666	10	0	0	3,904
Maine	0	0	0	0	0	0	0	0
Maryland	0	0	0	0	0	0	0	0
Massachusetts	0	0	0	0	0	0	0	0
Michigan	2	0	0	184	9	0	0	8,683
Minnesota	2	0	0	208	4	0	0	1,121
Mississippi	7	0	0	1,270	6	0	0	696
Missouri	2	0	0	2,017	2	0	0	859
Montana	0	0	0	0	0	0	0	0
Nebraska	2	0	0	518	1	0	0	3,404
Nevada	0	0	0	0	1	0	0	126
New Hampshire	0	0	0	0	0	0	0	0
New Jersey	1	0	0	0	1	0	0	207
New Mexico	2	0	0	121	0	0	0	0
New York	4	0	0	894	2	0	0	72
North Carolina	1	0	0	606	2	0	0	858
North Dakota	5	0	0	519	2	0	0	226
Ohio	1	0	0	1,501	3	0	0	544
Oklahoma	8	0	0	3,507	7	0	0	951
Oregon	0	0	0	0	0	0	0	0
Pennsylvania	2	0	0	564	2	0	0	358
Rhode Island	0	0	0	0	0	0	0	0
South Carolina	0	0	0	0	1	0	0	111
South Dakota	0	0	0	0	0	0	0	0
Tennessee	1	0	0	97	1	0	0	64
Texas	10	0	0	8,909	21	1	0	3,080
Utah	1	0	0	177	0	0	0	0
Vermont	0	0	0	0	0	0	0	0
Virginia	0	0	0	0	0	0	0	0
Washington	2	0	0	795	0	0	0	0
West Virginia	0	0	0	0	5	0	0	178
Wisconsin	1	0	0	230	1	0	0	297
Wyoming	1	0	0	257	1	0	0	523
United States, total[1]	111	0	2	50,940	141	1	1	55,888

[1]Incidents that have an "unknown" location are included in the U.S. total (15 Incidents causing $6,945,051 in property damage for 2013; and 18 incidents causing $9,981,646 in property damage for 2014).

NOTES: Data for 2013 are revised. Incidents are reported on Form RSPA F 7100.2. Incident means any of the following events:
I. An event that involves a release of gas from a pipeline or a liquefied natural gas (LNG) facility and a) a death or personal injury necessitating in-patient hospitalization or b) estimated property damage, including cost of gas lost, of the operator or others, or both, of $50,000 or more.
II. An event that results in an emergency shutdown of an LNG facility.
III. An event that is significant, in the judgment of the operator, even though it did not meet the criteria of I or II.
Historical totals may change as the Office of Pipeline Safety receives supplemental information on incidents.

SOURCE: U.S. Department of Transportation, Pipeline and Hazardous Materials Safety Administration, Office of Pipeline Safety, Incident Statistics, available at www.phmsa.dot.gov/pipeline/library/data-stats as of July 2015.

43

Table 2-23: Hazardous Liquid Pipeline Incidents: 2013 and 2014

State	2013 Number of incidents	2013 Number of fatalities	2013 Number of injuries	2013 Damages ($1000)[2]	2014 Number of incidents	2014 Number of fatalities	2014 Number of injuries	2014 Damages ($1000)[2]
Alabama	3	0	0	93	3	0	0	2,872
Alaska	1	0	0	55	1	0	0	7
Arizona	0	0	0	0	0	0	0	0
Arkansas	4	0	0	94,709	3	0	0	1,078
California	17	0	0	7,557	28	0	0	6,415
Colorado	2	0	0	2	8	0	0	2,067
Connecticut	1	0	0	1	0	0	0	0
Delaware	0	0	0	0	0	0	0	0
District of Columbia	0	0	0	0	0	0	0	0
Florida	0	0	0	0	3	0	0	174
Georgia	4	0	0	92	3	0	0	312
Hawaii	0	0	0	0	1	0	0	42
Idaho	1	0	0	224	0	0	0	0
Illinois	13	0	0	5,600	17	0	0	6,285
Indiana	10	0	0	9,386	15	0	0	1,647
Iowa	11	0	0	1,801	4	0	0	275
Kansas	22	0	0	1,076	26	0	0	900
Kentucky	3	0	0	89	4	0	0	345
Louisiana	17	1	0	13,998	31	0	0	18,923
Maine	0	0	0	0	0	0	0	0
Maryland	1	0	0	5	0	0	0	0
Massachusetts	0	0	0	0	0	0	0	0
Michigan	7	0	0	534	4	0	0	320
Minnesota	12	0	0	1,231	10	0	0	2,508
Mississippi	7	0	0	6,609	5	0	0	71
Missouri	8	0	0	769	5	0	0	1,613
Montana	2	0	0	1,991	6	0	0	70
Nebraska	3	0	0	95	2	0	0	59
Nevada	0	0	0	0	0	0	0	0
New Hampshire	0	0	0	0	0	0	0	0
New Jersey	9	0	0	161	9	0	0	1,220
New Mexico	12	0	0	1,258	11	0	0	363
New York	2	0	0	308	1	0	0	24
North Carolina	4	0	0	2,312	2	0	0	491
North Dakota	10	0	0	20,059	10	0	0	4,252
Ohio	7	0	0	166	13	0	0	9,736
Oklahoma	39	0	0	19,769	40	0	0	1,405
Oregon	0	0	0	0	0	0	0	0
Pennsylvania	9	0	0	1,601	4	0	0	1,555
Rhode Island	0	0	0	0	0	0	0	0
South Carolina	1	0	0	1	4	0	0	5,321
South Dakota	0	0	0	0	0	0	0	0
Tennessee	2	0	0	86	2	0	0	46
Texas	145	0	6	57,997	143	0	0	29,629
Utah	2	0	0	21,893	1	0	0	19
Vermont	0	0	0	0	0	0	0	0
Virginia	1	0	0	20	2	0	0	171
Washington	0	0	0	0	2	0	0	1,254
West Virginia	1	0	0	4,917	0	0	0	0
Wisconsin	1	0	0	31	4	0	0	377
Wyoming	7	0	0	167	16	0	0	1,083
United States, total	401	1	6	276,662	445	0	0	104,402

[1]Incidents that have an "unknown" location are included in the U.S. total (2 Incidents causing $1,475,149 in property damage for 2014).
[2]The Property damage category includes public and private Property damage, value of product loss, and the value of operator Property damage. It does not include the costs of emergency response, environmental remediation, other operator costs, and other public costs.

NOTES: Data for 2013 are revised. Historical totals may change as the Office of Pipeline Safety receives supplemental information on incidents. Incidents are reported on DOT Form 7000-1. An accident report is required for each failure in a pipeline system in which there is a release of the hazardous liquid or carbon dioxide transported resulting in any of the following: 1. Explosion or fire not intentionally set by the operator; 2. Loss of 5 or more gallons of hazardous liquid or carbon dioxide; 3. Escape to the atmosphere of more than 5 barrels (0.8 cubic meters) a day of highly volatile liquids; 4. Death of any person; 5. Bodily harm to any person resulting in: a. loss of consciousness; or b. necessity to carry the person from the scene; or c. necessity for medical treatment; or d. disability which prevents the discharge of normal duties or the pursuit of normal activities beyond the day of the accident; 6. Estimated property damage, including cost of clean-up and recovery, value of lost product, and damage to the property of the operator or others, or both, exceeding $50,000.

SOURCE: U.S. Department of Transportation, Pipeline and Hazardous Materials Safety Administration, Office of Pipeline Safety, Incident Statistics, available at www.phmsa.dot.gov/pipeline/library/data-stats as of July 2015.

Table 2-24: State Laws on Distracted Driving: June 2015

State	Ban on hand-held devices	Ban on text messaging
Alabama	no	yes
Alaska	no	yes
Arizona	no	no
Arkansas	no	yes
California	yes	yes
Colorado	no	yes
Connecticut	yes	yes
Delaware	yes	yes
District of Columbia	yes	yes
Florida	no	yes
Georgia	no	yes
Hawaii	yes	yes
Idaho	no	yes
Illinois	yes	yes
Indiana	no	yes
Iowa	no	yes
Kansas	no	yes
Kentucky	no	yes
Louisiana	no	yes
Maine	no	yes
Maryland	yes	yes
Massachusetts	no	yes
Michigan	no	yes
Minnesota	no	yes
Mississippi	no	yes
Missouri	no	no
Montana	no	no
Nebraska	no	yes
Nevada	yes	yes
New Hampshire	yes	yes
New Jersey	yes	yes
New Mexico[1]	no	yes
New York	yes	yes
North Carolina	no	yes
North Dakota	no	yes
Ohio	no	yes
Oklahoma	no	yes (eff. 11/15)
Oregon	yes	yes
Pennsylvania	no	yes
Rhode Island	no	yes
South Carolina	no	yes
South Dakota	no	yes
Tennessee	no	yes
Texas	no	no
Utah	no	yes
Vermont	no	yes
Virginia	no	yes
Washington	yes	yes
West Virginia	yes	yes
Wisconsin	no	yes
Wyoming	no	yes
Total	14	46

[1]Hand-held ban for drivers with in state vehicles.

NOTES: The totals are the sum of the individual state's data. In Florida, Iowa, Nebraska, Ohio, and South Dakota secondary enforcement is applied to texting while driving. The term "secondary enforcement" means that motorists must be stopped for another violation before they can be cited for texting or using a mobile phone.

SOURCE: U.S. Department of Transportation, National Highway Traffic Safety Administration, Distraction.gov, available at www.distraction.gov/content/get-the-facts/state-laws.html as of June 2015.

Table 2-25: Bus Involvement in Fatal Crashes: 2013

State	Number of vehicles involved in fatal crahes			Number of fatalities		
	Buses	All vehicles	Buses as percentage of all vehicles	Buses	All vehicles	Bus fatatlities as percentage of all fatalities
Alabama	7	1,116	0.6	9	852	1.1
Alaska	0	67	0.0	0	51	0.0
Arizona	3	1,173	0.3	3	849	0.4
Arkansas	1	638	0.2	1	483	0.2
California	27	4,125	0.7	27	3,000	0.9
Colorado	5	630	0.8	5	481	1.0
Connecticut	2	375	0.5	2	276	0.7
Delaware	2	150	1.3	3	99	3.0
District of Columbia	0	31	0.0	0	20	0.0
Florida	29	3,358	0.9	30	2,407	1.2
Georgia	11	1,636	0.7	11	1,179	0.9
Hawaii	1	123	0.8	1	102	1.0
Idaho	1	277	0.4	1	214	0.5
Illinois	9	1,353	0.7	9	991	0.9
Indiana	4	1,093	0.4	6	783	0.8
Iowa	4	434	0.9	6	317	1.9
Kansas	1	473	0.2	1	350	0.3
Kentucky	1	880	0.1	1	638	0.2
Louisiana	5	969	0.5	5	703	0.7
Maine	3	189	1.6	3	145	2.1
Maryland	7	648	1.1	7	465	1.5
Massachusetts	5	417	1.2	5	326	1.5
Michigan	4	1,363	0.3	4	947	0.4
Minnesota	6	563	1.1	6	387	1.6
Mississippi	3	781	0.4	3	613	0.5
Missouri	3	1,002	0.3	4	757	0.5
Montana	1	266	0.4	1	229	0.4
Nebraska	1	279	0.4	1	211	0.5
Nevada	6	372	1.6	6	262	2.3
New Hampshire	0	168	0.0	0	135	0.0
New Jersey	11	750	1.5	11	542	2.0
New Mexico	2	389	0.5	2	310	0.6
New York	26	1,579	1.6	28	1,199	2.3
North Carolina	7	1,756	0.4	7	1,289	0.5
North Dakota	1	215	0.5	1	148	0.7
Ohio	5	1,485	0.3	5	989	0.5
Oklahoma	5	972	0.5	5	678	0.7
Oregon	2	421	0.5	2	313	0.6
Pennsylvania	19	1,694	1.1	22	1,208	1.8
Rhode Island	0	83	0.0	0	65	0.0
South Carolina	7	1,030	0.7	9	767	1.2
South Dakota	1	184	0.5	1	135	0.7
Tennessee	6	1,400	0.4	14	995	1.4
Texas	18	4,651	0.4	22	3,382	0.7
Utah	2	289	0.7	2	220	0.9
Vermont	2	89	2.2	2	69	2.9
Virginia	6	1,001	0.6	6	740	0.8
Washington	2	593	0.3	3	436	0.7
West Virginia	2	431	0.5	2	332	0.6
Wisconsin	4	801	0.5	5	543	0.9
Wyoming	0	106	0.0	0	87	0.0
United States, total	280	44,868	0.6	310	32,719	0.9

NOTES: Fatal bus crashes involve school buses, cross country/inter-city buses, transit buses, van-based bus with gross vehicle weight rating greater than 10,000 lbs. and other/unknown bus types.

SOURCES: Fatal crashes: U.S. Department of Transportation, National Highway Traffic Safety Administration, Fatality Analysis Reporting System Encyclopedia, available at www-fars.nhtsa.dot.gov as of July 2015.

Table 2-26: Bicyclist Fatalities Involving Motor Vehicles: 2013

State	Total traffic fatalities	Bicyclists killed	Bicylist fatalities as percent of total	Population (thousands)	Bicyclist fatality rate per 100,000 population
Alabama	852	6	0.7	4,834	0.12
Alaska	51	1	2.0	737	0.14
Arizona	849	31	3.7	6,635	0.47
Arkansas	483	4	0.8	2,959	0.14
California	3,000	141	4.7	38,431	0.37
Colorado	481	12	2.5	5,272	0.23
Connecticut	276	3	1.1	3,599	0.08
Delaware	99	1	1.0	925	0.11
District of Columbia	20	1	5.0	649	0.15
Florida	2,407	133	5.5	19,600	0.68
Georgia	1,179	28	2.4	9,995	0.28
Hawaii	102	2	2.0	1,409	0.14
Idaho	214	3	1.4	1,613	0.19
Illinois	991	30	3.0	12,891	0.23
Indiana	783	14	1.8	6,571	0.21
Iowa	317	3	0.9	3,092	0.10
Kansas	350	6	1.7	2,896	0.21
Kentucky	638	3	0.5	4,400	0.07
Louisiana	703	14	2.0	4,629	0.30
Maine	145	4	2.8	1,329	0.30
Maryland	465	6	1.3	5,939	0.10
Massachusetts	326	6	1.8	6,709	0.09
Michigan	947	27	2.9	9,898	0.27
Minnesota	387	6	1.6	5,422	0.11
Mississippi	613	6	1.0	2,992	0.20
Missouri	757	4	0.5	6,045	0.07
Montana	229	1	0.4	1,015	0.10
Nebraska	211	0	0.0	1,869	0.00
Nevada	262	7	2.7	2,791	0.25
New Hampshire	135	4	3.0	1,323	0.30
New Jersey	542	14	2.6	8,912	0.16
New Mexico	310	4	1.3	2,087	0.19
New York	1,199	40	3.3	19,696	0.20
North Carolina	1,289	22	1.7	9,849	0.22
North Dakota	148	1	0.7	724	0.14
Ohio	989	19	1.9	11,572	0.16
Oklahoma	678	13	1.9	3,853	0.34
Oregon	313	3	1.0	3,928	0.08
Pennsylvania	1,208	11	0.9	12,781	0.09
Rhode Island	65	3	4.6	1,053	0.28
South Carolina	767	15	2.0	4,772	0.31
South Dakota	135	0	0.0	846	0.00
Tennessee	995	8	0.8	6,497	0.12
Texas	3,382	48	1.4	26,506	0.18
Utah	220	6	2.7	2,903	0.21
Vermont	69	0	0.0	627	0.00
Virginia	740	8	1.1	8,270	0.10
Washington	436	11	2.5	6,974	0.16
West Virginia	332	0	0.0	1,854	0.00
Wisconsin	543	10	1.8	5,743	0.17
Wyoming	87	0	0.0	583	0.00
United States, total	32,719	743	2.3	316,498	0.23

NOTE: Details may not add to totals due to rounding.

SOURCE: Fatalities: U.S. Department of Transportation, National Highway Traffic Safety Administration, Fatality Analysis Reporting System Encyclopedia, available at www-fars.nhtsa.dot.gov as of June 2015. Population: U.S. Department of Commerce, U.S. Census Bureau, Population Estimates, Vintage 2009 and 2012, available at www.census.gov/popest as of June 2015.

Chapter 3
Freight Transportation

Table 3-1: Freight Shipments by State of Origin: 2012

State	Value ($ millions)	Tons (thousands)	Ton-miles (millions)
Alabama	214,750	191,500	51,227
Alaska	19,848	23,958	3,108
Arizona	147,147	117,119	16,298
Arkansas	114,095	121,430	30,478
California	1,476,407	718,345	171,432
Colorado	158,800	169,335	50,450
Connecticut	271,125	179,846	32,455
Delaware	42,768	25,537	2,786
District of Columbia	2,509	3,049	S
Florida	440,516	414,015	61,698
Georgia	395,725	272,760	62,439
Hawaii	22,156	25,730	S
Idaho	41,405	44,001	24,417
Illinois	825,191	606,874	149,574
Indiana	393,998	324,668	66,176
Iowa	195,992	263,357	85,170
Kansas	218,973	193,929	70,888
Kentucky	268,530	285,812	88,294
Louisiana	349,658	438,166	138,352
Maine	38,545	44,888	9,628
Maryland	162,416	101,222	12,042
Massachusetts	235,932	109,368	13,472
Michigan	427,177	258,965	61,455
Minnesota	270,394	291,694	101,362
Mississippi	140,334	119,048	24,662
Missouri	242,404	197,077	47,770
Montana	30,561	90,511	73,468
Nebraska	109,147	146,474	66,851
Nevada	69,591	40,254	10,176
New Hampshire	42,805	26,554	3,474
New Jersey	450,795	219,863	35,599
New Mexico	48,793	48,681	7,472
New York	545,050	317,630	42,457
North Carolina	385,732	220,669	47,304
North Dakota	45,743	88,071	31,915
Ohio	587,929	449,851	81,668
Oklahoma	169,262	217,905	51,251
Oregon	147,065	106,742	31,974
Pennsylvania	550,644	418,478	76,704
Rhode Island	45,575	26,719	1,882
South Carolina	159,760	99,936	26,526
South Dakota	58,621	70,357	27,891
Tennessee	329,399	187,514	48,264
Texas	1,897,658	1,686,264	243,743
Utah	108,593	89,129	29,911
Vermont	24,980	17,862	3,324
Virginia	238,576	173,461	30,082
Washington	296,901	183,138	46,771
West Virginia	54,759	174,741	56,674
Wisconsin	311,937	234,984	53,485
Wyoming	25,470	421,925	461,804
United States, total	13,852,143	11,299,409	2,969,506

KEY: S = Estimate does not meet publication standards.

NOTE: Details may not add to total due to rounding. Ton-miles estimates are based on estimated distances traveled along a modeled transportation network. Value-of-shipments estimates have not been adjusted for price changes. For more information, visit www.census. gov/econ/cfs.

SOURCE: U.S. Department of Transportation, Bureau of Transportation Statistics and U.S. Department of Commerce, U.S. Census Bureau, Commodity Flow Survey, *United States,* table 14, Shipment Characteristics by Origin State for the United States: 2012, available at www.bts.gov/publications/commodity_flow_survey as of July 2015.

Table 3-2: Hazardous Material Shipments by Selected State of Origin: 2012
(Ranked by tons)

State	Value ($ millions)	Tons (thousands)	Ton-miles (millions)
Texas	802,054	911,558	86,339
Louisiana	185,958	228,855	50,821
California	155,608	161,487	15,608
Illinois	136,261	153,609	25,466
Connecticut	95,097	100,006	3,219
Florida	70,884	70,889	6,405
Ohio	55,777	58,051	5,572
New Jersey	61,025	56,241	2,401
Oklahoma	46,039	54,561	6,353
New York	46,688	50,714	3,277
Washington	41,895	50,681	2,636
Pennsylvania	44,756	49,486	6,214
Indiana	40,530	46,514	2,805
Wisconsin	33,804	36,144	3,540
Massachusetts	S	S	S
Georgia	33,686	34,770	2,958
Michigan	32,378	34,322	3,334
Kentucky	34,352	32,984	3,939
Tennessee	28,807	29,212	3,304
Kansas	25,159	26,423	2,561
United States, total	2,334,425	2,580,153	307,524

KEY: S = Estimate does not meet publication standards because of high sampling variability or poor response quality.

NOTES: Selected states shown had the highest estimated weight without considering sampling variability and are shown in descending order. Since an "All other states" line is not shown, estimates do not add to total. Ton-miles estimates are based on estimated distances traveled along a modeled transportation network. Value-of-shipments estimates have not been adjusted for price changes. For more information, visit www.census.gov/econ/cfs.

SOURCE: U.S. Department of Transportation, Bureau of Transportation Statistics and U.S. Department of Commerce, U.S. Census Bureau, Commodity Flow Survey, *Hazardous Materials*, table 5a, Hazardous Material Shipment Characteristics by Selected State of Origin, available at www.bts.gov/publications/commodity_flow_survey as of July 2015.

51

Table 3-3: Hazardous Material Shipments by Selected State of Destination: 2012
(Ranked by tons)

State	Value ($ millions)	Tons (thousands)	Ton-miles (millions)
Texas	804,751	919,634	64,672
California	157,704	164,829	32,530
Louisiana	126,128	153,886	10,417
Illinois	109,044	120,213	15,468
Connecticut	83,387	90,375	2,493
Florida	83,421	86,552	21,187
New Jersey	55,362	61,416	8,317
Ohio	58,051	60,834	8,365
Indiana	50,039	54,921	3,402
New York	54,866	54,116	8,788
Oklahoma	46,200	52,325	4,216
Washington	44,511	51,888	4,215
Pennsylvania	44,623	50,549	7,793
Massachusetts	45,765	44,176	1,976
Michigan	37,948	40,026	6,082
Georgia	36,623	37,916	6,290
Minnesota	28,419	33,476	3,163
Tennessee	28,971	31,829	8,896
North Carolina	30,888	31,565	S
Mississippi	26,270	30,182	3,389
United States, total	2,334,425	2,580,153	307,524

KEY: S = Estimate does not meet publication standards because of high sampling variability or poor response quality.

NOTES: Selected states shown had the highest estimated weight without considering sampling variability and are shown in descending order. Since an "All other states" line is not shown, estimates do not add to total. Ton-miles estimates are based on estimated distances traveled along a modeled transportation network. Value-of-shipments estimates have not been adjusted for price changes. For more information, visit www.census.gov/econ/cfs.

SOURCE: U.S. Department of Transportation, Bureau of Transportation Statistics and U.S. Department of Commerce, U.S. Census Bureau, Commodity Flow Survey, *Hazardous Materials*, table 5b, Hazardous Material Shipment Characteristics by Selected State of Destination, available at www.bts.gov/publications/commodity_flow_survey as of July 2015.

Table 3-4: Rail Shipments: 2012

State	Rail shipments terminating in state		Rail shipments originating in state	
	All commodities (thousands of tons)	Top commodity by weight	All commodities (thousands of tons)	Top commodity by weight
Alabama	51,082	Coal	38,161	Coal
Alaska	5,561	Stone, sand, gravel	5,561	Stone, sand, gravel
Arizona	26,052	Coal	3,281	Stone, sand, lime
Arkansas	27,429	Coal	14,493	Stone, sand, gravel
California	98,903	Intermodal	59,066	Intermodal
Colorado	29,703	Coal	30,647	Coal
Connecticut	1,324	Primary metal prod.	1,271	Waste & scrap
Delaware	4,442	Stone, sand, gravel	842	Coke & metal products
District of Columbia	17	All traffic	37	All traffic
Florida	66,677	Phospate rock	43,721	Phospate rock
Georgia	67,689	Coal	31,841	Stone, sand, gravel
Hawaii	NA	NA	NA	NA
Idaho	7,380	Chemicals	7,081	Food products
Illinois	157,810	Coal	115,899	Intermodal
Indiana	56,517	Coal	54,154	Coal
Iowa	35,389	Coal	46,269	Food products
Kansas	23,383	Coal	17,913	Farm products
Kentucky	36,761	Coal	59,158	Coal
Louisiana	44,592	Coal	29,344	Chemicals
Maine	2,573	Ground minerals	2,126	Pulp & paper
Maryland	35,538	Coal	5,815	Waste & scrap
Massachusetts	6,671	Intermodal	2,829	Empty containers
Michigan	32,653	Coal	21,874	Motor veh. & parts
Minnesota	70,254	Metallic ores	90,337	Metallic ores
Mississippi	13,579	Coal & metallic ores	7,699	Chemicals
Missouri	68,908	Coal	16,716	Food products
Montana	4,771	Prod. of petr. refining	38,320	Coal & coke
Nebraska	23,323	Coal	27,027	Farm products
Nevada	5,060	Coal	2,075	Concrete & gypsum prod.
New Hampshire	780	Coal & cement	321	Stone, sand, gravel
New Jersey	23,625	Chemicals	11,789	Intermodal
New Mexico	3,772	Food products	12,068	Coal
New York	20,575	Chemicals	7,439	Waste & scrap
North Carolina	47,903	Coal	10,362	Chemicals
North Dakota	22,003	Farm products	49,480	Farm products
Ohio	77,297	Coal	66,191	Coal
Oklahoma	34,810	Coal	18,299	Stone, sand, gravel
Oregon	19,304	Chemicals	10,187	Lumber & wood
Pennsylvania	54,495	Coal	51,550	Coal
Rhode Island	836	Chemicals	49	All traffic
South Carolina	27,757	Coal	12,114	Chemicals
South Dakota	4,813	Coal & cement	14,276	Farm products
Tennessee	26,558	Chemicals	15,695	Intermodal
Texas	206,591	Coal	92,892	Chemicals
Utah	10,752	Coal & cement	15,775	Coal
Vermont	1,552	Salt & ground miner.	659	Ground minerals
Virginia	77,551	Coal	32,231	Coal
Washington	48,340	Farm products	21,892	Intermodal
West Virginia	14,281	Coal	92,328	Coal
Wisconsin	57,490	Coal	20,625	Stone, sand, gravel
Wyoming	15,755	Coal	434,299	Coal
United States, total	1,800,883	Coal	1,764,078	Coal

KEY: NA = not applicable.

NOTE: The top commodity is based on the 38 two-digit Standard Transportation Commodity Code groupings and is determined by the tonnage either originating or terminating in the state (including intrastate shipments.) Commodity tonnage data are rounded estimates based on the Carload Waybill Sample. Individual state shipments may not add to total.

SOURCE: Association of American Railroads, *Railroad Ten-Year Trends*, available at www.aar.org/StatisticsAndPublications as of July 2015.

Table 3-5: Waterborne Shipments: 2012 and 2013
(Thousands of short tons)

State	2012						2013					
		Terminating in state		Originating in state				Terminating in state		Originating in state		
	Intrastate	Domestic	Foreign	Domestic	Foreign	Total	Intrastate	Domestic	Foreign	Domestic	Foreign	Total
Alabama	16,073	13,542	13,308	10,104	16,512	69,539	13,929	14,169	12,493	10,624	18,178	69,394
Alaska	3,776	3,142	1,763	28,103	4,258	41,041	5,398	3,171	1,044	28,246	3,740	41,599
Arkansas	1,932	6,918	0	7,580	0	16,430	2,035	6,697	0	8,676	0	17,409
California	12,505	16,310	120,470	5,662	65,889	220,836	12,746	15,400	124,222	5,061	68,745	226,174
Connecticut	730	6,884	2,027	472	532	10,645	694	7,544	2,417	371	341	11,368
Delaware	124	4,059	6,991	3,372	1,249	15,794	190	4,002	4,983	3,096	1,665	13,936
District of Columbia	0	113	0	0	0	113	0	128	0	0	0	128
Florida	876	39,987	28,017	4,695	18,510	91,501	615	38,495	30,274	6,530	18,013	93,925
Georgia	1,125	903	16,646	234	17,971	36,879	690	1,027	14,500	138	18,863	35,216
Hawaii	10,367	4,172	8,521	1,469	403	24,932	9,574	4,222	7,804	1,133	447	23,180
Idaho	0	0	0	867	0	868	0	0	0	825	0	825
Illinois	7,441	17,063	1,352	80,424	116	106,399	5,786	16,239	1,475	68,424	91	92,015
Indiana	2,288	46,265	1,443	18,211	116	68,322	1,930	43,215	1,033	18,722	21	64,922
Iowa	125	3,372	0	6,829	0	10,327	53	3,257	0	4,552	0	7,861
Kansas	0	0	0	346	0	346	0	0	0	391	0	391
Kentucky	20,657	25,357	0	48,674	0	94,688	25,608	23,828	0	50,887	0	100,232
Louisiana	51,561	136,948	92,973	86,780	142,523	510,788	54,212	134,938	91,850	86,737	133,340	501,077
Maine	109	1,136	13,179	168	536	15,127	130	1,156	12,322	87	382	14,078
Maryland	1,015	3,712	12,892	3,656	23,993	45,268	3,421	3,194	10,765	3,919	19,370	40,669
Massachusetts	381	5,028	10,206	223	1,459	17,298	274	6,488	10,482	180	1,442	18,866
Michigan	9,853	18,948	3,960	19,859	4,927	57,547	9,364	19,979	3,471	19,950	5,459	58,222
Minnesota	1,204	6,560	314	31,296	3,499	42,872	1,286	7,194	316	30,441	2,230	41,466
Mississippi	467	7,727	18,469	13,806	8,122	48,592	296	8,991	17,520	13,360	8,416	48,582
Missouri	4,253	5,853	0	23,960	0	34,066	3,883	6,197	0	26,899	0	36,979
Nebraska	0	10	0	12	0	22	0	6	0	3	0	9
New Hampshire	0	492	1,654	9	264	2,419	6	499	2,004	12	158	2,679
New Jersey	9,554	10,119	74,657	33,954	24,401	152,685	6,423	11,641	69,166	36,718	22,043	145,991
New York	5,179	13,279	9,507	8,325	2,585	38,875	4,710	14,414	7,362	10,233	1,988	38,706
North Carolina	1,385	1,612	5,314	160	2,557	11,028	1,688	1,731	5,155	180	2,878	11,632
Ohio	10,820	49,682	6,531	18,621	4,915	90,569	10,812	54,048	5,466	17,102	6,321	93,749
Oklahoma	6	2,632	0	3,478	0	6,116	3	2,905	0	3,869	0	6,777
Oregon	2,904	5,842	3,745	2,261	16,004	30,758	2,938	5,621	3,976	3,873	13,851	30,259
Pennsylvania	8,947	29,488	20,424	9,734	1,838	70,431	5,900	30,751	21,757	12,900	2,237	73,546
Puerto Rico	1,398	3,681	13,351	1,324	253	19,424	1,100	3,309	13,058	945	441	18,853
Rhode Island	112	2,721	3,795	363	575	7,567	140	2,526	5,194	531	681	9,072
South Carolina	456	1,629	10,614	403	6,437	19,539	332	1,700	9,610	360	6,914	18,916
Tennessee	1,656	25,378	0	7,042	0	34,076	1,808	25,508	0	7,439	0	34,755
Texas	75,043	26,494	218,616	37,957	127,774	485,884	76,260	23,489	201,524	45,605	145,781	492,659
Vermont	0	0	0	0	0	0	0	0	0	0	0	0
Virginia	2,650	3,080	9,205	3,765	61,121	79,821	2,784	3,525	9,996	3,549	63,980	83,834
Washington	9,257	18,906	23,857	11,396	52,182	115,598	9,548	19,996	22,157	10,826	49,685	112,212
West Virginia	11,822	15,420	0	37,742	0	64,984	12,180	14,576	0	35,873	0	62,629
Wisconsin	171	6,571	1,305	18,880	4,706	31,634	15	7,018	2,341	18,893	5,958	34,225
United States, total	288,507	596,369	804,514	596,369	617,381	2,306,770	288,781	602,371	758,743	602,371	624,883	2,274,778

NOTES: U.S. and state totals exclude duplication. U.S. total includes data for Guam, the Virgin Islands, the Pacific Islands, other territories, and transshipments, which are not individually provided in the table.

SOURCE: U.S. Army Corps of Engineers, Navigation Data Center, Waterborne Commerce Statistics Center, *Waterborne Commerce of the United States 2012 and 2013, Part 5 National Summaries*, Table 4-1, available at www.navigationdatacenter.us/wcsc as of July 2015.

Table 3-6: Top 50 U.S. Ports by Port Calls and Vessel Type[1]: 2013
(Capacity in thousands of dwt tons)

Port	Rank	Total Calls	Total Capacity	Tanker[3] Calls	Tanker[3] Capacity	Dry-bulk Calls	Dry-bulk Capacity	Containership Calls	Containership Capacity	Other general cargo[4] Calls	Other general cargo[4] Capacity
Houston, TX	1	8,321	331,539	4,977	225,256	803	36,894	722	34,078	1,819	35,312
Sabine-Neches Waterway, TX	2	7,462	431,098	5,111	356,464	1,016	46,558	0	0	1,335	28,076
New Orleans, LA	3	6,605	337,589	2,371	143,971	2,633	148,940	385	18,825	1,216	25,852
New York/New Jersey, NY	4	5,508	284,870	2,478	127,892	217	11,245	2,252	133,382	561	12,351
South Louisiana, LA	5	4,098	231,160	2,050	123,877	1,726	99,945	0	0	322	7,339
San Francisco Bay Area, CA	6	3,953	38,252	1,259	0	755	38,252	1,635	0	304	0
Philadelphia/Delaware River Ports, F	7	2,602	69,972	914	56,410	223	7,137	383	0	1,082	6,425
Savannah, GA	8	2,566	133,587	321	11,517	202	7,438	1,739	106,299	304	8,333
Hampton Roads, VA	9	2,176	143,713	99	3,311	734	64,340	1,134	71,211	209	4,850
Port Everglades, FL	10	2,001	51,588	386	17,933	56	1,591	1,170	28,942	389	3,123
Long Beach, CA	11	1,962	159,070	618	72,872	249	14,514	877	66,172	218	5,512
Los Angeles, CA	12	1,925	114,320	250	11,954	91	4,598	1,430	93,924	154	3,844
Baltimore, MD	13	1,498	70,125	91	2,735	323	28,845	298	19,779	786	18,766
Miami, FL	14	1,492	31,043	23	1,432	0	0	1,026	28,168	443	1,444
Jacksonville, FL	15	1,431	43,286	125	5,550	95	5,489	472	19,067	739	13,178
Corpus Christi, TX	16	1,415	79,679	946	61,944	286	15,152	0	0	183	2,584
Columbia River, OR	17	1,392	44,684	81	0	942	44,684	86	0	283	0
Charleston, SC	18	1,296	64,626	93	3,973	67	3,386	833	50,909	303	6,358
Texas City, TX	19	1,077	54,197	1,040	52,483	32	1,585	0	0	5	129
San Juan, PR	20	1,074	22,919	199	7,107	33	1,313	433	9,799	409	4,700
Mobile, AL	21	986	46,698	130	5,251	350	23,868	163	10,358	343	7,221
Tacoma, WA	22	873	41,493	12	935	90	5,321	483	29,140	288	6,096
Tampa, FL	23	834	28,618	259	9,305	316	12,800	38	1,829	221	4,684
Lake Charles, LA	24	807	48,916	557	40,315	121	6,257	0	0	129	2,345
Seattle, WA	25	669	38,949	20	896	54	2,685	512	33,483	83	1,884
Greater Baton Rouge, LA	26	616	29,427	449	22,937	120	5,787	0	0	47	703
Galveston, TX	27	547	14,217	123	4,797	107	3,739	0	0	317	5,682
Boston, MA	28	522	24,015	258	10,584	34	2,065	137	8,192	93	3,175
Pascagoula, MS	29	514	34,297	385	29,152	61	3,855	0	0	68	1,290
Freeport, TX	30	505	19,638	312	15,383	10	573	115	1,856	68	1,825
Brunswick, GA	31	489	10,782	3	116	52	1,834	0	0	434	8,832
Wilmington, NC, NC	32	452	16,962	132	4,704	47	2,749	172	7,126	101	2,383
Honolulu, HI	33	447	13,386	76	3,096	5	246	303	9,155	63	890
Wilmington, DE, DE	34	344	8,359	7	593	43	1,526	97	3,100	197	3,140
Cherry Point Refinery, WA	35	304	35,952	286	34,960	13	728	0	0	5	263
Apra Harbor, GU	36	302	6,933	72	2,128	13	616	126	3,147	91	1,042
Port Hueneme, CA	37	299	5,285	10	445	0	0	45	1,268	244	3,572
San Diego, CA	38	279	5,374	7	335	5	248	47	619	220	4,172
Dutch Harbor, AK	39	272	6,889	11	230	0	0	124	5,924	137	736
El Segundo Offshore Oil Terminal, C	40	272	27,904	272	27,904	0	0	0	0	0	0
Valdez, AK	41	267	32,720	266	32,719	0	0	0	0	1	1
Portland, ME	42	255	15,489	198	14,392	4	187	10	82	43	828
Point Comfort, TX	43	235	10,660	87	2,559	117	7,262	0	0	31	839
Louisiana Offshore Oil Port, LA	44	220	46,749	220	46,749	0	0	0	0	0	0
March Point, WA	45	209	19,335	209	19,335	0	0	0	0	0	0
Providence, RI	46	192	7,680	136	5,549	33	1,726	0	0	23	406
Palm Beach, FL	47	187	1,459	5	134	0	0	23	211	159	1,114
Anchorage, AK	48	185	4,189	3	170	5	188	84	1,755	93	2,077
Port Manatee, FL	49	167	4,315	9	501	58	2,432	0	0	100	1,382
Kalaeloa (Barbers Point), HI	50	152	10,349	123	8,682	25	1,593	0	0	4	73
Top 50 ports total		72,256	3,354,357	28,069	1,631,537	12,166	670,189	17,354	797,802	14,667	254,830
U.S. ports total[5]		74,188	3,418,774	28,679	1,657,892	12,648	693,076	17,540	801,170	15,321	266,636
Top 50 ports as percent of U.S. total		97.4	98.1	97.9	98.4	96.2	96.7	98.9	99.6	95.7	95.6

[1]Excludes calls by vessels under 10,000 dwt.
[2]Capacity is calculated as the sum for all calling vessels of calls multiplied by capacity in dwt.
[3]Includes petroleum and chemical tankers.
[4]Includes roll-on/roll-off, gas carrier, general cargo, and combination carriers.
[5]Includes Puerto Rico.

KEY: dwt = deadweight.

SOURCE: U.S. Department of Transportation, Maritime Administration, Vessel Calls at U.S. Ports by Vessel Type, available at http://www.marad.dot.gov/resources/data-statistics as of July 2015.

Table 3-7: Top 30 U.S. Containership Ports: 2013
(Thousands of TEUs)

Port	Rank	Total	Export	Import
Los Angeles, CA	1	5,662	1,737	3,925
Long Beach, CA	2	4,963	1,518	3,445
New York, NY	3	4,197	1410	2,788
Savannah, GA	4	2,363	1218	1146
Norfolk, VA	5	1,834	934	900
Oakland, CA	6	1,608	836	772
Houston, TX	7	1,572	917	655
Charleston, SC	8	1,292	626	666
Tacoma, WA	9	1,263	530	733
Seattle, WA	10	999	454	545
Jacksonville, FL	11	753	513	240
Miami, FL	12	711	360	352
Port Everglades, FL	13	695	386	309
Baltimore, MD	14	536	202	334
New Orleans, LA	15	301	220	81
Philadelphia, PA	16	281	94	187
Wilmington, NC	17	220	114	106
Wilmington, DE	18	194	27	167
San Juan, PR	19	185	22	162
Gulfport, MS	20	171	74	97
Mobile, AL	21	170	101	69
Boston, MA	22	161	64	97
West Palm Beach, FL	23	153	124	29
Portland, OR	24	144	71	73
Freeport, TX	25	74	27	47
Chester, PA	26	67	25	42
Honolulu, HI	27	60	40	20
Port Hueneme, CA	28	54	4	49
Pensauken, NJ	29	53	38	15
San Diego, CA	30	51	2	48
Top 30 ports, total		30,786	12,687	18,099
United States, all ports[1]		30,926	12,748	18,178
Top 30 ports as percent of U.S. total		99.5	99.5	99.6

[1]Includes Puerto Rico.

KEY: TEU = twenty-foot equivalent unit.

SOURCE: U.S. Department of Transportation, Maritime Administration, U.S. Waterborne Foreign Container Trade by U.S. Custom Ports, available at www.marad.dot.gov/library_landing_page/data_and_statistics/Data_and_Statistics.htm as of July 2015.

Table 3-8: Scheduled and Nonscheduled Air Freight and Mail Enplaned: 2013
(Short tons)

State	Freight		Mail	
	Scheduled	Nonscheduled	Scheduled	Nonscheduled
Alabama	22,062	39,916	12	0
Alaska	520,051	278,305	91,472	570
Arizona	148,769	1,978	12,468	0
Arkansas	9,137	114	167	0
California	1,682,268	108,476	69,873	134
Colorado	110,562	5,569	6,720	0
Connecticut	51,097	1,613	3,991	0
Delaware	0	514	0	0
District of Columbia	0	0	0	0
Florida	903,708	176,725	26,631	0
Georgia	290,000	6,808	27,372	0
Hawaii	221,125	49,624	21,401	1,850
Idaho	21,057	114	58	0
Illinois	629,829	56,097	32,608	0
Indiana	555,854	1,183	2,091	0
Iowa	54,407	15	3,911	0
Kansas	10,518	4,069	0	0
Kentucky	1,370,694	172,484	38,025	0
Louisiana	40,084	194	170	0
Maine	5,033	3	0	0
Maryland	50,515	898	3,067	0
Massachusetts	124,459	1,739	5,427	0
Michigan	127,005	1,780	10,345	0
Minnesota	104,996	3,876	11,962	0
Mississippi	3,342	40	3	0
Missouri	97,524	1,539	2,947	0
Montana	24,436	3	126	0
Nebraska	33,718	60	1,089	0
Nevada	84,557	274	1,732	4
New Hampshire	42,623	199	255	0
New Jersey	310,086	4,704	20,742	9,498
New Mexico	41,640	59	285	0
New York	603,751	33,202	19,938	13,058
North Carolina	130,207	1,286	12,659	0
North Dakota	12,532	247	3	0
Ohio	94,462	7,630	1,868	0
Oklahoma	43,829	215	0	0
Oregon	97,465	2,181	3,035	39
Pennsylvania	288,339	1,048	16,561	0
Rhode Island	5,113	28	1	0
South Carolina	47,993	5,793	117	0
South Dakota	27,938	2	28	0
Tennessee	2,335,611	1,352	3,324	1,983
Texas	756,042	37,189	27,481	0
Utah	86,375	2,459	10,431	0
Vermont	2,165	0	0	0
Virginia	162,850	1,238	5,916	0
Washington	235,757	9,514	10,931	54
West Virginia	2,765	25	1	0
Wisconsin	56,800	156	1,293	0
Wyoming	7,614	0	0	0
United States, total (including U.S. territories)	12,771,658	1,025,424	510,721	27,356

NOTE: Shipments by foreign carriers, destined for foreign airports and intrastate shipments are included.

SOURCE: U.S. Department of Transportation, Bureau of Transportation Statistics, TranStats Database, T-100 Market (All Carriers), available at www.transtats.bts.gov as of July 2015.

Table 3-9: Top 50 Airports by Landed Weight of All-Cargo Operations: 2008–2013
(In thousand short tons)

Airport	Rank in 2013	Landed weight					
		2008	2009	2010	2011	2012	2013
Memphis International (MEM)	1	9,750	9,464	9,772	10,152	10,492	10,946
Ted Stevens Anchorage International (ANC)	2	8,976	7,762	9,732	8,887	8,261	7,991
Louisville International-Standiford Field (SDF)	3	5,223	5,139	5,319	5,491	5,548	5,632
Miami International (MIA)	4	2,103	1,750	2,448	2,184	2,278	3,432
Indianapolis International (IND)	5	3,494	3,176	3,453	3,317	3,574	3,424
Chicago O'Hare International (ORD)	6	2,564	2,288	2,359	2,407	2,470	2,634
Los Angeles International (LAX)	7	2,876	1,884	1,977	2,022	2,102	2,100
John F Kennedy International (JFK)	8	104	564	1,216	1,410	1,594	1,711
Cincinnati/Northern Kentucky International (CVG)	9	2,222	1,591	1,962	1,972	1,747	1,686
Dallas/Fort Worth International (DFW)	10	1,614	1,436	1,516	1,532	1,544	1,531
Newark Liberty International (EWR)	11	1,742	1,341	1,324	1,340	1,323	1,362
Metropolitan Oakland International (OAK)	12	1,727	1,464	1,489	1,525	1,427	1,267
Ontario International (ONT)	13	1,350	1,168	1,121	1,157	1,181	1,186
Hartsfield - Jackson Atlanta International (ATL)	14	1,167	1,278	1,314	1,328	1,014	1,094
Honolulu International (HNL)	15	1,032	1,021	1,062	1,057	988	1,058
Philadelphia International (PHL)	16	1,264	1,132	994	975	942	942
George Bush Intercontinental/Houston (IAH)	17	754	784	763	808	788	852
Phoenix Sky Harbor International (PHX)	18	747	803	697	679	645	693
Seattle-Tacoma International (SEA)	19	675	610	607	620	650	688
Denver International (DEN)	20	625	624	619	605	602	630
San Francisco International (SFO)	21	775	747	652	622	599	596
Portland International (PDX)	22	656	545	531	567	581	569
Salt Lake City International (SLC)	23	521	449	424	428	438	467
Minneapolis-St Paul International/Wold-Chamberlain (MSP)	24	492	418	409	403	390	433
Luis Munoz Marin International (SJU)	25	431	543	441	434	425	424
Rafael Hernandez (BQN)	26	710	564	459	444	411	396
Chicago/Rockford International (RFD)	27	433	382	365	375	364	387
San Antonio International (SAT)	28	418	447	453	455	396	380
Boeing Field/King County International (BFI)	29	412	336	337	374	405	369
General Edward Lawrence Logan International (BOS)	30	562	474	512	484	438	366
Bradley International (BDL)	31	322	255	257	333	411	358
Orlando International (MCO)	32	425	391	398	403	363	349
Rickenbacker International (LCK)	33	365	323	342	327	347	348
San Diego International (SAN)	34	354	292	276	301	333	341
Detroit Metropolitan Wayne County (DTW)	35	333	319	315	325	341	339
Fort Worth Alliance (AFW)	36	449	299	350	449	317	318
Piedmont Triad International (GSO)	37	232	279	306	304	303	303
Albuquerque International Sunport (ABQ)	38	315	290	299	297	284	284
El Paso International (ELP)	39	227	166	249	261	260	257
Manchester (MHT)	40	228	235	236	242	244	247
Baltimore/Washington International Thurgood Marshall (BWI)	41	294	228	216	212	214	244
Washington Dulles International (IAD)	42	279	187	248	245	222	243
Laredo International (LRD)	43	224	196	264	267	277	240
Fort Lauderdale/Hollywood International (FLL)	44	285	215	225	223	233	239
General Mitchell International (MKE)	45	252	219	220	217	220	227
Spokane International (GEG)	46	336	251	238	213	224	223
Reno/Tahoe International (RNO)	47	296	199	199	208	210	221
Huntsville International-Carl T Jones Field (HSV)	48	234	168	175	186	219	214
Des Moines International (DSM)	49	213	223	186	192	175	214
Kansas City International (MCI)	50	298	240	217	213	216	208
Top 50 airports, total[1]		62,092	55,727	59,873	59,663	59,098	60,663
United States, all airports[2]		71,147	63,191	67,530	67,194	66,356	68,655
Top 50 airports as percent of U.S. total		87.27	88.19	88.66	88.79	89.06	88.36

[1]The sum of the top 50 airports in earlier years will not be equal to the total since some of the top 50 airports in earlier years are not in the top 50 list in 2013.
[2]Includes Puerto Rico and Guam.

SOURCE: U.S. Department of Transportation, Federal Aviation Administration, Passenger Boarding and All-Cargo Data, available at www.faa.gov/airports/planning_capacity/passenger_allcargo_stats as of July 2015.

Table 3-10: U.S. Surface Merchandise Trade with Canada and Mexico: 2014
(Millions of current dollars)

State	Exports to		Imports from	
	Canada	Mexico	Canada	Mexico
Alabama	4,183	1,499	2,151	1,499
Alaska	188	5	298	18
Arizona	1,417	8,238	905	7,171
Arkansas	1,409	665	861	600
California	14,932	22,133	24,449	38,207
Colorado	1,390	951	4,142	1,692
Connecticut	1,415	1,167	1,310	2,318
Delaware	569	86	1,603	59
District of Columbia	5	4	46	7
Florida	3,363	1,298	2,483	2,847
Georgia	6,059	2,620	4,111	4,860
Hawaii	5	1	42	5
Idaho	1,324	242	852	97
Illinois	20,238	7,358	38,983	12,247
Indiana	11,701	4,774	7,927	4,820
Iowa	4,494	2,006	3,245	1,704
Kansas	2,293	1,497	1,411	924
Kentucky	7,163	1,999	3,629	5,313
Louisiana	2,124	1,523	1,531	358
Maine	1,372	50	1,638	57
Maryland	1,503	347	1,611	1,429
Massachusetts	3,034	2,139	6,792	3,127
Michigan	24,553	10,664	47,685	41,302
Minnesota	4,930	1,960	12,777	2,082
Mississippi	1,717	1,020	1,248	1,177
Missouri	4,191	2,300	3,105	3,242
Montana	538	80	5,522	46
Nebraska	2,119	1,314	1,101	271
Nevada	896	233	703	384
New Hampshire	515	404	894	548
New Jersey	6,075	2,408	5,049	3,227
New Mexico	168	1,469	175	484
New York	13,015	2,296	17,315	2,934
North Carolina	6,453	2,702	3,272	4,278
North Dakota	3,977	311	2,545	145
Ohio	19,715	5,511	15,168	7,317
Oklahoma	1,751	576	6,357	1,016
Oregon	2,927	280	2,463	472
Pennsylvania	11,041	3,419	11,138	3,041
Rhode Island	468	168	359	208
South Carolina	3,373	1,731	2,635	2,799
South Dakota	683	336	471	71
Tennessee	8,720	4,477	5,282	6,021
Texas	19,038	85,139	14,661	67,060
Utah	1,168	649	1,494	2,250
Vermont	1,592	125	2,940	44
Virginia	2,990	1,108	1,641	666
Washington	6,567	1,201	14,147	713
West Virginia	1,775	159	1,058	240
Wisconsin	7,373	2,713	4,388	2,488
Wyoming	723	29	1,628	28
United States, total[1]	249,944	195,408	297,303	243,936

[1] United States total includes trade in which the state is unknown.

NOTE: Surface merchandise trade comprises all shipments of goods between the U.S. and Canada or Mexico by surface modes of transport (other than air or maritime vessel).

SOURCE: U.S. Department of Transportation, Bureau of Transportation Statistics, Transborder Freight Data, available at transborder.bts.gov/programs/international/transborder as of July 2015.

Table 3-11: U.S. Surface Merchandise Imports from Canada and Mexico: 2014
(Short tons)

State	Imports from Canada				Imports from Mexico			
	Total (short tons)	Truck (percent)	Rail (percent)	Other[1] (percent)	Total (short tons)	Truck (percent)	Rail (percent)	Other[1] (percent)
Alabama	2,095,981	14.3	85.7	Z	292,848	87.9	12.1	<0.05
Alaska	116,027	85.8	14.1	0.1	6,511	20.5	79.5	Z
Arizona	618,888	29.2	70.7	0.1	4,048,823	83.4	15.3	1.3
Arkansas	562,114	29.9	70.1	<0.05	114,958	94.4	5.6	<0.05
California	7,787,906	28.5	71.4	0.1	8,012,181	85.7	11.5	2.7
Colorado	6,539,586	4.1	8.7	87.2	174,456	89.0	11.0	<0.05
Connecticut	828,088	68.7	31.1	0.1	338,682	51.5	48.4	<0.05
Delaware	3,225,844	2.5	91.2	6.4	16,082	90.8	9.2	Z
District of Columbia	9,401	97.8	2.2	Z	8,389	100.0	0.0	Z
Florida	1,701,687	31.0	69.0	0.1	610,036	74.1	25.8	<0.05
Georgia	2,257,043	31.9	68.0	<0.05	1,171,752	89.2	10.8	Z
Hawaii	36,507	99.8	0.1	0.1	2,826	100.0	0.0	Z
Idaho	1,878,297	25.6	74.4	<0.05	36,495	92.3	7.7	Z
Illinois	71,574,177	3.7	6.8	89.5	4,997,040	38.5	61.4	0.1
Indiana	6,306,719	31.5	68.5	<0.05	767,003	82.4	17.6	Z
Iowa	2,956,674	22.2	77.8	Z	254,383	97.9	2.1	Z
Kansas	911,384	25.8	66.1	8.2	95,597	77.9	22.1	<0.05
Kentucky	1,936,680	45.4	54.6	<0.05	838,459	75.1	24.8	0.1
Louisiana	2,065,599	4.8	95.2	<0.05	217,679	23.4	76.6	<0.05
Maine	3,342,324	37.2	21.6	41.2	15,095	99.7	0.3	Z
Maryland	1,280,718	35.3	64.1	0.6	155,659	77.4	22.5	0.1
Massachusetts	2,971,809	56.6	43.4	<0.05	221,903	93.2	6.8	<0.05
Michigan	22,198,405	38.5	16.6	44.9	5,708,628	36.1	63.9	<0.05
Minnesota	23,208,863	7.3	17.1	75.6	356,736	92.3	7.7	Z
Mississippi	1,194,425	12.3	85.8	1.9	387,755	57.2	42.8	Z
Missouri	2,445,147	24.1	35.0	40.9	718,625	82.2	17.8	Z
Montana	10,567,106	13.1	3.6	83.3	8,240	60.3	0.0	39.7
Nebraska	948,149	35.5	63.9	0.6	50,602	98.9	1.1	Z
Nevada	547,733	34.0	65.9	<0.05	141,274	99.7	0.3	Z
New Hampshire	772,863	66.0	34.0	Z	26,451	100.0	0.0	Z
New Jersey	3,549,441	45.0	54.7	0.2	576,776	84.4	15.3	0.3
New Mexico	570,920	5.2	94.8	Z	363,366	81.6	17.7	0.6
New York	9,556,738	71.1	23.8	5.2	491,910	91.7	8.3	<0.05
North Carolina	2,422,742	30.1	69.9	<0.05	650,436	95.3	4.7	<0.05
North Dakota	4,271,094	63.6	36.3	0.1	15,099	81.1	18.9	Z
Ohio	16,494,347	23.2	18.7	58.1	1,126,851	75.3	20.9	3.9
Oklahoma	11,658,574	1.3	3.5	95.2	251,191	99.2	0.8	<0.05
Oregon	5,055,076	17.7	82.3	<0.05	133,915	90.7	9.3	Z
Pennsylvania	9,021,730	41.9	33.7	24.4	779,736	65.3	34.2	0.5
Rhode Island	269,484	56.7	43.3	Z	18,742	99.5	0.5	Z
South Carolina	1,709,278	31.5	68.0	0.5	407,898	75.2	4.1	20.7
South Dakota	473,781	56.2	43.8	<0.05	22,022	60.0	40.0	Z
Tennessee	2,825,456	30.1	69.9	0.1	830,491	87.8	6.1	6.1
Texas	12,288,801	14.2	43.1	42.6	18,243,650	82.7	15.0	2.3
Utah	862,793	45.2	54.7	<0.05	136,144	94.8	5.2	<0.05
Vermont	1,725,439	74.5	25.5	Z	4,659	97.8	2.2	Z
Virginia	1,245,348	41.9	55.0	3.1	100,475	81.6	18.4	0.1
Washington	14,279,588	21.2	23.9	54.9	153,704	74.0	26.0	Z
West Virginia	747,691	26.3	73.7	Z	160,532	13.6	86.4	<0.05
Wisconsin	4,940,644	24.7	72.2	3.1	636,356	87.8	12.2	<0.05
Wyoming	2,470,753	2.9	17.9	79.2	6,901	98.9	1.1	Z
United States, total[2]	289,348,903	20.6	28.4	50.9	54,909,985	73.8	24.6	1.6

[1]Includes pipeline, mail, imports into Foreign Trade Zones, and other imports by modes not elsewhere classified.
[2]The sum of states may not add to U.S. totals, because the totals include imports to unknown destinations.

KEY: Z = No activity.

NOTES: For "Other" category of Imports from Canada, approximately 90.0 percent of the weight arrives by pipeline. For the category "Other" Imports from Mexico, approximately 66.6 percent of the weight is via pipeline, and approximately 32.1 percent of the weight arrives by Foreign Trade Zones.

SOURCE: U.S. Department of Transportation, Bureau of Transportation Statistics, Transborder Freight Data, available at transborder.bts.gov/programs/international/transborder as of July 2015.

Table 3-12: Incoming Truck Crossings, U.S.-Canadian Border: 2009–2014

	2009	2010	2011	2012	2013	2014
Alaska	9,484	5,944	5,699	5,275	4,843	10,117
Idaho	58,390	63,927	64,992	69,633	69,125	71,408
Maine	335,671	344,612	334,310	328,974	321,728	305,326
Michigan	1,867,706	2,165,079	2,189,895	2,274,224	2,303,991	2,371,352
Minnesota	67,452	73,928	75,298	69,712	66,396	62,929
Montana	144,911	155,016	165,818	175,770	176,583	183,828
New York	1,398,201	1,451,605	1,463,269	1,474,122	1,476,360	1,514,443
North Dakota	363,076	380,838	386,711	412,873	396,412	422,452
Vermont	216,463	217,404	205,843	207,317	212,291	219,548
Washington	559,279	586,052	598,540	605,607	620,929	640,808
United States, total	5,020,633	5,444,405	5,490,375	5,623,507	5,648,658	5,802,211

NOTES: Truck crossings do not represent the number of unique vehicles and include both loaded and unloaded trucks. Crossings do not include privately owned pickup trucks. The data for incoming trucks exceeds the data for truck containers loaded and unloaded (empty) because some incoming trucks do not carry a container. The states listed in the table comprise all states with truck entries at U.S.–Canada border.

SOURCE: U.S. Department of Transportation, Bureau of Transportation Statistics, North American Border Crossing/Entry Data, available at transborder.bts.gov/programs/international/transborder/TBDR_BC/TBDR_BC_Index.html as of June 2015.

Table 3-13: Incoming Truck Container (Loaded) Crossings, U.S.-Canadian Border: 2009–2014

	2009	2010	2011	2012	2013	2014
Alaska	7,059	10,141	10,469	9,920	9,449	8,694
Idaho	49,723	49,573	46,726	48,556	44,768	53,133
Maine	189,200	199,200	176,215	183,831	180,242	172,495
Michigan	1,541,803	1,805,476	1,734,025	1,732,268	1,771,063	1,809,462
Minnesota	38,300	40,189	40,575	35,160	35,440	36,059
Montana	119,215	112,774	127,790	129,789	108,649	182,095
New York	1,118,436	1,144,885	1,091,610	1,100,864	1,094,797	1,211,479
North Dakota	262,108	273,137	259,135	277,270	279,550	312,787
Vermont	195,304	169,036	163,909	162,117	164,661	138,672
Washington	376,156	367,020	398,462	388,999	394,632	302,351
United States, total	3,897,304	4,171,431	4,048,916	4,068,774	4,083,251	4,227,227

NOTES: Truck crossings do not represent the number of unique vehicles and include both loaded and unloaded trucks. Crossings do not include privately owned pickup trucks. The data for incoming trucks exceeds the data for truck containers loaded and unloaded (empty) because some incoming trucks do not carry a container. The states listed in the table comprise all states with truck entries at U.S.–Canada border.

SOURCE: U.S. Department of Transportation, Bureau of Transportation Statistics, North American Border Crossing/Entry Data, available at transborder.bts.gov/programs/international/transborder/TBDR_BC/TBDR_BC_Index.html as of June 2015.

Table 3-14: Incoming Truck Container (Empty) Crossings, U.S.-Canadian Border: 2009–2014

	2009	2010	2011	2012	2013	2014
Alaska	1,044	4,579	4,356	3,856	3,770	3,882
Idaho	8,510	8,755	12,788	16,633	21,634	22,570
Maine	131,192	144,724	133,641	141,840	98,972	99,883
Michigan	280,601	288,006	274,300	388,933	509,246	477,666
Minnesota	29,320	35,226	37,381	36,699	31,623	27,194
Montana	23,092	26,071	35,776	44,047	43,575	35,183
New York	277,995	308,783	315,926	321,025	323,218	310,682
North Dakota	102,566	111,243	132,504	139,638	120,910	113,272
Vermont	40,867	48,576	40,927	41,455	39,084	28,557
Washington	161,951	163,753	175,823	172,773	181,333	126,971
United States, total	1,057,138	1,139,716	1,163,422	1,306,899	1,373,365	1,245,860

NOTES: Truck crossings do not represent the number of unique vehicles and include both loaded and unloaded trucks. Crossings do not include privately owned pickup trucks. The data for incoming trucks exceeds the data for truck containers loaded and unloaded (empty) because some incoming trucks do not carry a container. The states listed in the table comprise all states with truck entries at U.S.–Canada border.

SOURCE: U.S. Department of Transportation, Bureau of Transportation Statistics, North American Border Crossing/Entry Data, available at transborder.bts.gov/programs/international/transborder/TBDR_BC/TBDR_BC_Index.html as of June 2015.

Table 3-15: Incoming Train Crossings, U.S.-Canadian Border: 2009–2014

	2009	2010	2011	2012	2013	2014
Alaska	318	300	295	273	0	277
Idaho	967	1,205	1,233	1,188	1,267	1,389
Maine	743	726	593	923	981	998
Michigan	5,490	6,268	6,485	6,682	7,060	6,616
Minnesota	6,556	6,744	7,101	7,406	8,031	7,629
Montana	344	373	380	442	444	351
New York	4,042	3,984	4,023	4,238	4,455	4,556
North Dakota	2,887	3,311	3,048	3,509	3,085	3,199
Vermont	767	803	793	787	735	649
Washington	1,920	2,409	2,716	3,076	3,028	2,979
United States, total	24,034	26,123	26,667	28,524	29,086	28,643

NOTE: The states listed in the table comprise all states with rail crossings at the U.S.–Canada border.

SOURCE: U.S. Department of Transportation, Bureau of Transportation Statistics, North American Border Crossing/Entry Data, available at transborder.bts.gov/programs/international/transborder/TBDR_BC/TBDR_BC_Index.html as of June 2015.

Table 3-16: Incoming Rail Container (Loaded) Crossings, U.S.-Canadian Border: 2009–2014

	2009	2010	2011	2012	2013	2014
Alaska	NA	NA	NA	NA	NA	NA
Idaho	68,792	89,365	89,989	88,508	99,890	119,017
Maine	12,513	15,783	14,639	21,274	17,840	12,683
Michigan	325,594	385,873	401,959	401,374	406,646	383,480
Minnesota	224,202	267,534	302,829	382,975	420,956	472,546
Montana	14,405	16,985	13,725	14,700	14,469	8,373
New York	127,635	151,185	164,089	168,291	193,633	201,723
North Dakota	164,274	200,168	203,848	254,306	271,676	273,357
Vermont	24,665	25,004	25,964	26,337	26,491	22,993
Washington	60,852	57,143	70,485	74,077	82,560	80,676
United States, total	1,022,932	1,209,040	1,287,527	1,431,842	1,534,161	1,574,848

KEY: NA = not applicable.

NOTE: The states listed in the table comprise all states with rail crossings at the U.S.–Canada border.

SOURCE: U.S. Department of Transportation, Bureau of Transportation Statistics, North American Border Crossing/Entry Data, available at transborder.bts.gov/programs/international/transborder/TBDR_BC/TBDR_BC_Index.html as of June 2015.

Table 3-17: Incoming Rail Container (Empty) Crossings, U.S.-Canadian Border: 2009–2014

	2009	2010	2011	2012	2013	2014
Alaska	NA	NA	NA	NA	NA	NA
Idaho	6,338	8,153	9,266	8,799	7,590	8,443
Maine	12,005	13,670	14,816	27,948	26,752	14,334
Michigan	223,346	219,110	235,493	247,419	278,926	294,016
Minnesota	70,969	80,552	91,799	117,189	140,282	141,598
Montana	10,712	10,201	13,414	24,122	22,747	11,517
New York	49,459	45,577	48,654	48,322	44,259	56,615
North Dakota	107,998	122,251	106,968	127,611	109,575	132,729
Vermont	8,792	9,177	8,149	7,303	10,475	7,805
Washington	40,865	84,528	110,290	106,632	111,135	112,948
United States, total	530,484	593,219	638,849	715,345	751,741	780,005

KEY: NA = not applicable.

NOTE: The states listed in the table comprise all states with rail crossings at the U.S.–Canada border.

SOURCE: U.S. Department of Transportation, Bureau of Transportation Statistics, North American Border Crossing/Entry Data, available at transborder.bts.gov/programs/international/transborder/TBDR_BC/TBDR_BC_Index.html as of June 2015.

Table 3-18: Incoming Truck Crossings, U.S.-Mexican Border: 2009–2014

	2009	2010	2011	2012	2013	2014
Arizona	343,761	372,719	354,573	377,903	381,568	380,751
California	1,026,642	1,088,707	1,110,151	1,144,877	1,143,338	1,187,675
New Mexico	66,181	87,290	80,620	91,675	92,924	101,520
Texas	2,854,881	3,194,209	3,323,032	3,489,468	3,577,037	3,744,622
United States, total	4,291,465	4,742,925	4,868,376	5,103,923	5,194,867	5,414,568

NOTES: Truck crossings do not represent the number of unique vehicles and include both loaded and unloaded trucks. Crossings do not include privately owned pickup trucks. The data for incoming trucks exceeds the data for truck containers loaded and unloaded (empty) because some incoming trucks do not carry a container. The states listed in the table comprise all states with truck entries at U.S.–Mexico border.

SOURCE: U.S. Department of Transportation, Bureau of Transportation Statistics, North American Border Crossing/Entry Data, available at transborder.bts.gov/programs/international/transborder/TBDR_BC/TBDR_BC_Index.html as of June 2015.

Table 3-19: Incoming Truck Container (Loaded) Crossings, U.S.-Mexican Border: 2009–2014

	2009	2010	2011	2012	2013	2014
Arizona	264,579	290,773	272,641	286,742	288,249	294,686
California	620,758	677,959	700,750	734,214	740,345	815,257
New Mexico	46,243	56,625	57,813	55,144	67,912	67,729
Texas	1,797,123	2,148,778	2,245,799	2,383,492	2,402,516	2,601,672
United States, total	2,728,703	3,174,135	3,277,003	3,459,592	3,499,022	3,779,344

NOTES: Truck crossings do not represent the number of unique vehicles and include both loaded and unloaded trucks. Crossings do not include privately owned pickup trucks. The data for incoming trucks exceeds the data for truck containers loaded and unloaded (empty) because some incoming trucks do not carry a container. The states listed in the table comprise all states with truck entries at U.S.–Mexico border.

SOURCE: U.S. Department of Transportation, Bureau of Transportation Statistics, North American Border Crossing/Entry Data, available at transborder.bts.gov/programs/international/transborder/TBDR_BC/TBDR_BC_Index.html as of June 2015.

Table 3-20: Incoming Truck Container (Empty) Crossings, U.S.-Mexican Border: 2009–2014

	2009	2010	2011	2012	2013	2014
Arizona	80,732	84,826	87,021	92,096	91,408	87,197
California	398,773	410,314	408,855	427,693	382,724	373,282
New Mexico	19,819	27,809	22,345	24,228	22,658	31,888
Texas	1,050,714	1,012,053	1,002,716	1,079,517	1,035,971	1,042,072
United States, total	1,550,038	1,535,002	1,520,937	1,623,534	1,532,761	1,534,439

NOTES: Truck crossings do not represent the number of unique vehicles and include both loaded and unloaded trucks. Crossings do not include privately owned pickup trucks. The data for incoming trucks exceeds the data for truck containers loaded and unloaded (empty) because some incoming trucks do not carry a container. The states listed in the table comprise all states with truck entries at U.S.–Mexico border.

SOURCE: U.S. Department of Transportation, Bureau of Transportation Statistics, North American Border Crossing/Entry Data, available at transborder.bts.gov/programs/international/transborder/TBDR_BC/TBDR_BC_Index.html as of June 2015.

Table 3-21: Incoming Train Crossings, U.S.-Mexican Border: 2009–2014

	2009	2010	2011	2012	2013	2014
Arizona	563	602	709	657	866	795
California	506	469	481	467	504	457
New Mexico	NA	NA	NA	NA	NA	NA
Texas	6,406	6,596	7,176	7,833	7,971	9,161
United States, total	7,475	7,667	8,366	8,957	9,341	10,413

KEY: NA = not applicable.

NOTE: The states listed in the table comprise all states with rail crossings at the U.S.–Mexico border.

SOURCE: U.S. Department of Transportation, Bureau of Transportation Statistics, North American Border Crossing/Entry Data, available at transborder.bts.gov/programs/international/transborder/TBDR_BC/TBDR_BC_Index.html as of June 2015.

Table 3-22: Incoming Rail Container (Loaded) Crossings, U.S.-Mexican Border: 2009–2014

	2009	2010	2011	2012	2013	2014
Arizona	26,735	35,862	38,761	37,931	49,481	42,802
California	410	493	675	676	475	588
New Mexico	NA	NA	NA	NA	NA	NA
Texas	211,524	281,667	319,752	361,206	392,483	430,476
United States, total	238,669	318,022	359,188	399,813	442,439	473,866

KEY: NA = not applicable.

NOTE: The states listed in the table comprise all states with rail crossings at the U.S.–Mexico border.

SOURCE: U.S. Department of Transportation, Bureau of Transportation Statistics, North American Border Crossing/Entry Data, available at transborder.bts.gov/programs/international/transborder/TBDR_BC/TBDR_BC_Index.html as of June 2015.

Table 3-23: Incoming Rail Container (Empty) Crossings, U.S.-Mexican Border: 2009–2014

	2009	2010	2011	2012	2013	2014
Arizona	18,097	18,141	22,471	23,464	33,885	32,963
California	9,924	9785	11142	9846	9219	9649
New Mexico	NA	NA	NA	NA	NA	NA
Texas	307,609	360,119	378,164	394,640	351,783	393,515
United States, total	335,630	388,045	411,777	427,950	394,887	436,127

KEY: NA = not applicable.

NOTE: The states listed in the table comprise all states with rail crossings at the U.S.–Mexico border.

SOURCE: U.S. Department of Transportation, Bureau of Transportation Statistics, North American Border Crossing/Entry Data, available at transborder.bts.gov/programs/international/transborder/TBDR_BC/TBDR_BC_Index.html as of June 2015.

Table 3-24: Top 50 U.S. Foreign Trade Freight Gateways: 2013
(Ranked by value of shipments in billions of dollars)

Gateway[1]	Mode	Rank	Exports	Imports	Total
Los Angeles, CA	Water	1	42.6	170.2	212.9
New York, NY	Water	2	52.4	149.5	201.9
John F. Kennedy International Airport, NY	Air	3	96.4	93.4	189.7
Long Beach, CA	Water	4	37.3	143.6	180.9
Laredo, TX	Land	5	82.4	91.6	174.0
Houston, TX	Water	6	93.1	74.4	167.5
Detroit, MI	Land	7	64.0	58.9	122.9
Chicago, IL	Air	8	38.9	83.3	122.2
Los Angeles International Airport, CA	Air	9	41.8	45.8	87.6
Port Huron, MI	Land	10	40.2	41.6	81.8
Buffalo-Niagara Falls, NY	Land	11	43.4	37.5	80.9
Norfolk, VA	Water	12	33.8	37.5	71.3
Savannah, GA	Water	13	27.8	43.3	71.1
New Orleans, LA	Air	14	26.3	41.9	68.2
Miami International Airport, FL	Air	15	39.6	27.8	67.4
Charleston, SC	Water	16	24.4	40.7	65.2
El Paso, TX	Land	17	30.3	34.0	64.2
Baltimore, MD	Water	18	20.9	31.8	52.7
San Francisco International Airport, CA	Air	19	28.1	23.0	51.1
Tacoma, WA	Water	20	11.6	39.4	51.0
Dallas-Fort Worth, TX	Air	21	17.4	32.6	50.0
Oakland, CA	Water	22	19.9	27.5	47.4
Cleveland, OH	Air	23	25.7	18.1	43.8
Anchorage, AK	Air	24	9.5	31.5	41.0
New Orleans, LA	Water	25	24.0	15.3	39.3
Otay Mesa, CA	Land	26	13.1	22.9	36.0
Atlanta, GA	Air	27	12.8	21.9	34.7
Beaumont, TX	Water	28	6.6	25.9	32.6
Nogales, AZ	Land	29	10.3	17.4	27.7
Hidalgo, TX	Land	30	10.7	16.6	27.3
Seattle, WA	Water	31	7.4	19.6	27.0
Pembina, ND	Land	32	17.0	9.9	26.9
Miami, FL	Water	33	11.1	14.7	25.8
Corpus Christi, TX	Water	34	10.9	14.7	25.6
Morgan City, LA	Water	35	2.1	22.1	24.2
Port Everglades, FL	Water	36	13.5	10.4	23.9
Jacksonville, FL	Water	37	12.3	11.2	23.5
Gramercy, LA	Water	38	14.5	8.1	22.6
Champlain-Rouses Point, NY	Land	39	9.3	12.5	21.9
Texas City, TX	Water	40	9.6	12.0	21.7
Eagle Pass, TX	Land	41	7.1	14.3	21.4
Blaine, WA	Land	42	13.0	8.0	21.0
Philadelphia, PA	Water	43	2.8	17.0	19.8
Portal, ND	Land	44	12.3	7.1	19.4
Lake Charles, LA	Water	45	5.8	13.4	19.2
Brunswick, GA	Water	46	5.0	14.2	19.2
Port Arthur, TX	Water	47	7.9	10.7	18.6
Santa Teresa, NM	Land	48	8.3	10.2	18.6
Sweetgrass, MT	Land	49	9.9	7.3	17.2
Houston Intercontinental Airport, TX	Air	50	9.5	7.6	17.1
Total top 50 gateways			1,214.6	1,784.0	2,998.6

[1]Gateway is any port, airport, or border crossing that provides access for the import or export of goods.

NOTES: All data: Trade levels reflect the mode of transportation as a shipment enters or exits at a border port. Flows through individual ports are based on reported data collected from U.S. trade documents. Trade does not include low-value shipments. (In general, these are imports valued at less than $1,250 and exports that are valued at less than $2,500). Air: Data for all air gateways include a low level (generally less than 2%-3% of the total value) of small user-fee airports located in the same region. Air gateways not identified by airport name (e.g., Chicago, IL, and others) include major airport(s) in that geographic area in addition to small regional airports. In addition, due to U.S. Census Bureau confidentiality regulations, data for courier operations are included in the airport totals for JFK International Airport, Chicago, Los Angeles, Miami, New Orleans, Anchorage, and Cleveland.

SOURCES: Air-U.S. Department of Commerce, U.S. Census Bureau, Foreign Trade Division, USA Trade Online, available at www.usatradeonline.gov as of November 2014. **Land**-U.S. Department of Transportation, Bureau of Transportation Statistics, Transborder Freight Data available at transborder.bts.gov/programs/international/transborder as of March 2015. **Water**-U.S. Army Corps of Engineers, Navigation Data Center, personal communication as of March 2015.

Chapter 4
Passenger Travel

Table 4-1: Commuting to Work: 2013

State	Number of workers	Percent						Mean travel time to work (minutes)
		Car, truck, or van– drove alone	Car, truck, or van– carpooled	Public transportation (excluding taxicab)	Walked	Taxicab, motorcycle, bicycle or other means	Worked at home	
Alabama	1,983,610	86.4	8.5	0.5	1.0	1.0	2.5	23.6
Alaska	357,776	66.7	13.0	1.8	8.8	5.4	4.3	18.4
Arizona	2,754,451	76.3	11.0	2.4	2.1	2.8	5.5	23.4
Arkansas	1,223,214	83.4	10.1	0.5	1.7	1.5	2.8	20.8
California	16,745,843	73.2	10.9	5.3	2.7	2.6	5.2	26.4
Colorado	2,577,184	74.7	9.7	3.3	2.9	2.5	6.9	22.9
Connecticut	1,736,156	77.9	8.3	5.1	3.1	1.2	4.3	24.4
Delaware	423,542	80.3	9.1	3.5	2.1	1.2	3.7	24.5
District of Columbia	330,087	32.3	5.3	38.5	13.6	5.9	4.4	28.6
Florida	8,353,263	79.6	9.4	2.1	1.5	2.2	5.1	24.8
Georgia	4,291,263	79.6	10.3	2.1	1.5	1.7	4.9	25.7
Hawaii	672,446	67.6	13.5	6.1	4.2	4.2	4.4	25.6
Idaho	696,905	78.8	9.6	0.7	3.1	2.3	5.5	19.0
Illinois	5,973,263	73.6	8.3	9.1	3.1	1.6	4.2	26.9
Indiana	2,974,599	83.0	8.8	1.2	2.0	1.7	3.3	22.4
Iowa	1,547,508	80.9	8.6	1.1	3.7	1.6	4.2	18.1
Kansas	1,389,013	82.4	9.1	0.5	2.5	1.5	4.0	18.4
Kentucky	1,866,676	82.8	9.6	1.1	2.3	1.2	3.2	21.9
Louisiana	1,984,437	82.6	9.6	1.3	1.7	2.3	2.4	24.6
Maine	629,171	77.4	10.6	0.7	3.9	1.6	5.7	22.0
Maryland	2,946,590	74.0	9.0	9.1	2.4	1.2	4.2	31.1
Massachusetts	3,326,313	71.8	7.4	9.9	4.8	1.7	4.4	27.3
Michigan	4,274,964	82.4	8.8	1.5	2.2	1.3	3.8	23.1
Minnesota	2,773,626	78.4	8.6	3.6	2.9	1.6	4.9	21.9
Mississippi	1,181,081	84.0	10.3	0.4	1.5	1.7	1.9	23.2
Missouri	2,773,780	81.7	9.2	1.6	2.0	1.4	4.1	22.3
Montana	475,287	75.1	10.1	0.7	5.3	2.8	6.0	16.9
Nebraska	954,452	81.5	9.3	0.8	2.7	1.3	4.4	17.3
Nevada	1,246,513	78.4	10.5	3.4	2.2	1.9	3.6	22.8
New Hampshire	677,618	81.2	8.1	1.0	3.1	1.1	5.4	25.4
New Jersey	4,166,286	72.0	8.0	11.1	2.9	2.0	4.0	29.7
New Mexico	865,357	79.2	10.5	1.1	2.3	2.6	4.4	20.5
New York	9,024,559	52.8	6.9	27.9	6.4	2.0	4.0	30.8
North Carolina	4,348,669	81.1	10.0	1.1	1.9	1.3	4.5	22.8
North Dakota	387,697	79.0	10.1	0.4	4.5	1.6	4.4	17.1
Ohio	5,241,598	83.6	7.8	1.7	2.2	1.2	3.5	22.4
Oklahoma	1,703,568	83.4	9.7	0.5	1.7	1.4	3.4	20.6
Oregon	1,745,718	71.6	10.3	4.3	4.0	3.5	6.3	21.4
Pennsylvania	5,867,765	76.8	8.3	5.6	3.9	1.5	3.9	25.0
Rhode Island	505,361	80.3	8.0	2.7	4.1	1.8	3.1	23.2
South Carolina	2,064,944	82.9	9.0	0.7	2.5	1.6	3.3	22.9
South Dakota	427,117	79.7	9.2	0.3	4.2	1.4	5.2	16.1
Tennessee	2,837,090	83.9	9.2	0.7	1.4	1.3	3.5	23.7
Texas	11,939,372	80.2	10.7	1.6	1.6	1.8	4.1	24.4
Utah	1,307,408	76.0	11.8	2.3	2.6	2.1	5.1	20.1
Vermont	314,505	75.4	9.7	1.2	5.3	1.6	6.8	21.0
Virginia	4,018,400	77.4	9.4	4.4	2.5	1.8	4.5	26.4
Washington	3,204,510	72.7	10.1	6.3	3.5	2.2	5.3	24.6
West Virginia	738,848	81.5	10.8	0.7	2.8	1.2	3.1	25.0
Wisconsin	2,822,070	80.5	8.2	2.0	3.5	1.7	4.1	21.2
Wyoming	290,906	77.1	10.8	1.5	4.6	2.3	3.7	16.9
United States, total	142,962,379	76.4	9.4	5.2	2.8	1.9	4.4	24.7

NOTES: Data for workers age 16 years and over, based on state of residence.

SOURCE: U.S. Department of Commerce, U.S. Census Bureau, *2013 American Community Survey 1-Year Estimates*, available at www.census.gov/acs as of August 2015.

Table 4-2: Licensed Drivers: 2013

State	Number of licensed drivers[1]	Licensed drivers per registered vehicle	Resident population	Driving age population (16 and over)	Drivers per 1,000 total resident population	Drivers per 1,000 driving age population
Alabama	3,859,403	0.81	4,833,722	3,848,576	798	1,003
Alaska	528,873	0.69	735,132	567,372	719	932
Arizona	4,791,450	0.90	6,626,624	5,189,383	723	923
Arkansas	2,097,201	0.89	2,959,373	2,328,418	709	901
California	24,390,236	0.89	38,332,521	30,218,651	636	807
Colorado	3,837,488	0.83	5,268,367	4,162,832	728	922
Connecticut	2,534,090	0.90	3,596,080	2,908,694	705	871
Delaware	723,657	0.77	925,749	744,154	782	972
District of Columbia	405,555	1.30	646,449	545,368	627	744
Florida	13,670,441	0.92	19,552,860	15,996,284	699	855
Georgia	6,607,016	0.86	9,992,167	7,775,850	661	850
Hawaii	915,033	0.70	1,404,054	1,128,884	652	811
Idaho	1,111,485	0.66	1,612,136	1,230,965	689	903
Illinois	8,261,582	0.82	12,882,135	10,208,958	641	809
Indiana	4,500,403	0.81	6,570,902	5,164,988	685	871
Iowa	2,143,665	0.61	3,090,416	2,447,740	694	876
Kansas	2,017,759	0.78	2,893,957	2,248,518	697	897
Kentucky	3,019,283	0.76	4,395,295	3,493,897	687	864
Louisiana	3,278,143	0.85	4,625,470	3,633,574	709	902
Maine	1,011,385	0.85	1,328,302	1,099,524	761	920
Maryland	4,140,105	1.10	5,928,814	4,737,568	698	874
Massachusetts	4,765,586	0.97	6,692,824	5,466,929	712	872
Michigan	6,986,587	0.86	9,895,622	7,922,631	706	882
Minnesota	3,330,725	0.64	5,420,380	4,283,605	614	778
Mississippi	1,968,907	0.96	2,991,207	2,334,928	658	843
Missouri	4,280,438	0.74	6,044,171	4,804,108	708	891
Montana	766,716	0.50	1,015,165	816,492	755	939
Nebraska	1,374,529	0.75	1,868,516	1,453,480	736	946
Nevada	1,756,095	0.81	2,790,136	2,202,901	629	797
New Hampshire	1,061,433	0.76	1,323,459	1,087,125	802	976
New Jersey	6,081,386	0.87	8,899,339	7,115,472	683	855
New Mexico	1,456,500	0.79	2,085,287	1,632,983	698	892
New York[2]	11,210,783	1.07	19,651,127	15,907,539	570	705
North Carolina	6,822,902	0.88	9,848,060	7,812,833	693	873
North Dakota	513,838	0.62	723,393	577,967	710	889
Ohio	8,030,421	0.79	11,570,808	9,230,566	694	870
Oklahoma	2,418,307	0.71	3,850,568	3,004,270	628	805
Oregon	2,773,373	0.78	3,930,065	3,170,882	706	875
Pennsylvania	8,896,590	0.86	12,773,801	10,381,760	696	857
Rhode Island	749,232	0.90	1,051,511	863,702	713	867
South Carolina	3,536,404	0.91	4,774,839	3,813,523	741	927
South Dakota	603,643	0.61	844,877	659,321	714	916
Tennessee	4,605,100	0.87	6,495,978	5,171,538	709	890
Texas	15,447,273	0.79	26,448,193	20,165,608	584	766
Utah	1,661,219	0.81	2,900,872	2,095,086	573	793
Vermont	543,057	0.90	626,630	519,298	867	1,046
Virginia	5,602,765	0.81	8,260,405	6,602,567	678	849
Washington	5,301,630	0.84	6,971,406	5,553,636	760	955
West Virginia	1,177,136	0.83	1,854,304	1,516,395	635	776
Wisconsin	4,171,427	0.80	5,742,713	4,585,087	726	910
Wyoming	421,473	0.51	582,658	459,841	723	917
United States, total	212,159,728	0.84	316,128,839	250,892,271	671	846

[1]Includes restricted drivers and graduated driver licenses.
[2]State did not provide current data, estimated by FHWA.

SOURCE: U.S. Department of Transportation, Federal Highway Administration, Highway Statistics, DL-1C, available at www.fhwa.dot.gov/policyin-formation/statistics.cfm as of June 2015.

Table 4-3: Transit Ridership in the 50 Largest Urbanized Areas: 2012 and 2013

Urbanized area	Population (2010)	Rank by population	Annual unlinked passenger trips (thousands)		Percent in 2013					Percent in 2012				
			2013	2012	Motor bus	Heavy rail	Light rail	Commuter rail	Other	Motor bus	Heavy rail	Light rail	Commuter rail	Other
New York-Newark, NY-NJ-CT	18,351,295	1	4,299,316	4,178,127	27.7	63.6	0.4	6.1	0.9	28.8	63.6	0.5	6.2	0.9
Los Angeles-Long Beach-Anaheim, CA	12,150,996	2	681,565	679,932	77.9	7.3	9.3	2.0	1.8	80.1	7.2	8.9	2.1	1.8
Chicago, IL-IN	8,608,208	3	648,055	664,108	51.6	35.4	0.0	11.9	1.1	52.4	34.8	0.0	11.7	1.1
Miami, FL	5,502,379	4	171,635	168,182	77.3	12.4	0.0	2.4	7.9	78.3	11.4	0.0	2.4	7.8
Philadelphia, PA-NJ-DE-MD	5,441,567	5	380,981	371,544	51.2	29.3	0.0	9.9	2.4	50.2	29.7	7.8	9.9	2.4
Dallas-Fort Worth-Arlington, TX	5,121,892	6	80,648	80,607	56.4	0.0	36.5	2.6	3.9	57.6	0.0	35.4	2.7	4.2
Houston, TX	4,944,332	7	84,791	82,223	71.8	0.0	13.4	0.0	5.2	80.9	0.0	13.8	0.0	5.2
Washington, DC-VA-MD	4,586,770	8	473,403	479,674	40.0	57.8	0.0	1.0	0.5	40.3	58.2	0.0	1.0	0.5
Atlanta, GA	4,515,419	9	140,132	139,959	46.8	49.7	0.0	0.0	1.4	48.3	50.4	0.0	0.0	1.3
Boston, MA-NH-RI	4,181,019	10	403,160	408,893	30.2	41.8	17.4	8.7	1.8	30.3	40.7	18.3	8.8	1.9
Detroit, MI	3,734,090	11	45,838	46,479	88.1	0.0	0.0	0.0	11.9	90.5	0.0	0.0	0.0	9.5
Phoenix-Mesa, AZ	3,629,114	12	76,807	75,431	78.6	0.0	18.6	0.0	2.8	78.6	0.0	18.6	0.0	2.8
San Francisco-Oakland, CA	3,281,212	13	449,674	440,217	38.8	28.1	10.1	3.6	17.5	39.0	28.0	11.8	3.1	18.1
Seattle, WA	3,059,393	14	201,644	196,621	57.7	0.0	4.8	1.5	25.6	67.3	0.0	5.3	1.4	25.9
San Diego, CA	2,956,746	15	154,010	102,031	54.0	0.0	41.3	1.1	2.2	62.6	0.0	33.0	1.6	2.8
Minneapolis-St. Paul, MN-WI	2,650,890	16	95,088	94,674	85.9	0.0	10.7	0.8	2.5	85.8	0.0	11.1	0.7	2.4
Tampa-St. Petersburg, FL	2,441,770	17	30,945	30,511	96.2	0.0	0.0	0.0	2.5	96.6	0.0	1.0	0.0	2.4
Denver-Aurora, CO	2,374,203	18	101,684	98,716	75.1	0.0	23.4	0.0	1.5	77.7	0.0	20.9	0.0	1.4
Baltimore, MD	2,203,663	19	108,096	107,991	63.8	14.1	8.0	8.4	1.9	67.6	14.3	8.2	8.1	1.9
St. Louis, MO-IL	2,150,706	20	49,900	50,287	64.0	0.0	34.2	0.0	1.8	64.1	0.0	34.1	0.0	1.9
Riverside-San Bernardino, CA	1,932,666	21	25,790	25,566	94.2	0.0	0.0	0.0	4.4	95.9	0.0	0.0	0.0	4.1
Las Vegas-Henderson, NV	1,886,011	22	65,874	65,867	84.9	0.0	0.0	0.0	8.4	91.7	0.0	0.0	0.0	8.3
Portland, OR-WA	1,849,898	23	111,675	113,365	57.7	0.0	35.1	0.0	1.3	59.1	0.0	39.7	0.0	1.2
Cleveland, OH	1,780,673	24	50,067	49,115	69.3	12.8	5.8	0.0	2.0	79.5	12.7	5.8	0.0	2.0
San Antonio, TX	1,758,210	25	46,963	47,508	96.9	0.0	0.0	0.0	3.1	96.9	0.0	0.0	0.0	3.1
Pittsburgh, PA	1,733,853	26	65,462	67,410	83.4	0.0	12.3	0.0	3.2	83.5	0.0	11.5	0.0	5.0
Sacramento, CA	1,723,634	27	31,867	31,087	53.2	0.0	42.4	0.0	2.1	54.7	0.0	43.7	0.0	1.6
San Jose, CA	1,664,496	28	44,221	43,741	74.1	0.0	24.3	0.0	1.7	74.3	0.0	24.0	0.0	1.7
Cincinnati, OH-KY-IN	1,624,827	29	21,067	21,445	97.9	0.0	0.0	0.0	1.9	98.2	0.0	0.0	0.0	1.8
Kansas City, MO-KS	1,519,417	30	17,010	17,189	86.1	0.0	0.0	0.0	3.5	96.3	0.0	0.0	0.0	3.7
Orlando, FL	1,510,516	31	29,853	29,531	93.8	0.0	0.0	0.0	3.4	96.5	0.0	0.0	0.0	3.5
Indianapolis, IN	1,487,483	32	10,527	10,243	97.4	0.0	0.0	0.0	2.6	97.4	0.0	0.0	0.0	2.6
Virginia Beach, VA	1,439,666	33	18,811	18,839	86.2	0.0	9.4	0.0	4.4	86.5	0.0	8.8	0.0	4.7
Milwaukee, WI	1,376,476	34	128,516	47,497	66.4	0.0	0.0	0.0	0.5	98.4	0.0	0.0	0.0	1.6
Columbus, OH	1,368,035	35	18,917	18,692	97.8	0.0	0.0	0.0	2.2	98.6	0.0	0.0	0.0	1.4
Austin, TX	1,362,416	36	36,402	36,275	93.7	0.0	0.0	0.0	2.3	96.1	0.0	1.6	0.0	2.3
Charlotte, NC-SC	1,249,442	37	29,046	28,610	80.2	0.0	16.9	0.0	2.9	80.9	0.0	17.4	0.0	1.7
Providence, RI-MA	1,190,956	38	21,660	21,349	95.2	0.0	0.0	0.0	4.3	95.6	0.0	0.0	0.0	4.4
Jacksonville, FL	1,065,219	39	12,678	12,549	88.5	0.0	0.0	0.0	11.5	89.4	0.0	0.0	0.0	10.6
Memphis, TN-MS-AR	1,060,061	40	10,460	10,267	83.6	0.0	0.0	0.0	2.4	83.0	0.0	14.5	0.0	2.4
Salt Lake City-West Valley City, UT	1,021,243	41	44,281	42,347	42.7	0.0	42.9	8.6	4.0	49.7	0.0	41.4	4.4	4.4
Louisville/Jefferson County, KY-IN	972,546	42	17,089	17,162	95.9	0.0	0.0	0.0	4.1	96.0	0.0	0.0	0.0	4.0
Nashville-Davidson, TN	969,587	43	10,545	10,500	90.0	0.0	0.0	2.4	6.1	91.3	0.0	0.0	2.5	6.2
Richmond, VA	953,556	44	9,369	9,458	91.9	0.0	0.0	0.0	8.1	92.7	0.0	0.0	0.0	7.3
Buffalo, NY	935,906	45	29,750	29,937	78.2	0.0	21.2	0.0	0.6	77.8	0.0	21.6	0.0	0.6
Hartford, CT	924,859	46	18,784	17,724	87.3	0.0	0.0	4.6	5.9	90.4	0.0	0.0	3.5	6.1
Bridgeport-Stamford, CT-NY	923,311	47	12,130	12,115	96.5	0.0	0.0	0.0	3.5	97.2	0.0	0.0	0.0	2.8
New Orleans, LA	899,703	48	27,191	27,349	55.6	0.0	0.0	0.0	12.6	64.0	0.0	26.4	0.0	9.5
Raleigh, NC	884,891	49	10,008	6,929	95.5	0.0	0.0	0.0	4.5	93.7	0.0	0.0	0.0	6.3
Oklahoma City, OK	861,505	50	2,912	2,943	97.8	0.0	0.0	0.0	2.2	97.8	0.0	0.0	0.0	2.2
Top 50 urbanized area, total	141,816,726		9,656,298	9,388,820	45.4	39.4	5.1	4.9	2.9	46.9	39.7	5.5	5.0	3.0
United States, urbanized area total[1]	209,569,050		10,574,238	10,214,018	49.2	36.1	4.6	4.5	3.2	50.7	36.5	5.0	4.6	3.2
Top 50 as percent of U.S. total	67.7		91.3	91.9	84.3	99.7	100.0	99.5	84.4	85.0	100.0	99.9	99.4	85.5

[1]Excludes territories (Puerto Rico and Virgin Islands)

NOTES: This table includes data from urban transit agencies that are required to report information to the federal government because they applied for or are direct beneficiaries of urbanized area formula grants (49 USC 5307). Beginning in 2012, data include estimated industry totals for agencies with a Small Systems Waiver in place and Rural reporters. Details may not add to totals due to rounding. Other includes autmoated guideway, cable car, demand response, ferry boat, inclined plane, monorail, trolley bus, and van pool.

SOURCE: U.S. Department of Transportation, Federal Transit Adminstration, National Transit Database, Monthly Database, available at www. ntdprogram.gov as of July 2015.

Table 4-4: Urban Transit Ridership by State and Transit Mode: 2013

State	Number of agencies reporting	Annual unlinked passenger trips (thousands)	Percent				
			Motor bus	Heavy rail	Light rail	Commuter rail	Other
Alabama	14	7,514	84.8	0.0	0.0	0.0	15.2
Alaska	4	5,079	87.9	0.0	0.0	0.0	9.1
Arizona	16	100,261	82.9	0.0	14.2	0.0	2.8
Arkansas	7	5,862	95.8	0.0	1.6	0.0	2.6
California	102	1,434,266	65.2	12.3	12.1	2.3	7.0
Colorado	10	109,704	76.5	0.0	21.7	0.0	1.9
Connecticut	18	44,809	93.0	0.0	0.0	1.9	4.2
Delaware	1	11,195	91.0	0.0	0.0	0.0	9.0
District of Columbia	2	413,652	33.3	66.2	0.0	0.0	0.5
Florida	34	285,579	83.9	7.4	0.1	1.5	6.8
Georgia	20	161,115	53.1	43.2	0.0	0.0	1.8
Hawaii	2	73,078	97.8	0.0	0.0	0.0	2.0
Idaho	6	2,677	90.1	0.0	0.0	0.0	9.9
Illinois	18	674,192	53.9	34.0	0.0	10.9	1.2
Indiana	24	34,656	86.1	0.0	0.0	10.4	3.3
Iowa	13	22,724	95.6	0.0	0.0	0.0	4.4
Kansas	9	7,459	88.6	0.0	0.0	0.0	9.1
Kentucky	11	27,075	95.5	0.0	0.0	0.0	4.3
Louisiana	15	38,411	67.8	0.0	22.5	0.0	9.7
Maine	10	5,445	62.4	0.0	0.0	10.2	27.4
Maryland	14	143,586	72.3	10.6	6.0	6.3	1.9
Massachusetts	16	424,702	33.2	39.7	16.5	8.3	2.1
Michigan	23	98,694	91.9	0.0	0.0	0.0	7.9
Minnesota	8	103,567	86.8	0.0	9.8	0.8	2.5
Mississippi	3	1,981	86.3	0.0	0.0	0.0	13.7
Missouri	10	68,235	70.7	0.0	25.0	0.0	2.0
Montana	4	2,466	95.6	0.0	0.0	0.0	4.4
Nebraska	3	6,594	96.6	0.0	0.0	0.0	3.4
Nevada	4	74,479	86.1	0.0	0.0	0.0	7.9
New Hampshire	7	3,865	67.4	0.0	0.0	0.0	1.6
New Jersey	33	391,480	46.4	20.7	5.4	20.5	2.2
New Mexico	5	16,426	90.5	0.0	0.0	6.6	2.6
New York	47	3,966,731	26.4	67.1	0.2	4.6	0.8
North Carolina	40	73,295	87.7	0.0	6.7	0.0	5.6
North Dakota	4	2,509	87.0	0.0	0.0	0.0	13.0
Ohio	30	112,620	82.1	5.7	2.6	0.0	5.0
Oklahoma	5	7,831	95.5	0.0	0.0	0.0	3.7
Oregon	12	124,644	59.7	0.0	34.8	0.0	1.9
Pennsylvania	27	461,149	58.8	21.9	7.7	8.2	2.9
Rhode Island	1	20,483	96.6	0.0	0.0	0.0	3.4
South Carolina	13	11,469	93.3	0.0	0.0	0.0	5.1
South Dakota	2	1,554	85.4	0.0	0.0	0.0	14.6
Tennessee	17	31,473	86.5	0.0	4.7	0.8	7.5
Texas	45	290,399	76.9	0.0	14.7	0.7	4.3
Utah	3	46,769	45.7	0.0	40.6	8.2	3.9
Vermont	1	2,740	91.1	0.0	0.0	0.0	2.0
Virginia	22	73,559	83.8	0.0	2.4	6.2	3.1
Washington	22	243,626	62.6	0.0	4.7	1.2	23.1
West Virginia	8	8,525	71.0	0.0	0.0	0.0	29.0
Wisconsin	21	70,584	96.7	0.0	0.1	0.0	2.6
Wyoming	2	487	84.4	0.0	0.0	0.0	15.6
United States, total[1]	788	10,351,277	49.1	36.8	5.0	4.6	3.2

[1]Excludes territories (Puerto Rico and Virgin Islands)

NOTES: This table includes data from urban transit agencies that are required to report information to the federal government because they applied for or are direct beneficiaries of urbanized area formula grants (49 USC 5307). Beginning in 2012, data include estimated industry totals for agencies with a Small Systems Waiver in place and Rural reporters. Data are assigned to the state of a transit agency's mailing address. Details may not add to totals due to rounding. Light rail includes light rail, street car, and hybrid rail modes. Motorbus includes motorbus, commuter bus, and bus rapid transit. Other includes automated guideway, cable car, demand response, ferry boat, inclined plane, monorail, trolley bus, and van pool.

SOURCE: U.S. Department of Transportation, Federal Transit Adminstration, National Transit Database, table 19, available at www. ntdprogram.gov as of July 2015.

Table 4-5: Top 50 Amtrak Stations by Number of Passengers[1]: Fiscal Years 2013 and 2014

Station	Fiscal Year 2013		Fiscal Year 2014	
	Rank	Number of passengers	Rank	Number of passengers
New York City (Penn Station), DC	1	9,556,424	1	10,024,474
Washington, DC	2	5,033,392	2	5,028,928
Philadelphia 30th Street, PA	3	4,125,503	3	4,083,704
Chicago, IL	4	3,522,388	4	3,377,259
Los Angeles, CA	5	1,643,706	5	1,551,090
Boston-South Station, MA	6	1,434,148	6	1,491,095
Baltimore, MD	8	1,065,576	7	1,032,527
Sacramento, CA	7	1,132,750	8	1,022,322
Albany-Rensselaer, NY	9	764,898	9	781,597
New Haven, CT	10	745,530	10	714,146
Wilmington, DE	11	738,313	11	704,523
San Diego, CA	13	686,953	12	700,107
BWI Thurgood Marshall Airport, MD	12	710,513	13	692,268
Newark, NJ	15	656,822	14	677,175
Providence, RI	14	660,267	15	665,670
Seattle, WA	17	640,054	16	626,623
Milwaukee, WI	18	617,153	17	596,415
Portland, OR	16	652,455	18	585,828
Emeryville, CA	19	598,859	19	578,386
Boston-Back Bay, MA	23	540,770	20	566,892
Lancaster, PA	20	578,731	21	529,409
Bakersfield, CA	22	546,439	22	521,423
Harrisburg, PA	21	571,940	23	498,995
Boston-North Station, MA	24	475,447	24	433,060
Trenton, NJ	28	425,075	25	419,477
Oceanside, CA	34	384,786	26	412,711
Irvine, CA	29	425,041	27	406,451
Stamford, CT	33	388,733	28	401,414
Fresno, CA	32	399,141	29	389,543
Solana Beach, CA	26	428,841	30	384,547
Metropark, NJ	35	383,353	31	381,178
Martinez, CA	25	473,836	32	359,755
Richmond - Staples Mill, VA	37	372,592	33	358,615
Davis, CA	30	424,114	34	358,350
St. Louis, MO	36	378,146	35	350,866
Fullerton, CA	40	313,949	36	336,265
Santa Barbara, CA	39	322,410	37	319,245
Oakland, CA	31	405,627	38	303,431
Stockton (San Joaquin St.), CA	41	295,344	39	292,818
Sanford (Auto Train Station), FL	43	265,274	40	274,445
Lorton (Auto Train), VA	44	265,274	41	274,445
Bloomington/Normal, IL	45	263,235	42	261,631
Anaheim, CA	38	342,284	43	254,066
Richmond, CA	37	372,592	44	241,962
San Juan Capistrano, CA	47	242,722	45	226,515
Hanford, CA	48	225,708	46	220,144
San Jose, CA	46	258,776	47	210,297
New Orleans, LA	49	212,426	48	201,476
San Diego-Old Town, CA	76	135,749	49	196,795
Springfield, IL	51	202,095	50	194,762
Top 50 stations, total		46,490,906		45,515,120
United States, all stations		62,841,683		61,557,072
Top 50 stations as percent of U.S. total		74.0		73.9

[1]Includes the number of boarding and alighting passengers (on & off the train).

NOTES: Amtrak's fiscal year ends on September 30. Ranking is based on the 2014 data. The total for the top 50 stations in 2013 is not the sum of stations in this table since some of the 2013 top 50 stations are not in the top 50 list in 2014.

SOURCE: National Passenger Railroad Corporation (Amtrak) available at http://www.amtrak.com/servlet/ContentServer?c=Page&pagename=am%2FLayout&cid=1246041980432 as of June 2015.

Table 4-6: Top 50 Airports by Passengers Enplaned on Large U.S. Carriers: 2003, 2012, 2013

Airport	Rank in 2013	Number of enplanements		
		2003	2012	2013
Atlanta, GA (Hartsfield-Jackson Atlanta International)	1	38,256,038	45,192,870	44,675,318
Chicago, IL (Chicago O'Hare International)	2	30,835,241	29,983,544	29,991,861
Dallas/Fort Worth, TX (Dallas/Fort Worth International)	3	24,724,519	27,555,896	28,490,680
Los Angeles, CA (Los Angeles International)	4	20,939,293	24,982,954	25,859,720
Denver, CO (Denver International)	5	17,744,834	25,511,455	25,184,634
Charlotte, NC (Charlotte Douglas International)	6	11,414,356	19,928,299	21,241,895
Phoenix, AZ (Phoenix Sky Harbor International)	7	18,030,517	19,221,241	19,156,769
San Francisco, CA (San Francisco International)	8	12,231,791	18,567,216	18,853,118
Las Vegas, NV (McCarran International)	9	16,898,813	18,467,290	18,480,027
Houston, TX (George Bush Intercontinental/Houston)	10	15,692,910	18,155,248	17,945,713
New York, NY (John F. Kennedy International)	11	10,821,004	17,107,144	17,038,558
Minneapolis, MN (Minneapolis-St Paul International)	12	16,047,432	15,892,286	16,200,673
Seattle, WA (Seattle/Tacoma International)	13	12,799,019	15,460,449	15,979,235
Newark, NJ (Newark Liberty International)	14	13,154,602	15,370,482	15,879,280
Detroit, MI (Detroit Metro Wayne County)	15	15,603,940	15,424,226	15,507,719
Miami, FL (Miami International)	16	11,288,952	15,316,047	15,442,379
Orlando, FL (Orlando International)	17	12,579,440	15,594,968	15,278,563
Philadelphia, PA (Philadelphia International)	18	11,511,273	14,362,474	14,508,927
Boston, MA (Logan International)	19	9,897,699	12,857,791	13,257,406
New York, NY (LaGuardia)	20	11,049,194	12,313,701	12,820,980
Baltimore, MD (Baltimore/Washington International Thurgood Marshall)	21	9,548,075	11,096,463	11,040,598
Fort Lauderdale, FL (Fort Lauderdale-Hollywood International)	22	8,276,957	10,644,055	10,693,964
Washington, DC (Washington Dulles International)	23	6,733,062	9,359,654	9,748,489
Chicago, IL (Chicago Midway International)	24	8,680,635	9,264,895	9,726,623
Salt Lake City, UT (Salt Lake City International)	25	8,932,998	9,579,427	9,666,707
Washington, DC (Ronald Reagan Washington National)	26	6,956,596	9,137,164	8,740,399
San Diego, CA (San Diego International)	27	7,466,727	8,479,221	8,662,314
Honolulu, HI (Honolulu International)	28	7,658,719	7,961,154	8,138,354
Tampa, FL (Tampa International)	29	7,475,654	8,005,320	8,036,590
Portland, OR (Portland International)	30	5,963,210	7,076,710	7,400,965
St. Louis, MO (Lambert-St. Louis International)	31	9,931,995	6,178,781	6,193,661
Houston, TX (William P Hobby)	32	3,703,830	5,040,709	5,371,820
Nashville, TN (Nashville International)	33	3,927,389	4,777,315	5,022,777
Austin, TX (Austin - Bergstrom International)	34	3,165,554	4,605,401	4,898,886
Kansas City, MO (Kansas City International)	35	4,825,282	4,856,267	4,820,972
Oakland, CA (Metropolitan Oakland International)	36	6,520,138	4,851,495	4,692,991
New Orleans, LA (Louis Armstrong New Orleans International)	37	4,589,037	4,273,944	4,554,142
Raleigh/Durham, NC (Raleigh-Durham International)	38	3,885,536	4,458,715	4,448,169
Santa Ana, CA (John Wayne Airport-Orange County)	39	4,265,963	4,300,976	4,424,745
Cleveland, OH (Cleveland-Hopkins International)	40	4,989,325	4,327,344	4,355,885
San Jose, CA (Norman Y. Mineta San Jose International)	41	5,041,304	4,028,860	4,235,676
Sacramento, CA (Sacramento International)	42	4,367,111	4,326,178	4,202,425
Dallas, TX (Dallas Love Field)	43	2,796,140	3,900,854	4,019,531
San Juan, PR (Luis Munoz Marin International)	44	4,619,347	4,073,344	4,000,152
San Antonio, TX (San Antonio International)	45	3,066,242	3,863,661	3,825,514
Pittsburgh, PA (Pittsburgh International)	46	7,035,578	3,868,672	3,786,479
Fort Myers, FL (Southwest Florida International)	47	2,815,861	3,507,186	3,637,929
Indianapolis, IN (Indianapolis International)	48	3,662,734	3,570,149	3,517,235
Milwaukee, WI (General Mitchell International)	49	3,083,674	3,698,097	3,203,231
Columbus, OH (Port Columbus International)	50	3,033,475	3,087,239	3,043,372
Top 50 airports, total[1]		508,751,314	573,729,606	579,904,050
United States, all airports		656,709,814	692,369,957	696,930,821
Top 50 as percent of all enplanements		77.5	82.9	83.2

[1]The total for the top 50 airports will not sum from the individual airports because some top 50 airports in 2012 were not in the top 50 in the earlier years.

NOTES: Data for 2013 are revised. Rank order by total enplaned passengers on large certificated U.S. air carriers (Majors, Nationals, Large Regionals, and Medium Regionals), scheduled and nonscheduled operations, at all airports served within the 50 states, the District of Columbia, and other U.S. areas designated by the Federal Aviation Administration.   Large certificated air carriers hold Certificates of Public Convenience and Necessity issued by the U.S. Department of Transportation authorizing the performance of air transportation. Large certificated air carriers operate at least one aircraft with seating capacity of more than 60 seats or a maximum payload capacity of more than 18,000 pounds. Data for commuter, small-certificated and foreign-flag air carriers are not included.

SOURCE: U.S. Department of Transportation, Bureau of Transportation Statistics, TranStats Database, T3: U.S. Air Carrier Airport Activity Statistics, available at www.transtats.bts.gov as of July 2015.

Table 4-7: Major Airports by On-Time Arrival Performance: 2013 and 2014
(Percent on-time)

Airport	2013		2014	
	Rank	On-time percentage	Rank	On-time percentage
Salt Lake City, UT (SLC)	1	85.0	1	85.6
Detroit, MI (DTW)	5	82.9	2	82.3
Seattle, WA (SEA)	3	83.4	3	81.9
Minneapolis/St. Paul, MN (MSP)	4	83.2	4	81.4
Charlotte, NC (CLT)	9	80.7	5	81.4
Atlanta, GA (ATL)	8	80.9	6	81.2
Miami, FL (MIA)	6	82.0	7	81.0
Phoenix, AZ (PHX)	2	83.8	8	80.8
Portland, OR (PDX)	7	82.0	9	79.6
Washington, DC (DCA)	17	78.7	10	78.0
Las Vegas, NV (LAS)	10	80.4	11	77.8
Boston, MA (BOS)	18	78.3	12	77.6
Baltimore, MD (BWI)	13	79.4	13	77.4
Los Angeles, CA (LAX)	12	79.6	14	77.1
San Diego, CA (SAN)	15	79.1	15	77.0
Tampa, FL (TPA)	16	78.8	16	76.8
Houston, TX (IAH)	11	79.8	17	76.8
Orlando, FL (MCO)	14	79.4	18	76.8
Denver, CO (DEN)	22	76.8	19	76.5
Philadelphia, PA (PHL)	23	76.0	20	76.2
Washington, DC (IAD)	20	77.5	21	75.6
Dallas/Fort Worth, TX (DFW)	19	78.2	22	75.4
New York, NY (JFK)	25	75.0	23	75.1
Chicago, IL (MDW)	21	77.2	24	74.4
Fort Lauderdale, FL (FLL)	24	75.3	25	74.0
New York, NY (LGA)	28	72.2	26	71.3
Newark, NJ (EWR)	29	70.4	27	70.2
San Francisco, CA (SFO)	27	72.7	28	69.2
Chicago, IL (ORD)	26	73.5	29	67.6
At all U.S. airports		78.3		76.3

NOTES: Major airports are those designated by the Office of Airline Information as having at least 1% of enplanements in the 48 contiguous states. Carriers reporting on-time data may change each year due to changes in carriers that are required to report and in carriers that report voluntarily. In 2013, the reporting carriers were AirTran Airways, Alaska Airlines, American Airlines, American Eagle Airlines, Delta Airlines, Endeavor Air, ExpressJet Airlines, Frontier Airlines, Hawaiian Airlines, JetBlue Airways, Mesa Airlines, SkyWest Airlines, Southwest Airlines, United Airlines, US Airways, Virgin America. The percentage of on-time arrivals is based on the number of scheduled operations. Flights that are cancelled, diverted or arrived at the gate more than 15 minutes after the scheduled arrival are excluded from on-time arrivals. Effective January 2012, data of the merged operations of United Airlines and Continental Airlines are combined. Effective January 2012, data of the merged operations of ExpressJet Airlines and Atlantic Southeast Airlines are combined.

SOURCE: U.S. Department of Transportation, Bureau of Transportation Statistics, Airline On-time Tables, available at www.rita.dot.gov/bts/sites/rita.dot.gov.bts/files/subject_areas/airline_information/airline_ontime_tables/index.html as of June 2015.

Table 4-8: Top 15 Cruise Ship Ports by Port of Departure: 2010 and 2011

Port	2010			2011		
	Rank	Passengers (thousands)	Cruises	Rank	Passengers (thousands)	Cruises
Miami, FL	1	2,151	779	1	1,970	731
Fort Lauderdale, FL	2	1,759	649	2	1,826	611
Port Canaveral, FL	3	1,299	448	3	1,496	485
New York, NY	4	562	219	4	612	242
San Juan, PR	5	522	227	5	522	222
Galveston, TX	7	440	152	6	462	149
Tampa, FL	8	425	192	7	458	199
Seattle, WA	6	469	217	8	439	183
Long Beach, CA	9	414	150	9	405	144
New Orleans, LA	11	261	89	10	373	136
Los Angeles, CA	10	378	140	11	311	130
Baltimore, MD	13	215	90	12	254	104
Cape Liberty, NJ	14	198	67	13	217	73
Jacksonville, FL	16	172	71	14	190	77
Charleston, SC	18	117	49	15	165	68
All other ports[1]		700	348		706	390
Top 15 ports, total[1]		9,516	3,618		9,702	3,554
Total U.S. ports		10,216	3,966		10,409	3,944
Top 15 as percent of total[1]		93.2	91.2		93.2	90.1

[1]Data for 2010 are based on the top 15 cruise ship ports in that year.

NOTES: Cruise passenger statistics for this table are based on the passenger data provided by 20 major cruise lines that offered North American cruises with a U.S. port of call. Details may not add to totals due to rounding.

SOURCE: U.S. Department of Transportation, Maritime Administration, Cruise Summary Tables, available at www.marad.dot.gov/library_landing_page/data_and_statistics/Data_and_Statistics.htm as of June 2013.

Table 4-9: Incoming Personal Vehicle Crossings, U.S.-Canadian Border: 2009–2014

State	2009	2010	2011	2012	2013	2014
Alaska	97,832	97,879	92,911	91,014	90,780	89,997
Idaho	244,118	262,244	286,310	270,114	278,175	279,732
Maine	2,747,309	3,051,111	3,194,976	3,208,951	3,098,861	2,874,542
Michigan	6,439,995	6,565,627	6,966,265	7,133,003	7,170,429	6,944,792
Minnesota	1,036,727	1,192,351	1,284,589	1,287,040	1,259,588	1,238,024
Montana	555,911	659,358	696,532	737,724	763,866	759,832
New York	8,253,468	8,581,980	9,072,685	9,386,897	9,175,000	8,689,968
North Dakota	638,750	761,960	760,514	853,493	846,334	841,472
Vermont	1,249,939	1,334,432	1,447,109	1,532,179	1,563,982	1,608,154
Washington	5,442,781	6,377,325	7,793,878	8,583,221	9,586,373	8,653,223
United States, total	26,706,830	28,884,267	31,595,769	33,083,636	33,833,388	31,979,736

SOURCE: U.S. Department of Transportation, Bureau of Transportation Statistics, North American Border Crossing/Entry Data, available at transborder.bts.gov/programs/international/transborder/TBDR_BC/TBDR_BC_Index.html as of June 2015

Table 4-10: Incoming Passengers in Personal Vehicles, U.S.-Canadian Border: 2009–2014

State	2009	2010	2011	2012	2013	2014
Alaska	205,504	207,433	213,009	229,786	229,863	214,766
Idaho	457,231	534,176	518,557	515,368	527,659	512,404
Maine	4,530,838	4,991,191	4,844,899	4,939,243	4,754,379	4,510,849
Michigan	12,012,710	12,251,134	12,732,327	13,103,922	13,189,897	12,659,396
Minnesota	2,068,739	2,302,687	2,031,845	2,046,631	1,991,269	1,946,510
Montana	1,147,465	1,314,802	1,219,337	1,300,642	1,365,943	1,353,302
New York	18,050,422	18,208,480	19,215,414	19,936,696	19,465,181	18,301,361
North Dakota	1,288,031	1,560,246	1,602,572	1,720,789	1,670,263	1,591,154
Vermont	2,704,002	2,622,861	2,586,654	2,738,342	2,832,460	2,731,851
Washington	11,063,399	12,795,860	14,227,082	15,476,759	16,320,145	15,842,599
United States, total	53,528,341	56,788,870	59,191,696	62,008,178	62,347,059	59,664,192

SOURCE: U.S. Department of Transportation, Bureau of Transportation Statistics, North American Border Crossing/Entry Data, available at transborder.bts.gov/programs/international/transborder/TBDR_BC/TBDR_BC_Index.html as of June 2015.

Table 4-11: Incoming Train Passengers, U.S.-Canadian Border: 2009–2014

State	2009	2010	2011	2012	2013	2014
Alaska	64,751	71,970	73,307	74,844	81,526	81,393
Idaho	1,987	2,410	2,466	2,376	2,718	2,775
Maine	1,476	1,403	1,006	1,775	1,870	1,928
Michigan	13,214	16,084	17,367	18,078	19,062	17,579
Minnesota	13,283	13,916	14,434	15,767	13,390	16,538
Montana	2,064	2,238	2,280	2,651	2,664	2,106
New York	65,685	73,985	79,787	77,801	74,433	73,561
North Dakota	7,658	8,691	7,772	8,878	8,099	8,307
Vermont	1,639	1,633	1,641	1,613	1,491	1,273
Washington	46,076	62,206	76,670	65,265	74,224	77,693
United States, total	217,833	254,536	276,730	269,048	279,477	283,153

SOURCE: U.S. Department of Transportation, Bureau of Transportation Statistics, North American Border Crossing/Entry Data, available at transborder.bts.gov/programs/international/transborder/TBDR_BC/TBDR_BC_Index.html as of June 2015.

Table 4-12: Incoming Bus Crossings, U.S.-Canadian Border: 2009–2014

State	2009	2010	2011	2012	2013	2014
Alaska	11,015	10,830	11,102	12,197	12,543	13,002
Idaho	204	205	216	152	168	87
Maine	1,415	1,464	1,215	1,021	903	837
Michigan	36,843	35,928	34,635	29,633	30,017	27,966
Minnesota	2,661	2,628	2,647	2,463	2,137	2,082
Montana	630	684	646	843	597	381
New York	40,386	39,148	39,051	37,302	36,274	35,495
North Dakota	1,947	1,977	1,760	1,631	1,627	1,663
Vermont	3,577	5,215	5,440	5,260	5,282	5,520
Washington	17,677	17,985	17,220	17,519	16,604	16,716
United States, total	116,355	116,064	113,932	108,021	106,152	103,749

SOURCE: U.S. Department of Transportation, Bureau of Transportation Statistics, North American Border Crossing/Entry Data, available at transborder.bts.gov/programs/international/transborder/TBDR_BC/TBDR_BC_Index.html as of June 2015.

Table 4-13: Incoming Passengers on Buses, U.S.-Canadian Border: 2009–2014

State	2009	2010	2011	2012	2013	2014
Alaska	170,065	157,102	158,466	168,851	164,685	189,989
Idaho	6,763	7,849	7,750	5,510	6,540	4,728
Maine	34,674	38,505	39,353	35,204	30,006	28,827
Michigan	415,144	364,721	344,371	388,623	445,974	379,061
Minnesota	47,332	43,613	45,824	38,937	37,789	35,085
Montana	14,801	17,847	19,066	21,342	10,757	15,404
New York	1,258,049	1,214,441	1,223,422	1,193,677	1,104,610	1,032,034
North Dakota	57,707	58,529	56,461	52,740	51,989	48,147
Vermont	107,886	159,213	178,357	164,776	164,082	165,109
Washington	390,996	389,406	379,359	365,948	359,512	345,398
United States, total	2,503,417	2,451,226	2,452,429	2,435,608	2,375,944	2,243,782

SOURCE: U.S. Department of Transportation, Bureau of Transportation Statistics, North American Border Crossing/Entry Data, available at transborder.bts.gov/programs/international/transborder/TBDR_BC/TBDR_BC_Index.html as of June 2015.

Table 4-14: Incoming Pedestrians, U.S.-Canadian Border: 2009–2014

State	2009	2010	2011	2012	2013	2014
Alaska	2,836	2,745	2,781	2,486	2,640	2,066
Idaho	437	1,560	2,570	2,443	2,617	2,916
Maine	24,569	15,194	17,208	23,032	26,845	27,872
Michigan	16,529	17,302	20,913	16,214	0	0
Minnesota	15,788	22,198	18,849	16,506	14,710	15,946
Montana	5,048	3,073	3,588	5,145	5,391	4,355
New York	246,766	262,172	285,129	293,405	283,492	277,104
North Dakota	3,545	3,534	2,597	2,933	3,943	4,490
Vermont	3,632	2,897	4,063	4,282	4,996	5,626
Washington	60,752	64,428	48,987	60,535	72,460	83,230
United States, total	379,902	395,103	406,685	426,981	417,094	423,605

NOTE: Incoming pedestrians for Michigan were participants in the annual Detroit Marathon and were not counted in 2013 and 2014.

SOURCE: U.S. Department of Transportation, Bureau of Transportation Statistics, North American Border Crossing/Entry Data, available at transborder.bts.gov/programs/international/transborder/TBDR_BC/TBDR_BC_Index.html as of June 2015.

Table 4-15: Incoming Personal Vehicle Crossings, U.S.-Mexican Border: 2009–2014

State	2009	2010	2011	2012	2013	2014
Arizona	7,387,953	6,650,691	6,713,284	7,472,683	8,172,192	8,518,851
California	26,536,413	25,259,609	24,678,930	25,104,487	26,033,552	27,593,261
New Mexico	795,249	785,757	704,848	661,277	757,794	821,490
Texas	35,585,141	31,348,795	29,083,206	29,464,056	31,584,131	32,690,091
United States, total	70,304,756	64,044,852	61,180,268	62,702,503	66,547,669	69,623,693

SOURCE: U.S. Department of Transportation, Bureau of Transportation Statistics, North American Border Crossing/Entry Data, available at transborder.bts.gov/programs/international/transborder/TBDR_BC/TBDR_BC_Index.html as of June 2015.

Table 4-16: Incoming Passengers in Personal Vehicles, U.S.-Mexican Border: 2009–2014

State	2009	2010	2011	2012	2013	2014
Arizona	17,579,271	14,726,256	12,879,043	14,015,636	15,462,699	16,367,308
California	48,911,130	45,611,407	43,567,956	44,095,817	46,084,882	49,326,532
New Mexico	2,253,766	2,056,321	1,430,089	1,446,681	1,557,628	1,712,213
Texas	72,272,826	63,355,537	53,084,820	55,491,451	59,019,742	61,837,785
United States, total	141,016,993	125,749,521	110,961,908	115,049,585	122,124,951	129,243,838

SOURCE: U.S. Department of Transportation, Bureau of Transportation Statistics, North American Border Crossing/Entry Data, available at transborder.bts.gov/programs/international/transborder/TBDR_BC/TBDR_BC_Index.html as of June 2015.

Table 4-17: Incoming Train Passengers, U.S.-Mexican Border: 2009–2014

State	2009	2010	2011	2012	2013	2014
Arizona	2,252	2,408	2,836	2,628	3,466	3,180
California	1,935	875	787	691	733	1,572
New Mexico	U	U	U	U	U	U
Texas[1]	U	U	U	U	U	6,903
United States, total	4,187	3,283	3,623	3,319	4,199	11,655

[1]Customs and Border Protection has not provided data on train passengers and crew entering the United States in Texas between 2009 and 2013.

KEY: U = data are unavailable.

SOURCE: U.S. Department of Transportation, Bureau of Transportation Statistics, North American Border Crossing/Entry Data, available at transborder.bts.gov/programs/international/transborder/TBDR_BC/TBDR_BC_Index.html as of June 2015.

Table 4-18: Incoming Bus Crossings, U.S.-Mexican Border: 2009–2014

State	2009	2010	2011	2012	2013	2014
Arizona	14,035	12,624	11,586	10,557	11,294	12,236
California	109,718	107,305	98,924	108,667	105,000	101,415
New Mexico	2,590	2,073	1,762	1,651	1,512	1,624
Texas	102,111	96,752	96,052	91,336	92,394	98,505
United States, total	228,454	218,754	208,324	212,211	210,200	213,780

SOURCE: U.S. Department of Transportation, Bureau of Transportation Statistics, North American Border Crossing/Entry Data, available at transborder.bts.gov/programs/international/transborder/TBDR_BC/TBDR_BC_Index.html as of June 2015.

Table 4-19: Incoming Passengers on Buses, U.S.-Mexican Border: 2009–2014

State	2009	2010	2011	2012	2013	2014
Arizona	194,159	185,071	178,395	182,114	182,845	185,376
California	644,907	753,801	726,541	841,614	796,173	794,812
New Mexico	33,530	26,641	20,785	19,797	18,080	19,057
Texas	1,556,594	1,714,194	1,794,382	1,823,112	1,825,858	1,783,650
United States, total	2,429,190	2,679,707	2,720,103	2,866,637	2,822,956	2,782,895

SOURCE: U.S. Department of Transportation, Bureau of Transportation Statistics, North American Border Crossing/Entry Data, available at transborder.bts.gov/programs/international/transborder/TBDR_BC/TBDR_BC_Index.html as of June 2015.

Table 4-20: Incoming Pedestrians, U.S.-Mexican Border: 2009–2014

State	2009	2010	2011	2012	2013	2014
Arizona	8,066,921	7,648,107	7,440,332	7,048,474	7,154,131	6,310,951
California	14,124,387	14,740,276	16,859,463	18,140,671	17,729,194	17,762,847
New Mexico	276,090	370,988	357,675	368,717	445,498	442,904
Texas	18,847,287	17,155,610	15,363,746	15,583,778	15,870,112	16,706,590
United States, total	41,314,685	39,914,981	40,021,216	41,141,640	41,198,935	41,223,292

SOURCE: U.S. Department of Transportation, Bureau of Transportation Statistics, North American Border Crossing/Entry Data, available at transborder.bts.gov/programs/international/transborder/TBDR_BC/TBDR_BC_Index.html as of June 2015.

Table 4-21: Overseas Visitors to the United States by Destination State and Territory[1]: 2003, 2008, 2012, and 2013

State	2003 Rank	2003 Visitors (thousands)	2003 Percent of U.S. total	2008 Rank	2008 Visitors (thousands)	2008 Percent of U.S. total	2012 Rank	2012 Visitors (thousands)	2012 Percent of U.S. total	2013 Rank	2013 Visitors (thousands)	2013 Percent of U.S. total
New York	1	4,200	23.3	1	8,413	33.2	1	9,315	31.3	1	9,804	30.6
Florida	1	4,200	23.3	3	5,246	20.7	2	6,577	22.1	2	7,209	22.5
California	3	3,984	22.1	2	5,296	20.9	3	6,012	20.2	3	6,472	20.2
Hawaii	4	1,947	10.8	5	1,825	7.2	4	2,827	9.5	4	3,172	9.9
Nevada	5	1,370	7.6	4	2,103	8.3	5	2,768	9.3	5	2,915	9.1
Texas	7	829	4.6	9	1,090	4.3	6	1,339	4.5	6	1,570	4.9
Guam	6	847	4.7	8	1,191	4.7	7	1,399	4.7	7	1,474	4.6
Illinois	7	829	4.6	6	1,419	5.6	8	1,399	4.7	8	1,442	4.5
Massachusetts	7	829	4.6	7	1,267	5.0	9	1,339	4.5	9	1,378	4.3
Pennsylvania	11	613	3.4	11	1,014	4.0	10	952	3.2	10	993	3.1
New Jersey	10	685	3.8	10	1,039	4.1	11	863	2.9	11	929	2.9
Arizona	12	487	2.7	12	710	2.8	12	804	2.7	12	833	2.6
Georgia	13	451	2.5	13	634	2.5	13	744	2.5	13	705	2.2
Washington	14	342	1.9	14	456	1.8	14	446	1.5	14	513	1.6
Utah	18	252	1.4	15	380	1.5	15	476	1.6	15	481	1.5
North Carolina	18	252	1.4	17	355	1.4	16	387	1.3	16	384	1.2
Colorado	17	288	1.6	15	380	1.5	17	446	1.5	17	384	1.2
Ohio	16	324	1.8	20	304	1.2	18	357	1.2	18	352	1.1
Virginia	21	234	1.3	18	329	1.3	19	387	1.3	19	352	1.1
Louisiana	22	216	1.2	U	U	U	21	298	1.0	20	352	1.1
Maryland	23	198	1.1	21	253	1.0	20	298	1.0	21	320	1.0
Connecticut	18	252	1.4	18	329	1.3	22	268	0.9	U	U	U
Michigan	14	361	2.0	U	U	U	U	U	U	U	U	U
Tennessee	24	162	0.9	U	U	U	U	U	U	U	U	U
Minnesota	29	90	0.5	U	U	U	U	U	U	U	U	U
Oregon	24	162	0.9	U	U	U	U	U	U	U	U	U
South Carolina	26	144	0.8	U	U	U	U	U	U	U	U	U
Indiana	26	144	0.8	U	U	U	U	U	U	U	U	U
New Hampshire	29	90	0.5	U	U	U	U	U	U	U	U	U
Wisconsin	28	108	0.6	U	U	U	U	U	U	U	U	U
Kentucky	34	72	0.4	U	U	U	U	U	U	U	U	U
Missouri	29	90	0.5	U	U	U	U	U	U	U	U	U
New Mexico	29	90	0.5	U	U	U	U	U	U	U	U	U
Alabama	29	72	0.4	U	U	U	U	U	U	U	U	U
Rhode Island	34	72	0.4	U	U	U	U	U	U	U	U	U
United States, total[2]		18,026			25,341			29,761			32,038	

[1]International travelers to the United States from Canada and Mexico are not included.
[2]Includes U.S. territories.

KEY: U = data are unavailable.

NOTES: A visitor may visit more than one state. Percent of U.S. total represents the percent of overseas visitors visiting the state. These columns, therefore, do not sum to 100. Some states are not shown due to low sampling size of overseas visitors. The Office of Travel and Tourism Industries instituted a new policy for data quality in 2006. As a result, data is published for fewer states in subsequent years. The District of Columbia is included, together with the rest of its metropolitan area, in table 4-22.

SOURCE: U.S. Department of Commerce, International Trade Administration, Office of Travel and Tourism Industries, Overseas Visitors Estimates for U.S. States, July 2015.

Table 4-22: Overseas Visitors to the United States by Destination City[1]: 2003, 2008, 2012, and 2013

City	2003 Rank	2003 Visitors (thousands)	2003 Percent of U.S. total	2008 Rank	2008 Visitors (thousands)	2008 Percent of U.S. total	2012 Rank	2012 Visitors (thousands)	2012 Percent of U.S. total	2013 Rank	2013 Visitors (thousands)	2013 Percent of U.S. total
New York City, NY	1	3,984	22.1	1	8,211	32.4	1	9,107	30.6	1	9,579	29.9
Miami, FL	3	2,073	11.5	4	2,585	10.2	2	3,482	11.7	2	4,005	12.5
Los Angeles, CA	2	2,127	11.8	2	2,788	11.0	3	3,393	11.4	3	3,781	11.8
Orlando, FL	4	1,767	9.8	5	2,433	9.6	4	3,184	10.7	4	3,716	11.6
San Francisco, CA	5	1,694	9.4	3	2,610	10.3	5	2,798	9.4	5	3,044	9.5
Las Vegas, NV	7	1,298	7.2	6	2,027	8.0	6	2,708	9.1	6	2,851	8.9
Honolulu/Oahu, HI	6	1,622	9.0	7	1,495	5.9	7	2,232	7.5	7	2,563	8.0
Washington, DC-MD-VA	8	865	4.8	8	1,470	5.8	8	1,756	5.9	8	1,698	5.3
Chicago, IL	9	775	4.3	9	1,368	5.4	9	1,369	4.6	9	1,378	4.3
Boston, MA	10	757	4.2	10	1,115	4.4	10	1,250	4.2	10	1,282	4.0
San Diego, CA	11	433	2.4	12	684	2.7	11	774	2.6	11	833	2.6
Houston, TX	12	397	2.2	14	481	1.9	12	655	2.2	12	801	2.5
Philadelphia, PA	12	397	2.2	11	710	2.8	13	595	2.0	13	673	2.1
Atlanta, GA	14	379	2.1	13	532	2.1	14	655	2.2	14	577	1.8
Flagstaff-G. Canyon-Sedona	U	U	U	15	431	1.7	15	536	1.8	15	545	1.7
Anaheim, CA	20	288	1.6	19	355	1.4	16	476	1.6	16	481	1.5
Seattle, WA	18	306	1.7	16	405	1.6	18	417	1.4	16	481	1.5
Tampa/St. Petersburg, FL	16	324	1.8	17	380	1.5	18	417	1.4	18	449	1.4
Dallas/Ft. Worth, TX	18	306	1.7	17	380	1.5	16	417	1.4	18	449	1.4
San Jose, CA	16	324	1.8	19	355	1.4	20	417	1.4	20	416	1.3
Ft. Lauderdale, FL	15	342	1.9	U	U	U	21	506	1.7	U	U	U
Florida Keys, FL	21	252	1.4	U	U	U	U	U	U	U	U	U
Detroit, MI	22	234	1.3	U	U	U	U	U	U	U	U	U
New Orleans, LA	23	198	1.1	U	U	U	U	U	U	U	U	U
Newark, NJ	23	198	1.1	U	U	U	U	U	U	U	U	U
Phoenix, AZ	23	198	1.1	U	U	U	U	U	U	U	U	U
Denver, CO	26	180	1.0	U	U	U	U	U	U	U	U	U
Maui, HI	26	180	1.0	U	U	U	U	U	U	U	U	U
Monterey, CA	28	144	0.8	U	U	U	U	U	U	U	U	U
Sacramento, CA	28	144	0.8	U	U	U	U	U	U	U	U	U
West Palm Beach, FL	28	144	0.8	U	U	U	U	U	U	U	U	U
Ft. Myers, FL	31	126	0.7	U	U	U	U	U	U	U	U	U
Portland, OR	31	126	0.7	U	U	U	U	U	U	U	U	U
Riverside/San Bernadino, CA	31	126	0.7	U	U	U	U	U	U	U	U	U
Baltimore, MD	34	108	0.6	U	U	U	U	U	U	U	U	U
Buffalo-Niagara Falls, NY	34	108	0.6	U	U	U	U	U	U	U	U	U
Oakland, CA	34	108	0.6	U	U	U	U	U	U	U	U	U
Pittsburgh, PA	34	108	0.6	U	U	U	U	U	U	U	U	U
Santa Barbara, CA	34	108	0.6	U	U	U	U	U	U	U	U	U
Sarasota, FL	34	108	0.6	U	U	U	U	U	U	U	U	U
Cincinnati, OH	40	90	0.5	U	U	U	U	U	U	U	U	U
Hawaii, HI	40	90	0.5	U	U	U	U	U	U	U	U	U
Minn./St. Paul, MN	40	90	0.5	U	U	U	U	U	U	U	U	U
Nassau, NY	40	90	0.5	U	U	U	U	U	U	U	U	U
Salt Lake City, UT	40	90	0.5	U	U	U	U	U	U	U	U	U
San Antonio, TX	40	90	0.5	U	U	U	U	U	U	U	U	U
Austin, TX	46	72	0.4	U	U	U	U	U	U	U	U	U
Charlotte, NC	46	72	0.4	U	U	U	U	U	U	U	U	U
Cleveland, OH	46	72	0.4	U	U	U	U	U	U	U	U	U
Columbus, OH	46	72	0.4	U	U	U	U	U	U	U	U	U
Daytona Beach, FL	46	72	0.4	U	U	U	U	U	U	U	U	U
Indianapolis, IN	46	72	0.4	U	U	U	U	U	U	U	U	U
Jacksonville, FL	46	72	0.4	U	U	U	U	U	U	U	U	U
Kauai, HI	46	72	0.4	U	U	U	U	U	U	U	U	U
Melbourne, FL	46	72	0.4	U	U	U	U	U	U	U	U	U
Nashville, TN	46	72	0.4	U	U	U	U	U	U	U	U	U
Raleigh-Durham, NC	46	72	0.4	U	U	U	U	U	U	U	U	U
St. Louis, MO	46	72	0.4	U	U	U	U	U	U	U	U	U
Tucson, AZ	58	54	0.3	U	U	U	U	U	U	U	U	U
United States, total[2]		18,026			25,341			29,761			32,038	

[1]International travelers to the United States from Canada and Mexico are not included.
[2]Includes U.S. territories.

KEY: U = data are unavailable.

NOTES: A visitor may visit more than one city. Percent of U.S. total represents the percent of visitors visiting the city. These columns, therefore, do not sum to 100. Some cities are not shown due to low sampling size of overseas visitors. The Office of Travel and Tourism Industries instituted a new policy for data quality in 2006. As a result, data is published for fewer cities in subsequent years.

SOURCE: U.S. Department of Commerce, International Trade Administration, Office of Travel and Tourism Industries, *Overseas Visitors Estimates for U.S. States, Cities, and Census Regions* available at tinet.ita.doc.gov/outreachpages/inbound.general_information.inbound_overview.html as of July 2015.

Chapter 5

Registered Vehicles and
Vehicle-Miles Traveled

Table 5-1: Motor-Vehicle Registrations: 2013

(Thousands)

State	Private and commercial				Partial classification of trucks[1]				
	Automobiles	Motorcycles[2]	Buses	Trucks	Truck tractors	Pickups	Vans	Sport utilities	Other light[3]
Alabama	2,057	117	1	2,566	36	1,153	265	973	3
Alaska	197	32	2	538	5	228	55	208	0
Arizona	2,235	188	16	2,874	44	1,033	371	1,131	4
Arkansas[3]	822	74	1	1,454	39	691	132	509	1
California	13,598	785	34	13,038	263	4,122	1,890	5,902	10
Colorado	1,800	184	8	2,637	30	865	269	1,316	3
Connecticut	1,458	91	4	1,253	7	287	191	691	1
Delaware	447	30	3	461	3	131	75	231	0
District of Columbia	204	4	3	101	0	11	21	66	0
Florida	7,310	543	25	6,985	67	2,103	1,104	3,354	3
Georgia[3]	3,405	199	10	4,066	63	1,498	516	1,754	3
Hawaii	557	40	2	712	3	279	108	303	0
Idaho	594	65	3	1,020	22	473	103	351	1
Illinois[3]	4,750	352	4	4,959	142	1,218	928	2,400	2
Indiana	2,257	219	9	3,074	227	1,027	484	1,120	1
Iowa[3]	1,356	183	4	1,957	70	795	288	674	1
Kansas	1,017	99	3	1,473	46	613	192	510	1
Kentucky[3]	1,699	110	2	2,177	29	929	281	811	2
Louisiana[3]	1,466	113	22	2,269	32	1,098	186	839	1
Maine[3]	482	63	1	639	8	257	76	255	0
Maryland	1,893	99	6	1,773	11	444	303	890	1
Massachusetts[4]	2,483	125	8	2,311	13	521	358	1,292	0
Michigan	3,562	267	3	4,283	66	1,285	764	1,966	1
Minnesota[3]	2,191	237	5	2,732	67	906	460	1,124	2
Mississippi[3]	868	28	2	1,159	29	561	107	401	1
Missouri	2,462	185	3	3,116	67	1,210	452	1,196	2
Montana	442	171	4	916	24	437	88	282	1
Nebraska	704	56	2	1,082	58	423	135	385	1
Nevada[3]	968	71	1	1,138	8	404	126	539	1
New Hampshire[5]	620	74	2	702	4	232	91	332	0
New Jersey[4]	3,604	152	14	3,214	40	558	595	1,820	1
New Mexico	705	65	1	1,077	14	507	101	386	1
New York[5]	5,120	345	15	5,020	38	1,014	928	2,731	2
North Carolina[6]	3,463	195	12	4,061	61	1,490	563	1,712	2
North Dakota	249	36	1	542	36	234	52	163	0
Ohio	4,806	402	17	4,993	98	1,547	881	2,162	2
Oklahoma[3]	1,359	127	1	1,939	67	804	213	690	1
Oregon	1,505	90	1	1,968	24	771	268	774	3
Pennsylvania	4,764	400	52	5,124	67	1,425	806	2,484	2
Rhode Island[4]	452	32	0	353	2	91	58	182	0
South Carolina	1,709	113	5	2,063	20	783	264	892	1
South Dakota[3]	326	86	0	578	25	248	67	185	0
Tennessee[3]	2,248	164	2	2,895	41	1,178	361	1,145	2
Texas[3]	7,810	440	18	11,393	239	4,700	1,069	4,749	4
Utah	869	65	4	1,105	27	403	135	444	1
Vermont	256	29	1	318	4	119	33	139	0
Virginia	3,226	189	7	3,495	32	1,118	536	1,630	2
Washington[3]	2,772	227	12	3,308	41	1,220	455	1,366	5
West Virginia	516	57	1	839	8	362	83	335	1
Wisconsin[3]	2,240	323	1	2,679	63	869	470	1,111	1
Wyoming[3]	227	31	1	567	10	282	40	188	1
United States, total	112,128	8,375	361	130,998	2,443	44,958	18,395	57,091	76

[1]Data estimated by FHWA from state reported data and other sources. Farm trucks data are as reported by states.
[2]Many states do not maintain records on publicly owned motorcycles. Total may not represent an accurate count of the total number of publicly-owned motorcycles.
[3]State did not report active registrations and registers vehicles annually. Annual transaction data shown.
[4]State data estimated from Department of Motor Vehicles published data.
[5]State did not report current year data. Previous year data shown for private vehicles.
[6]State data estimated from North Carolina Department of Transportation published data and other data sources.

SOURCE: U.S. Department of Transportation, Federal Highway Administration, *Highway Statistics*, MV-1 and MV-9, available at www.fhwa.dot.gov/policyinformation/statistics.cfm as of June 2015.

Table 5-2: Trailer and Semi-Trailer Registrations: 2012[1]

State	Private and commercial				Publicly owned	
	Commercial trailers[2]	Light farm trailers, car trailers, etc.	House trailers[3]	Total	State, county, municipal government	Total
Alabama	66,267	242,849	51,649	360,765	U	360,765
Alaska	11,489	115,934	U	127,423	2,315	129,738
Arizona	766,697	U	90,236	856,933	53	856,986
Arkansas	92,899	35,229	7,700	135,828	U	135,828
California	1,000,747	954,211	330,696	2,285,654	68,286	2,353,940
Colorado	7,181	478,720	97,410	583,311	7,237	590,548
Connecticut	34,165	U	153,460	187,625	U	187,625
Delaware	18,628	60,895	56,100	135,623	U	135,623
District of Columbia	870	U	U	870	U	870
Florida	57,208	1,519,616	1	1,576,825	1,070	1,577,895
Georgia[4]	U	U	U	1,058,038	U	1,058,038
Hawaii[4]	U	U	U	28,958	1,694	30,652
Idaho	42,505	336,048	72,376	450,929	578	451,507
Illinois	297,154	501,446	89,989	888,589	U	888,589
Indiana	236,267	401,015	U	637,282	U	637,282
Iowa	254,677	434,035	87,759	776,471	3,670	780,141
Kansas	10,790	144,109	19,550	174,449	U	174,449
Kentucky	277,710	16,926	27,845	322,481	U	322,481
Louisiana	184,692	109,377	17,467	311,536	842	312,378
Maine	111,006	193,544	U	304,550	U	304,550
Maryland	871,889	U	U	871,889	U	871,889
Massachusetts	22,855	242,086	U	264,941	223	265,164
Michigan	369,869	U	288,974	658,843	U	658,843
Minnesota	242,098	43,395	119,901	405,394	U	405,394
Mississippi	30,174	65,253	9,619	105,046	340	105,386
Missouri[4]	U	U	U	985,159	U	985,159
Montana	30,461	445,733	68,745	544,939	221	545,160
Nebraska	205,396	170,037	U	375,433	6,835	382,268
Nevada	7,031	164,724	34,943	206,698	U	206,698
New Hampshire[5]	U	U	U	171,735	U	171,735
New Jersey	3,640	264,353	22,103	290,096	U	290,096
New Mexico	35,946	208,912	56,950	301,808	U	301,808
New York[6]	141,211	202,234	11,130	354,575	903	355,478
North Carolina	923,989	U	19,638	943,627	20,535	964,162
North Dakota	109,378	U	23,510	132,888	137	133,025
Ohio	250,775	524,734	94,591	870,100	842	870,942
Oklahoma	139,001	84,845	5,525	229,371	U	229,371
Oregon	753	135,515	84,505	220,773	U	220,773
Pennsylvania	1,110,355	U	U	1,110,355	14,836	1,125,191
Rhode Island	6,301	45,402	5,387	57,090	1,240	58,330
South Carolina	124,425	39,726	5	164,156	3,934	168,090
South Dakota	6,343	205,278	694	212,315	4,120	216,435
Tennessee	1,390,266	U	13	1,390,279	U	1,390,279
Texas	863,216	1,220,141	207,876	2,291,233	57,306	2,348,539
Utah	152,692	10,212	67,821	230,725	2,950	233,675
Vermont	94,360	U	U	94,360	U	94,360
Virginia	308,970	507,557	38,313	854,840	618	855,458
Washington	59,738	638,082	U	697,820	U	697,820
West Virginia	174,199	123,530	U	297,729	7,269	304,998
Wisconsin	428,507	2,266	72,439	503,212	5,194	508,406
Wyoming	126,483	161,090	37,877	325,450	169	325,619
United States, total[7]	11,701,273	11,049,059	2,372,797	27,367,019	213,417	27,580,436

[1]The completeness of data on trailer registrations varies greatly. Data are reported to the extent available from State reports.
[2]This column includes all commercial type vehicles and semiltrailers that are in a private or for-hire use.
[3]Mobile homes and house trailers are shown in this column for States that require them to be registered and are able to separate them from other trailers. In States where this classification is not available, house trailers are included with light car trailers.
[4]State indicated data by type was not available.
[5]State did not file a 2012 report, 2011 data used.
[6]State did not file a 2012 report, data estimated by FHWA from website report.
[7]As data has been estimated, or not included in some cases, totals should be considered estitmates at best.

KEY: U = data are unavailable.

SOURCE: U.S. Department of Transportation, Federal Highway Administration, *Highway Statistics*, MV-11, available at www.fhwa.dot.gov/policy-information/statistics.cfm as of August 2015.

Table 5-3: Highway Vehicle-Miles Traveled (VMT): 2008, 2013

State	2008 Total VMT[1] (millions)	2008 Estimated Population	2008 VMT per capita	2013 Total VMT[2] (millions)	2013 Estimated Population	2013 VMT per capita
Alabama	59,303	4,661,900	12,721	65,046	4,833,996	13,456
Alaska	4,865	686,293	7,089	4,848	737,259	6,576
Arizona	61,628	6,500,180	9,481	60,586	6,634,997	9,131
Arkansas	33,163	2,855,390	11,614	33,493	2,958,765	11,320
California	327,286	36,756,666	8,904	329,534	38,431,393	8,575
Colorado	47,860	4,939,456	9,689	46,968	5,272,086	8,909
Connecticut	31,737	3,501,252	9,064	30,941	3,599,341	8,596
Delaware	8,976	873,092	10,281	9,308	925,240	10,060
District of Columbia	3,611	591,833	6,101	3,527	649,111	5,434
Florida	198,616	18,328,340	10,837	192,702	19,600,311	9,832
Georgia	109,057	9,685,744	11,260	109,355	9,994,759	10,941
Hawaii	10,278	1,288,198	7,979	10,099	1,408,987	7,168
Idaho	15,251	1,523,816	10,008	15,980	1,612,843	9,908
Illinois	106,079	12,901,563	8,222	105,297	12,890,552	8,169
Indiana	70,973	6,376,792	11,130	78,311	6,570,713	11,918
Iowa	30,713	3,002,555	10,229	31,641	3,092,341	10,232
Kansas	29,727	2,802,134	10,609	30,208	2,895,801	10,432
Kentucky	47,534	4,269,245	11,134	46,996	4,399,583	10,682
Louisiana	45,091	4,410,796	10,223	47,758	4,629,284	10,316
Maine	14,559	1,316,456	11,059	14,129	1,328,702	10,634
Maryland	55,023	5,633,597	9,767	56,688	5,938,737	9,545
Massachusetts	54,505	6,497,967	8,388	56,311	6,708,874	8,394
Michigan	101,825	10,003,422	10,179	95,132	9,898,193	9,611
Minnesota[3]	57,995	5,220,393	11,109	56,974	5,422,060	10,508
Mississippi	43,711	2,938,618	14,875	38,758	2,992,206	12,953
Missouri	68,273	5,911,605	11,549	69,458	6,044,917	11,490
Montana	10,812	967,440	11,176	12,033	1,014,864	11,856
Nebraska	19,170	1,783,432	10,749	19,322	1,868,969	10,338
Nevada	20,780	2,600,167	7,992	24,649	2,791,494	8,830
New Hampshire	13,040	1,315,809	9,910	12,903	1,322,616	9,756
New Jersey	73,629	8,682,661	8,480	74,530	8,911,502	8,363
New Mexico	26,279	1,984,356	13,243	25,086	2,086,895	12,021
New York	134,085	19,490,297	6,880	129,737	19,695,680	6,587
North Carolina	101,712	9,222,414	11,029	105,213	9,848,917	10,683
North Dakota	7,820	641,481	12,191	10,100	723,857	13,953
Ohio	108,302	11,485,910	9,429	112,767	11,572,005	9,745
Oklahoma	48,499	3,642,361	13,315	47,999	3,853,118	12,457
Oregon	33,468	3,790,060	8,830	33,706	3,928,068	8,581
Pennsylvania	107,848	12,448,279	8,664	98,628	12,781,296	7,717
Rhode Island	8,187	1,050,788	7,791	7,775	1,053,354	7,381
South Carolina	49,597	4,479,800	11,071	48,986	4,771,929	10,266
South Dakota	8,986	804,194	11,174	9,122	845,510	10,789
Tennessee	69,469	6,214,888	11,178	71,067	6,497,269	10,938
Texas[4]	235,382	24,326,974	9,676	244,525	26,505,637	9,225
Utah	25,974	2,736,424	9,492	27,005	2,902,787	9,303
Vermont	7,312	621,270	11,769	7,116	626,855	11,352
Virginia	82,278	7,769,089	10,590	80,767	8,270,345	9,766
Washington	55,558	6,549,224	8,483	57,211	6,973,742	8,204
West Virginia	20,774	1,814,468	11,449	19,232	1,853,595	10,376
Wisconsin	57,462	5,627,967	10,210	59,486	5,742,953	10,358
Wyoming	9,447	532,668	17,735	9,309	583,223	15,961
United States, total	2,973,509	304,059,724	9,779	2,988,323	316,497,531	9,442

[1]Travel for all systems are FHWA estimates based on State provided HPMS data.
[2]Travel for the rural minor collector and rural/urban local functional systems is estimated by the States based on a model or other means and provided to the FHWA on a summary basis. Travel for all other systems are estimated from State-provided data in the Highway Performance Monitoring System.
[3]2008 Data excludes 788 miles of Federal agency owned roads.
[4]2008 State has revised their adjusted urbanized area boundaries and/or functional classifications.

NOTES: Population estimates are for July 1st of given year.

SOURCES: VMT: U.S. Department of Transportation, Federal Highway Administration, *Highway Statistics*, VM-2, available at www. fhwa.dot.gov/policyinformation/statistics.cfm as of July 2015. Population: U.S. Department of Commerce, U.S. Census Bureau, Population Estimates, available at www.census.gov/popest as of July 2015.

Table 5-4: Highway, Demographic, and Geographic Characteristics of 30 Largest Urbanized Areas: 2013

Federal-aid urbanized area[1]	State(s)	Estimated population (thousands)	Net land area (square miles)	Persons per square mile	Total roadway miles	Miles of roadway per thousand persons	Total DVMT (thousands)	Total DVMT per capita	Total estimated freeway lane miles[2]	Average daily traffic per freeway lane mile
New York-Newark	NY, NJ, CT	17,800	4,868	3,657	44,675	2.5	120,723	16.6	7,437	16,233
Los Angeles-Long Beach-Santa Ana	CA	11,789	1,971	5,981	25,207	2.1	119,806	22.3	5,246	22,837
Chicago	IL, IN	8,308	3,535	2,350	31,162	3.8	56,433	21.6	3,123	18,067
Philadelphia	PA, NJ, DE, MD	5,149	2,401	2,145	20,377	4.0	35,794	19.8	2,565	13,957
Miami	FL	4,919	1,499	3,282	15,569	3.2	41,175	25.5	2,256	18,250
Dallas-Fort Worth-Arlington	TX	4,146	2,375	1,746	22,223	5.4	64,670	30.5	3,880	16,667
Boston	MA, NH, RI	4,032	2,430	1,659	17,578	4.4	41,470	23.9	2,603	15,930
Washington	DC, VA, MD	3,934	1,279	3,076	12,620	3.2	37,786	25.2	2,113	17,886
Detroit	MI	3,903	1,603	2,435	15,342	3.9	32,689	23.5	2,049	15,957
Houston	TX	3,823	1,824	2,096	17,256	4.5	51,518	27.8	3,137	16,425
Atlanta	GA	3,500	3,649	959	25,046	7.2	49,469	41.2	2,881	17,174
San Francisco-Oakland	CA	2,996	1,054	2,842	7,688	2.6	27,612	19.9	1,475	18,722
Phoenix-Mesa	AZ	2,907	1,614	1,801	11,929	4.1	29,401	28.0	1,992	14,758
Seattle	WA	2,712	1,199	2,262	11,719	4.3	28,553	24.8	1,730	16,503
San Diego	CA	2,674	984	2,718	5,964	2.2	39,540	26.5	2,115	18,692
Minneapolis-St. Paul	MN - WI	2,651	1,593	1,664	13,389	5.1	29,550	26.0	1,863	15,857
St. Louis	MO, IL	2,078	1,476	1,408	11,892	5.7	30,557	32.3	2,467	12,388
Baltimore	MD	2,076	683	3,040	7,558	3.6	28,327	26.8	1,637	17,309
Tampa-St. Petersburg	FL	2,062	1,072	1,924	9,695	4.7	14,318	29.8	903	15,858
Denver-Aurora	CO	1,985	814	2,438	8,505	4.3	21,242	25.3	1,280	16,597
Cleveland	OH	1,787	855	2,090	7,389	4.1	17,868	23.1	1,539	11,607
Pittsburgh	PA	1,753	1,215	1,443	9,478	5.4	8,820	18.8	1,263	6,985
Portland	OR, WA	1,583	591	2,679	7,202	4.5	13,536	22.1	795	17,026
San Jose	CA	1,538	353	4,358	3,869	2.5	27,039	31.4	1,338	20,204
Riverside-San Bernardino	CA	1,507	747	2,017	5,286	3.5	32,744	37.2	1,525	21,476
Cincinnati	OH, KY, IN	1,503	910	1,652	7,106	4.7	18,070	30.7	1,260	14,337
Virginia Beach	VA	1,394	1,409	990	6,761	4.8	13,003	25.6	907	14,337
Sacramento	CA	1,393	446	3,124	5,245	3.8	15,607	27.8	872	17,901
Kansas City	MO, KS	1,362	1,202	1,133	9,836	7.2	22,187	33.4	2,098	10,574
San Antonio	TX	1,328	574	2,313	6,436	4.8	21,185	29.6	1,249	16,955

[1]A "Federal-Aid Urbanized Area" is an area with 50,000 or more persons that at a minimum encompasses the land area delineated as the urbanized area by the Bureau of the Census. Areas are in sort by population. Some areas may be missing, unreported, or included in other areas.
[2]Lane miles estimated by the Federal Highway Administration (FHWA).

KEY: DVMT = daily vehicle-miles of travel.

NOTE: Ratios are based on unrounded numbers.

SOURCE: U.S. Department of Transportation, Federal Highway Administration, *Highway Statistics*, HM-72, available at www.fhwa.dot.gov/policy-information/statistics.cfm as of June 2015.

Table 5-5: Highway Congestion in the 50 Largest Urban Areas: 2014

Urban area	Rank	Population (thousands)	Hours of delay (thousands)	Hours of delay per commuter	Cost of congestion ($ millions)	Cost of congestion per commuter ($)
Washington DC-VA-MD	1	4,920	204,375	82	4,560	1,834
Los Angeles-Long Beach-Anaheim CA	2	12,635	622,509	80	13,318	1,711
San Francisco-Oakland CA	3	3,480	146,013	78	3,143	1,675
New York-Newark NY-NJ-CT	4	19,040	628,241	74	14,712	1,739
San Jose CA	5	1,950	104,559	67	2,230	1,422
Boston MA-NH-RI	6	4,440	153,994	64	3,363	1,388
Seattle WA	7	3,325	139,842	63	3,294	1,491
Chicago IL-IN	8	8,700	302,609	61	7,222	1,445
Houston TX	8	5,000	203,173	61	4,924	1,490
Riverside-San Bernardino CA	10	2,020	99,058	59	2,201	1,316
Dallas-Fort Worth-Arlington TX	11	5,485	186,535	53	4,202	1,185
Miami FL	12	5,860	195,946	52	4,444	1,169
Detroit MI	12	3,825	155,358	52	3,514	1,183
Atlanta GA	12	4,500	148,666	52	3,214	1,130
Portland OR-WA	12	1,990	72,341	52	1,763	1,273
Austin TX	12	1,500	51,116	52	1,140	1,159
Phoenix-Mesa AZ	17	3,925	155,730	51	3,641	1,201
Denver-Aurora CO	19	2,615	91,479	49	2,061	1,101
Oklahoma City OK	19	1,000	45,652	49	1,030	1,110
Bridgeport-Stamford CT-NY	19	955	37,119	49	898	1,174
Philadelphia PA-NJ-DE-MD	22	5,560	157,183	48	3,669	1,112
Minneapolis-St. Paul MN-WI	23	2,815	99,710	47	2,196	1,035
Baltimore MD	23	2,600	87,620	47	2,075	1,115
Las Vegas-Henderson NV	27	1,975	63,693	46	1,375	984
Orlando FL	27	1,615	52,723	46	1,207	1,044
Virginia Beach VA	29	1,460	48,274	45	1,020	953
New Orleans LA	29	975	39,159	45	1,014	1,161
Nashville-Davidson TN	29	1,200	38,977	45	1,013	1,168
San Antonio TX	33	1,935	64,328	44	1,462	1,002
St. Louis MO-IL	35	2,200	69,350	43	1,637	1,020
San Juan PR	35	2,055	60,301	43	1,605	1,150
Sacramento CA	35	1,810	60,220	43	1,334	958
Indianapolis IN	35	1,555	46,435	43	1,142	1,060
Memphis TN-MS-AR	35	1,085	37,824	43	939	1,080
Providence RI-MA	35	1,180	37,809	43	846	951
Louisville-Jefferson County KY-IN	35	1,110	35,622	43	860	1,048
Charlotte NC-SC	35	1,200	34,153	43	770	963
San Diego CA	43	3,090	79,412	42	1,658	887
Tampa-St. Petersburg FL	45	2,540	71,628	41	1,589	907
Cincinnati OH-KY-IN	45	1,640	48,485	41	1,159	989
Columbus OH	45	1,455	40,025	41	921	933
Buffalo NY	49	945	26,851	40	620	918
Kansas City MO-KS	51	1,600	45,570	39	1,085	933
Pittsburgh PA	51	1,765	44,758	39	1,030	889
Cleveland OH	55	1,765	45,051	38	1,046	887
Milwaukee WI	55	1,410	37,659	38	984	987
Jacksonville FL	55	1,085	29,680	38	659	842
Salt Lake City-West Valley City UT	66	1,100	26,925	37	779	1,059
Richmond VA	77	1,000	26,104	34	558	729
Raleigh NC	77	965	23,128	34	504	734

NOTES: Ranked by annual hours of delay per commuter. TTI's methodology changes periodically. When changes do occur, the methods are applied to all years, resulting in changes possibly over the entire period of data available. Consequently, the most recently published figures may not be comparable to those in past editions.

SOURCE: Texas A&M University, Texas Transportation Institute, *Urban Mobility Report 2015*, available at mobility.tamu.edu/ums as of August 2015.

Table 5-6: Recreational Boat Registrations by Propulsion Type: 2014

State	Powered[1]	Nonpowered[2]	Other[3]	Total
Alabama	259,000	1,960	1,966	262,926
Alaska	49,390	448	285	50,123
Arizona	124,380	0	45	124,425
Arkansas	180,629	573	25,081	206,283
California	675,250	29,534	23,895	728,679
Colorado	78,926	3,226	1,531	83,683
Connecticut	99,250	305	103	99,658
Delaware	57,272	0	2,065	59,337
District of Columbia	1,529	339	95	1,963
Florida	825,019	20,918	27,570	873,507
Georgia	308,572	3,259	9,909	321,740
Hawaii	11,522	386	125	12,033
Idaho	83,419	650	2,201	86,270
Illinois	232,849	36,380	5,677	274,906
Indiana	210,930	733	803	212,466
Iowa	179,561	37,708	4,670	221,939
Kansas	78,514	2,628	874	82,016
Kentucky	160,296	0	14,062	174,358
Louisiana	307,059	0	0	307,059
Maine	105,550	0	778	106,328
Maryland	171,801	294	6,478	178,573
Massachusetts	124,507	0	11,243	135,750
Michigan	737,372	48,969	3,117	789,458
Minnesota	598,195	197,283	13,814	809,292
Mississippi	132,812	594	0	133,406
Missouri	291,771	2,174	64	294,009
Montana	46,374	297	756	47,427
Nebraska	82,915	1	3,862	86,778
Nevada	42,700	220	1,276	44,196
New Hampshire	88,869	3,389	0	92,258
New Jersey	149,529	3,360	0	152,889
New Mexico	33,610	964	73	34,647
New York	450,761	9	1,092	451,862
North Carolina	375,192	1,763	3,715	380,670
North Dakota	52,576	651	333	53,560
Ohio	303,511	156,148	119	459,778
Oklahoma	214,468	0	0	214,468
Oregon	157,558	0	5,800	163,358
Pennsylvania	283,321	19,150	19,724	322,195
Rhode Island	34,772	50	1,469	36,291
South Carolina	436,917	22,927	2,836	462,680
South Dakota	52,967	3,925	317	57,209
Tennessee	255,595	1,267	0	256,862
Texas	556,554	3,010	7,333	566,897
Utah	65,920	884	0	66,804
Vermont	27,861	0	0	27,861
Virginia	231,824	308	4,389	236,521
Washington	226,662	0	0	226,662
West Virginia	48,139	0	0	48,139
Wisconsin	601,514	19,555	6,283	627,352
Wyoming	26,279	614	224	27,117
United States, total[4]	10,960,861	627,056	216,085	11,804,002

[1]Powered boats include traditional power boats, sailboats with auxiliary engines and personal watercraft (such as jet-skis).
[2]Nonpowered boats include row boats, sail boats, canoes and kayaks.
[3]Other boats are those not included elsewhere.
[4]U.S. totals include Guam, Puerto Rico, the Virgin Islands, American Samoa, and the Northern Mariana Islands.

NOTES: Data are derived from reports of states and other jurisdictions with varying registration categories. The U.S. totals do not include sailboards, which are registered in some states.

SOURCE: U.S. Department of Homeland Security, U.S. Coast Guard, Office of Boating Safety, personal communication in July 2015.

Table 5-7: General Aviation and Air Taxi Aircraft and Hours Flown: 2013
(Excludes commuter aircraft)

State	Active aircraft	Hours flown (thousands)
Alabama	3,635	244
Alaska	8,161	675
Arizona	7,470	718
Arkansas	3,750	328
California	26,141	2,331
Colorado	6,819	611
Connecticut	1,681	175
Delaware	2,081	349
District of Columbia	52	13
Florida	18,162	1,868
Georgia	7,198	571
Hawaii	700	141
Idaho	3,731	322
Illinois	7,021	530
Indiana	4,489	359
Iowa	4,056	236
Kansas	4,806	378
Kentucky	2,197	142
Louisiana	4,177	757
Maine	1,606	80
Maryland	2,983	245
Massachusetts	2,944	218
Michigan	6,965	410
Minnesota	6,308	437
Mississippi	2,672	243
Missouri	4,855	328
Montana	2,968	211
Nebraska	2,750	194
Nevada	3,153	323
New Hampshire	1,645	103
New Jersey	3,508	434
New Mexico	3,629	137
New York	6,989	477
North Carolina	7,175	559
North Dakota	2,053	275
Ohio	6,830	537
Oklahoma	5,476	862
Oregon	6,535	569
Pennsylvania	7,144	510
Rhode Island	415	43
South Carolina	2,855	186
South Dakota	1,834	167
Tennessee	4,478	411
Texas	22,851	2,243
Utah	2,511	284
Vermont	666	22
Virginia	6,446	499
Washington	9,507	513
West Virginia	1,031	66
Wisconsin	7,046	318
Wyoming	1,466	156
United States, total (excluding territories)	265,621	22,807
United States, total (including territories)	265,989	22,876

NOTES: These data are derived from a sample survey of general aviation and air taxi aircraft. The estimates are subject to sampling and nonsampling error. Beginning in 2007, the survey asked the state in which the aircraft was primarily flown rather than where the aircraft was based. Columns may not add to totals due to rounding procedures.

SOURCE: U.S. Department of Transportation, Federal Aviation Administration, General Aviation and Part 135 Activity Surveys, available at www.faa.gov/data_research/aviation_data_statistics/general_aviation as of July 2015.

Table 5-8: Active Aviation Pilots and Flight Instructors: 2014[1]

State	Total	Students	Airplane pilots[2] Private	Commercial	Airline transport	Misc.[3]	Flight instructor[4]
Alabama	7,260	1,500	2,377	1,930	1,390	63	1,469
Alaska	8,032	1,144	2,877	1,772	2,187	52	1,374
Arizona	18,029	3,738	5,070	3,579	5,509	133	3,763
Arkansas	4,957	1,082	1,777	1,146	881	71	746
California	59,213	12,234	23,092	11,570	11,925	392	9,587
Colorado	17,382	2,861	5,138	3,184	6,089	110	3,615
Connecticut	5,023	866	1,889	821	1,422	25	847
Delaware	1,343	337	383	211	403	9	256
District of Columbia	572	152	222	92	98	8	82
Florida	52,967	12,501	13,437	9,786	16,770	473	9,592
Georgia	18,131	2,964	4,959	2,704	7,359	145	3,267
Hawaii	3,134	624	633	707	1,158	12	661
Idaho	4,850	919	1,869	1,043	948	71	840
Illinois	16,307	3,034	5,568	2,712	4,744	249	3,349
Indiana	9,558	1,805	3,612	1,720	2,229	192	1,662
Iowa	5,154	990	2,293	1,062	719	90	834
Kansas	6,866	1,333	2,748	1,411	1,301	73	1,414
Kentucky	5,629	1,003	1,598	875	2,096	57	1,060
Louisiana	5,650	1,215	1,857	1,320	1,196	62	898
Maine	2,415	420	921	487	541	46	387
Maryland	7,664	1,902	2,461	1,372	1,847	82	1,361
Massachusetts	7,784	1,728	3,088	1,345	1,564	59	1,227
Michigan	13,672	2,445	5,292	2,516	3,216	203	2,446
Minnesota	12,172	1,929	4,240	2,089	3,821	93	2,547
Mississippi	4,108	1,034	1,246	854	943	31	640
Missouri	8,986	1,751	3,232	1,692	2,180	131	1,642
Montana	3,681	671	1,449	916	613	32	661
Nebraska	3,550	824	1,389	713	595	29	496
Nevada	6,841	1,126	1,921	1,334	2,413	47	1,389
New Hampshire	3,632	514	1,117	603	1,357	41	704
New Jersey	8,787	1,819	3,059	1,507	2,363	39	1,615
New Mexico	4,527	908	1,728	1,127	701	63	638
New York	15,949	4,069	5,771	2,910	3,056	143	2,617
North Carolina	13,935	2,529	4,678	2,356	4,238	134	2,456
North Dakota	3,535	794	1,128	1,313	288	12	492
Ohio	15,137	2,815	5,487	2,568	4,002	265	2,975
Oklahoma	7,825	2,074	2,756	1,475	1,472	48	1,287
Oregon	8,573	1,587	3,485	1,989	1,436	76	1,581
Pennsylvania	15,187	2,889	5,336	2,610	4,154	198	2,726
Rhode Island	975	215	363	161	229	7	153
South Carolina	6,498	1,154	2,196	1,203	1,883	62	1,091
South Dakota	2,234	408	878	516	381	51	422
Tennessee	11,540	1,971	3,312	1,959	4,201	97	2,118
Texas	49,614	9,951	14,514	8,534	16,265	350	8,728
Utah	7,998	1,727	2,371	1,525	2,317	58	1,584
Vermont	1,221	203	523	246	238	11	171
Virginia	14,126	2,739	4,271	2,757	4,216	143	2,732
Washington	18,665	3,358	6,052	3,330	5,744	181	3,518
West Virginia	1,756	426	666	332	296	36	274
Wisconsin	9,073	1,604	3,768	1,430	2,043	228	1,579
Wyoming	1,852	374	790	366	304	18	288
United States, total	543,569	108,260	180,887	101,780	147,341	5,301	97,861

[1]An active pilot is a person who holds a pilot certificate and a valid medical certificate issued within the last 25 months.
[2]Includes pilots with an airplane only certificate and those with an airplane and a helicopter and/or glider certificate.
[3]Includes helicopter, glider, and recreational pilots. Does not include pilots holding an airplane certificate. A recreational pilot may fly no more than one passenger in a light, single engine aircraft with no more than four seats during good weather and daylight hours and, unless authorized, no more than 50 miles from the home airport.
[4]Not included in total. A flight instructor must hold a flight instructor certificate in addition to a pilot certificate.

NOTE: Excludes U.S. military personnel holding civilian certificates who are stationed in a foreign country and pilots in U.S. territories.

SOURCE: U.S. Department of Transportation, Federal Aviation Administration, U.S. Civil Airmen Statistics, available at www.faa.gov/data_research/aviation_data_statistics/civil_airmen_statistics as of June 2015.

Chapter 6
Economy and Finance

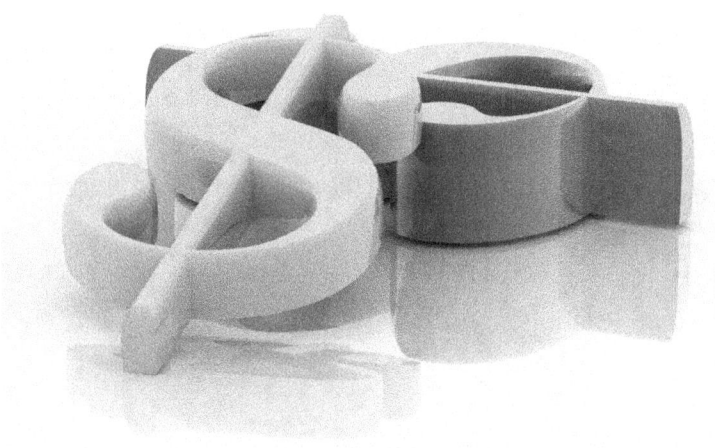

Table 6-1: Transportation and Warehousing Establishments and Employment: 2013

State	Number of establishments	Number of paid employees	Annual payroll ($ thousands)
Alabama	2,845	58,471	2,490,950
Alaska	1,084	19,097	1,345,399
Arizona	3,161	81,274	3,693,380
Arkansas	2,364	49,665	2,159,077
California	21,397	445,742	20,797,494
Colorado	3,457	63,219	3,086,311
Connecticut	1,611	40,491	1,729,350
Delaware	637	11,804	486,891
District of Columbia	157	2,845	141,502
Florida	13,517	209,498	9,223,123
Georgia	6,102	164,898	7,549,952
Hawaii	851	27,868	1,239,320
Idaho	1,735	16,858	610,622
Illinois	13,636	225,959	10,274,004
Indiana	5,082	122,587	4,753,813
Iowa	3,485	55,443	2,129,910
Kansas	2,492	49,763	2,006,261
Kentucky	2,826	83,574	3,998,594
Louisiana	3,830	69,766	3,876,909
Maine	1,195	14,649	574,154
Maryland	3,393	64,301	2,747,431
Massachusetts	3,553	77,211	3,371,837
Michigan	5,734	100,454	4,720,501
Minnesota	4,620	77,561	3,271,392
Mississippi	2,030	33,202	1,356,791
Missouri	4,479	81,996	3,291,794
Montana	1,434	12,387	501,434
Nebraska	2,293	27,758	1,164,097
Nevada	1,403	46,119	1,789,598
New Hampshire	804	12,309	465,939
New Jersey	7,171	158,946	7,746,426
New Mexico	1,389	17,620	748,953
New York	12,364	233,149	10,107,169
North Carolina	5,407	107,649	4,507,539
North Dakota	1,683	18,846	1,100,936
Ohio	7,000	158,169	6,928,667
Oklahoma	2,685	46,789	2,341,925
Oregon	2,940	50,836	2,215,373
Pennsylvania	8,227	206,938	8,240,126
Rhode Island	609	10,103	376,680
South Carolina	2,472	52,756	2,144,466
South Dakota	1,185	9,686	381,443
Tennessee	3,988	125,010	5,403,271
Texas	17,501	390,221	20,622,776
Utah	2,205	47,856	2,124,148
Vermont	489	6,266	222,453
Virginia	4,801	95,463	4,307,669
Washington	4,883	86,375	4,453,992
West Virginia	1,205	13,857	592,686
Wisconsin	5,171	93,997	3,747,073
Wyoming	965	9,935	495,120
United States, total	215,547	4,287,236	193,656,721

NOTES: The Transportation and Warehousing sector, North American Industrial Classification System (NAICS) 48, includes industries providing transportation of passengers and cargo, warehousing and storage for goods, scenic and sightseeing transportation, and support activities related to modes of transportation. Establishments in these industries use transportation equipment or transportation related facilities as a productive asset. The type of equipment depends on the mode of transportation. The industries included are: air transportation, water transportation, truck transportation, transit and ground passenger transportation, pipeline transportation, scenic and sightseeing transportation, support activities for transportation, postal service, couriers and messengers, and warehousing and storage. These data do not include government, railroad transportation (NAICS 482), or self-employed persons.

SOURCE: U.S. Department of Commerce, U.S. Census Bureau, County Business Patterns, available at www.census.gov/econ/cbp as of June 2015.

Table 6-2: Air Transportation Establishments and Employment: 2013

State	Number of establishments	Number of paid employees	Annual payroll ($ thousands)
Alabama	45	629	33,508
Alaska	196	5,773	315,963
Arizona	110	W	W
Arkansas	39	423	16,825
California	552	44,075	2,880,699
Colorado	103	15,614	907,706
Connecticut	42	1,400	83,677
Delaware	26	190	11,352
District of Columbia	15	W	W
Florida	533	22,099	1,266,728
Georgia	125	30,665	2,008,440
Hawaii	62	8,377	473,553
Idaho	49	1,082	47,841
Illinois	187	W	W
Indiana	71	W	126,704
Iowa	31	278	8,842
Kansas	34	406	16,300
Kentucky	49	4,191	247,294
Louisiana	103	4,654	277,909
Maine	20	184	5,458
Maryland	40	W	W
Massachusetts	87	7,683	410,361
Michigan	106	12,545	888,907
Minnesota	57	W	W
Mississippi	39	285	10,160
Missouri	62	W	W
Montana	64	779	33,929
Nebraska	30	577	31,424
Nevada	58	W	W
New Hampshire	25	W	W
New Jersey	101	14,846	1,281,137
New Mexico	38	611	31,855
New York	332	32,918	2,084,308
North Carolina	101	W	W
North Dakota	16	135	4,174
Ohio	102	10,906	877,901
Oklahoma	49	W	W
Oregon	80	5,242	333,669
Pennsylvania	124	W	W
Rhode Island	10	W	W
South Carolina	47	998	40,655
South Dakota	25	163	6,038
Tennessee	69	4,299	227,449
Texas	449	W	W
Utah	39	7,910	410,861
Vermont	7	91	3,053
Virginia	125	W	W
Washington	106	11,431	823,326
West Virginia	9	W	1,886
Wisconsin	51	1,381	51,099
Wyoming	24	W	W
United States, total[1]	4,864	418,936	26,921,123

[1]Values for states not reported individually are included in U.S. totals.

KEY: W = data withheld to avoid disclosure.

NOTES: The Air Transportation subsector (NAICS 481) includes industries providing air transportation of passengers and/or cargo using aircraft, such as airplanes and helicopters. These data do not include scenic and sightseeing air transportation (NAICS 4879, part), support activities for air transportation (NAICS 4881), or air courier services (NAICS 4921, part).

SOURCE: U.S. Department of Commerce, U.S. Census Bureau, County Business Patterns, available at www.census.gov/econ/cbp as of June 2015.

Table 6-3: Water Transportation Establishments and Employment: 2013

State	Number of establishments	Number of paid employees	Annual payroll ($ thousands)
Alabama	22	920	62,337
Alaska	78	W	98,156
Arizona	4	W	W
Arkansas	2	W	W
California	98	5,522	429,882
Colorado	2	W	W
Connecticut	29	966	85,969
Delaware	8	55	4,060
District of Columbia	W	W	W
Florida	214	14,667	939,639
Georgia	15	W	7,475
Hawaii	10	W	W
Idaho	1	W	W
Illinois	44	1,283	83,102
Indiana	8	W	W
Iowa	4	W	W
Kansas	1	W	W
Kentucky	23	2,234	139,188
Louisiana	263	11,958	948,669
Maine	12	52	2,102
Maryland	28	183	12,525
Massachusetts	36	445	45,441
Michigan	38	468	39,640
Minnesota	11	W	W
Mississippi	16	1,104	75,697
Missouri	11	504	29,451
Montana	W	W	W
Nebraska	W	W	W
Nevada	3	W	W
New Hampshire	1	W	W
New Jersey	63	887	62,710
New Mexico	5	W	W
New York	125	2,361	191,651
North Carolina	30	W	W
North Dakota	W	W	W
Ohio	18	W	W
Oklahoma	1	W	W
Oregon	16	W	W
Pennsylvania	34	1,176	60,852
Rhode Island	7	77	3,591
South Carolina	13	W	W
South Dakota	W	W	W
Tennessee	13	2,439	158,654
Texas	119	4,986	427,694
Utah	4	W	W
Vermont	4	W	W
Virginia	33	1,319	104,135
Washington	79	5,585	346,877
West Virginia	4	W	W
Wisconsin	5	W	3,888
Wyoming	1	W	W
United States, total[1]	1,556	66,672	4,737,874

[1]Values for states not reported individually are included in U.S. totals.

KEY: W = data withheld to avoid disclosure.

NOTES: The Water Transportation subsector (NAICS 483) includes industries providing water transportation of passengers and cargo using water craft, such as ships, barges, and boats. The subsector is composed of two industry groups: one for deep sea, coastal, and Great Lakes; and one for inland water transportation. This split typically reflects the difference in equipment used. These data do not include scenic and sightseeing water transportation services (NAICS 4872) and support activities for water transportation (NAICS 4883).

SOURCE: U.S. Department of Commerce, U.S. Census Bureau, County Business Patterns, available at www.census.gov/econ/cbp as of June 2015.

Table 6-4: Truck Transportation Establishments and Employment: 2013

State	Number of establishments	Number of paid employees	Annual payroll ($ thousands)
Alabama	1,692	25,591	1,000,439
Alaska	228	3,071	169,662
Arizona	1,397	22,134	866,289
Arkansas	1,503	31,703	1,438,892
California	9,304	105,264	4,655,923
Colorado	1,911	19,875	937,482
Connecticut	571	5,717	293,298
Delaware	231	3,086	123,526
District of Columbia	14	106	4,789
Florida	5,244	45,730	1,860,840
Georgia	3,133	48,472	2,042,001
Hawaii	195	3,325	134,010
Idaho	1,223	9,811	371,260
Illinois	8,801	68,952	3,176,110
Indiana	3,353	53,874	2,298,505
Iowa	2,612	36,065	1,361,041
Kansas	1,569	19,325	842,120
Kentucky	1,656	21,151	883,363
Louisiana	1,653	17,928	750,524
Maine	699	5,428	211,147
Maryland	1,447	15,479	678,264
Massachusetts	1,353	15,763	749,918
Michigan	3,407	42,509	1,963,534
Minnesota	2,866	26,402	1,172,656
Mississippi	1,234	13,771	557,601
Missouri	2,714	37,296	1,548,015
Montana	909	6,348	286,224
Nebraska	1,716	14,624	614,711
Nevada	558	6,287	284,980
New Hampshire	396	3,449	147,365
New Jersey	3,259	38,200	1,815,635
New Mexico	753	7,606	374,207
New York	4,501	39,800	1,734,713
North Carolina	3,014	40,340	1,687,003
North Dakota	1,327	13,887	874,076
Ohio	4,110	59,256	2,680,696
Oklahoma	1,725	20,021	912,162
Oregon	1,560	18,316	770,317
Pennsylvania	4,428	60,941	2,799,016
Rhode Island	277	2,663	126,949
South Carolina	1,213	17,269	740,298
South Dakota	859	4,952	208,026
Tennessee	1,963	48,710	2,243,234
Texas	8,639	130,575	6,123,275
Utah	1,435	21,185	1,016,095
Vermont	297	2,918	108,990
Virginia	2,554	29,254	1,228,829
Washington	2,438	22,925	1,016,832
West Virginia	794	6,262	252,846
Wisconsin	3,458	48,066	2,162,852
Wyoming	656	4,952	254,515
United States, total	112,849	1,366,634	60,555,055

NOTES: The Truck Transportation subsector (NAICS 484) includes industries providing over-the-road transportation of cargo using motor vehicles, such as trucks and tractor trailers. The subsector is divided into two industry groups for general freight trucking and specialized freight trucking. This distinction reflects differences in equipment used, type of load carried, scheduling, terminal, and other networking services. These data do not include support activities for road transportation (NAICS 4884), freight transportation arrangement services (NAICS 4885, part), the Postal Service (NAICS 491), or courier services (NAICS 492, part).

SOURCE: U.S. Department of Commerce, U.S. Census Bureau, County Business Patterns, available at www.census.gov/econ/cbp as of June 2015.

Table 6-5: Transit and Ground Passenger Transportation Establishments and Employment: 2013

State	Number of establishments	Number of paid employees	Annual payroll ($ thousands)
Alabama	95	1,677	31,776
Alaska	74	1,633	36,683
Arizona	266	9,132	238,928
Arkansas	61	1,083	21032
California	2,083	43,539	1,257,956
Colorado	219	4,944	142,502
Connecticut	383	14,009	383,207
Delaware	135	1,894	29396
District of Columbia	45	1,119	38,291
Florida	1043	13,248	342,405
Georgia	332	5,187	128,732
Hawaii	111	4,526	162,884
Idaho	81	1,803	30,327
Illinois	1104	26,994	550,168
Indiana	236	11,457	169,245
Iowa	104	1,707	45,146
Kansas	144	8,302	132,248
Kentucky	110	1,984	43,596
Louisiana	180	3,812	103,655
Maine	92	1,458	26,385
Maryland	703	11,340	280,892
Massachusetts	807	23,457	718,763
Michigan	349	7,003	155,992
Minnesota	503	14,383	295,800
Mississippi	82	1,828	34,120
Missouri	301	9,010	172,062
Montana	89	1,319	19,674
Nebraska	70	1,842	28,045
Nevada	149	15,577	385,585
New Hampshire	122	3,689	73,897
New Jersey	1,038	29,055	694,391
New Mexico	131	3,691	67,300
New York	2,976	73,467	2,188,905
North Carolina	296	4,551	103,498
North Dakota	66	1,038	20419
Ohio	400	9,829	182,182
Oklahoma	92	1,433	26384
Oregon	249	4,937	96,300
Pennsylvania	1,140	35,200	642,005
Rhode Island	99	2,948	56,923
South Carolina	148	1,632	38,433
South Dakota	86	1,148	21,095
Tennessee	276	4,803	136,872
Texas	716	19,091	503,392
Utah	80	1,581	27,416
Vermont	61	1,439	28,584
Virginia	426	8,523	258,332
Washington	288	5,576	159,583
West Virginia	42	400	5,952
Wisconsin	492	13,832	243,014
Wyoming	23	267	6676
United States, total[1]	19,198	473,397	11,587,048

[1]Values for states not reported individually are included in U.S. totals.

KEY: W = data withheld to avoid disclosure.

NOTES: The Transit and Ground Passenger Transportation subsector (NAICS 485) includes industries providing a variety of passenger transportation activities, such as urban transit systems; chartered bus, school bus, and interurban bus transportation; and taxis. These activities are distinguished based primarily on such production process factors as vehicle types, routes, and schedules. These data do not include scenic and sightseeing transportation (NAICS 4871, part), support activities for road transportation (NAICS 4884), or arrangement for car pools and vanpools (NAICS 4889, part).

SOURCE: U.S. Department of Commerce, U.S. Census Bureau, County Business Patterns, available at www.census.gov/econ/cbp as of June 2015.

Table 6-6: Pipeline Transportation Establishments and Employment: 2013

State	Number of establishments	Number of paid employees	Annual payroll ($ thousands)
Alabama	69	W	97,520
Alaska	16	1,456	267,975
Arizona	50	W	W
Arkansas	60	W	W
California	106	W	W
Colorado	102	W	W
Connecticut	15	164	19,255
Delaware	2	W	W
District of Columbia	7	W	W
Florida	53	W	W
Georgia	66	W	W
Hawaii	1	W	W
Idaho	5	W	6,876
Illinois	124	W	W
Indiana	64	538	50,929
Iowa	59	442	38,090
Kansas	143	1,716	162,111
Kentucky	60	954	83,197
Louisiana	335	W	314,489
Maine	13	W	7,307
Maryland	14	W	9,786
Massachusetts	30	343	39,208
Michigan	82	606	61,020
Minnesota	71	645	61,447
Mississippi	118	W	90,501
Missouri	66	W	29,221
Montana	30	252	23,218
Nebraska	57	698	65,061
Nevada	7	W	6,210
New Hampshire	11	36	3,851
New Jersey	40	333	34,797
New Mexico	88	925	85,905
New York	76	W	143,492
North Carolina	33	284	25,251
North Dakota	46	684	60,361
Ohio	87	W	W
Oklahoma	167	2,300	230,693
Oregon	13	131	13,716
Pennsylvania	147	1,987	172,273
Rhode Island	3	W	W
South Carolina	20	172	16,019
South Dakota	16	122	11,972
Tennessee	77	W	W
Texas	812	18,182	2,624,906
Utah	21	W	W
Vermont	3	W	W
Virginia	58	W	32,213
Washington	28	331	32,942
West Virginia	80	W	W
Wisconsin	50	W	39,833
Wyoming	90	839	77,380
United States, total[1]	3,791	52,021	6,070,358

[1]Values for states not reported individually are included in U.S. totals.

KEY: W = data withheld to avoid disclosure.

NOTES: The Pipeline Transportation subsector (NAICS 486) includes industries using transmission pipelines to transport products, such as crude oil, natural gas, refined petroleum products, and slurry. Industry groups are determined based on the products transported (i.e., crude oil, natural gas, and other). Gas industry data include the storage of natural gas because the storage is usually done by the pipeline establishment and because a pipeline is inherently a network in which all the nodes are interdependent. These data do not include activities classified under the Utilities sector, such as natural gas distribution (NAICS 2212) or water and air distribution and collection (NAICS 2213).

SOURCE: U.S. Department of Commerce, U.S. Census Bureau, County Business Patterns, available at www.census.gov/econ/cbp as of June 2015.

Table 6-7: Freight Railroad Employment, Retirement, and Wages: 2012[1]

State	Number of employees	Wages ($ millions)	Number of retirement beneficiaries	Retirement payments ($ millions)
Alabama	3,711	387	9,232	189
Alaska	525	48	229	5
Arizona	2,854	322	9,148	188
Arkansas	3,390	365	9,749	200
California	8,877	997	26,826	550
Colorado	2,973	337	7,735	159
Connecticut	117	11	2,562	53
Delaware	196	20	1,973	40
District of Columbia	12	1	418	9
Florida	4,981	529	28,642	587
Georgia	7,178	748	16,309	334
Hawaii	0	0	174	4
Idaho	1,390	151	4,423	91
Illinois	13,152	1,482	32,710	671
Indiana	6,223	659	15,227	312
Iowa	3,746	411	8,874	182
Kansas	5,427	626	13,575	278
Kentucky	4,195	446	14,340	294
Louisiana	3,083	339	7,178	147
Maine	650	65	2,574	53
Maryland	1,535	165	8,438	173
Massachusetts	823	75	3,664	75
Michigan	3,194	350	13,615	279
Minnesota	4,566	517	14,518	298
Mississippi	1,833	211	5,780	118
Missouri	7,333	832	18,593	381
Montana	2,805	321	5,629	115
Nebraska	12,010	1,364	12,781	262
Nevada	676	75	3,236	66
New Hampshire	242	20	834	17
New Jersey	1,132	118	8,469	174
New Mexico	1,671	196	4,242	87
New York	3,487	361	20,897	428
North Carolina	2,434	252	9,923	203
North Dakota	2,026	213	2,904	60
Ohio	7,619	791	24,606	504
Oklahoma	1,991	225	4,991	102
Oregon	2,026	220	7,747	159
Pennsylvania	7,056	718	32,481	666
Rhode Island	61	6	517	11
South Carolina	1,749	184	6,649	136
South Dakota	869	102	1,473	30
Tennessee	4,274	463	11,945	245
Texas	16,826	1,908	33,307	683
Utah	1,659	179	5,032	103
Vermont	172	14	744	15
Virginia	5,737	593	16,767	344
Washington	3,967	463	10,634	218
West Virginia	2,861	303	8,174	168
Wisconsin	3,128	358	9,118	187
Wyoming	2,822	323	3,114	64
United States, total	181,264	19,861	522,720	10,716

[1]Includes Class I, Regional, Switching and Terminal, and Local freight railroads.

NOTE: Wages are estimated by multiplying average wage by number of employees in each state. For Class I railroads, average wages are estimated based on aggregate data which incorporates fringe benefits, assumed to be 37.5 percent of wages.

SOURCE: Association of American Railroads, *Railroad Ten-Year Trends*, available at www.aar.org/StatisticsAndPublications as of July 2015.

Table 6-8: Transportation Expenditures by State and Local Governments: 2012
(Millions of current dollars)

State	Total	Highway	Transit	Air	Water
Alabama	2,649	2,265	77	185	123
Alaska	1,813	1,285	60	362	106
Arizona	3,595	2,343	670	582	Z
Arkansas	1,583	1,444	28	108	4
California	32,312	17,080	10,452	3,519	1,261
Colorado	3,543	2,410	581	550	2
Connecticut	2,517	1,742	716	57	2
Delaware	898	724	136	7	32
District of Columbia	2,832	548	2,284	Z	Z
Florida	12,221	8,110	1,696	1,961	454
Georgia	4,887	3,110	792	727	259
Hawaii	1,593	605	647	284	58
Idaho	951	881	17	51	2
Illinois	12,226	7,250	3,757	1,202	16
Indiana	3,209	2,842	185	166	17
Iowa	2,626	2,405	113	109	<0.5
Kansas	1,928	1,810	47	71	Z
Kentucky	2,903	2,577	143	163	19
Louisiana	3,619	2,766	222	289	342
Maine	999	893	16	69	21
Maryland	6,728	5,123	1,259	246	99
Massachusetts	5,718	2,627	2,449	557	85
Michigan	4,432	3,350	612	464	5
Minnesota	4,225	3,638	184	368	36
Mississippi	1,933	1,738	16	107	72
Missouri	3,760	2,962	449	342	7
Montana	1,161	1,058	35	67	1
Nebraska	1,375	1,229	40	106	Z
Nevada	2,698	1,686	361	651	Z
New Hampshire	824	750	15	59	<0.5
New Jersey	6,730	4,246	2,401	67	16
New Mexico	1,266	1,044	135	87	Z
New York	32,310	10,368	19,762	1,767	413
North Carolina	4,919	3,955	562	372	31
North Dakota	1,363	1,296	13	54	Z
Ohio	6,613	5,409	736	449	20
Oklahoma	2,550	2,330	72	138	11
Oregon	3,086	1,878	821	225	162
Pennsylvania	11,914	8,894	2,403	435	182
Rhode Island	647	441	150	53	3
South Carolina	1,985	1,585	91	160	148
South Dakota	1,016	949	10	58	Z
Tennessee	3,138	2,489	254	384	11
Texas	16,030	11,348	2,783	1,528	371
Utah	2,696	1,962	624	111	Z
Vermont	733	678	24	31	Z
Virginia	6,545	4,248	523	1,378	396
Washington	7,528	4,153	2,432	447	496
West Virginia	1,412	1,301	50	60	1
Wisconsin	4,499	3,874	363	247	15
Wyoming	823	761	3	59	Z
United States, total	249,562	160,459	62,270	21,533	5,300

KEY: Z = Data not available, no activity, value of zero, or value too small to report.

NOTES: Data are for fiscal year 2012. Most state government fiscal years end on June 30, except for four states with other ending dates: Alabama and Michigan (September 30), New York (March 31), and Texas (August 31). Not all agencies of a government necessarily have a fiscal period that coincides with the central organization. Totals for an individual government, in those instances, are the summation of finances for all agencies with a fiscal period ending between July 1, 2011, and June 30, 2012. Details may not add to totals due to rounding and values that are too small to report.

SOURCE: U.S. Department of Commerce, U.S. Census Bureau, State and Local Government Finance, available at www.census.gov/govs/local as of July 2015.

Table 6-9: Transportation Revenues Collected by State and Local Governments: 2012
(Millions of current dollars)

State	Total	Highway[1]	Transit	Air	Water
Alabama	1,118	868	6	99	145
Alaska	371	190	7	115	58
Arizona	1,661	1,099	116	446	Z
Arkansas	705	630	3	68	3
California	16,188	10,176	1,987	2,737	1,289
Colorado	2,232	1,301	140	791	Z
Connecticut	859	758	54	46	1
Delaware	510	453	17	6	34
District of Columbia	997	93	904	Z	Z
Florida	8,495	5,887	303	1,915	390
Georgia	2,532	1,368	174	707	284
Hawaii	1,064	530	59	380	94
Idaho	442	407	3	30	2
Illinois	5,948	3,904	907	1,118	19
Indiana	1,452	1,215	46	180	11
Iowa	1,103	1,012	25	66	<0.5
Kansas	786	739	6	41	Z
Kentucky	1,309	1,057	22	209	20
Louisiana	1,089	767	27	137	158
Maine	511	469	3	35	3
Maryland	2,186	1,752	168	211	55
Massachusetts	2,881	1,589	604	605	83
Michigan	2,616	2,070	85	458	2
Minnesota	1,983	1,617	21	334	11
Mississippi	648	562	1	51	33
Missouri	1,470	1,044	73	351	3
Montana	417	382	3	31	1
Nebraska	634	567	6	61	Z
Nevada	1,031	553	78	400	Z
New Hampshire	444	400	4	39	Z
New Jersey	3,733	2,707	986	20	19
New Mexico	462	365	15	82	Z
New York	15,415	6,799	5,640	2,690	287
North Carolina	3,057	2,543	74	408	32
North Dakota	362	339	4	19	Z
Ohio	3,275	2,834	131	280	30
Oklahoma	1,466	1,358	13	86	8
Oregon	1,603	1,159	126	242	76
Pennsylvania	5,309	4,179	599	520	11
Rhode Island	288	196	33	56	3
South Carolina	1,091	831	17	112	132
South Dakota	240	226	2	12	Z
Tennessee	1,600	1,272	38	286	4
Texas	8,868	6,631	292	1,575	369
Utah	813	574	47	192	Z
Vermont	205	182	5	18	Z
Virginia	2,951	1,660	116	875	299
Washington	3,411	2,039	417	527	428
West Virginia	545	499	11	34	Z
Wisconsin	1,923	1,676	84	153	10
Wyoming	184	162	1	22	Z
United States, total	120,481	81,692	14,505	19,876	4,408

[1]Highway revenues include state and local government receipts from motor fuel taxes and motor vehicle license taxes, regular and toll highway charges, and receipts from parking facilities.

KEY: Z = Data not available, no activity, value of zero, or value too small to report.

NOTES: Data are for fiscal year 2012. Most state government fiscal years end on June 30, except for four states with other ending dates: Alabama and Michigan (September 30), New York (March 31), and Texas (August 31). Not all agencies of a government necessarily have a fiscal period that coincides with the central organization. Totals for an individual government, in those instances, are the summation of finances for all agencies with a fiscal period ending between July 1, 2011, and June 30, 2012. Details may not add to totals due to rounding and values that are too small to report.

SOURCE: U.S. Department of Commerce, U.S. Census Bureau, State and Local Government Finance, available at www.census.gov/govs/local as of July 2015.

Table 6-10: Federal and State Funding of Public Transit: 2008, 2010, and 2012
(Thousands of current dollars)

State	2008 Federal	2008 State	2010 Federal	2010 State	2012 Federal	2012 State
Alabama	62,505	0	46,559	0	44,278	0
Alaska	77,703	86,815	71,954	98,132	62,886	179,978
Arizona	186,106	11,780	169,253	0	142,128	0
Arkansas	27,933	3,790	26,364	4,023	26,459	3,477
California	1,191,982	2,299,579	1,298,998	1,731,333	1,514,724	1,849,194
Colorado	189,078	23,048	260,467	12,673	254,446	12,350
Connecticut	151,637	267,500	143,886	307,342	182,299	453,476
Delaware	17,894	86,233	24,168	81,526	15,343	82,731
District of Columbia	193,160	272,724	283,671	322,038	194,810	484,166
Florida	336,576	146,339	386,206	184,516	397,708	217,310
Georgia	162,810	6,141	184,225	2,173	174,445	2,920
Hawaii	60,973	0	77,183	0	259,158	0
Idaho	20,869	312	17,354	312	19,350	312
Illinois	548,007	519,300	570,978	589,000	509,332	814,448
Indiana	99,438	55,733	85,528	54,671	86,504	56,019
Iowa	40,623	13,281	50,744	10,889	38,947	12,899
Kansas	33,260	5,762	28,802	6,000	28,193	6,000
Kentucky	51,200	3,502	70,868	1,412	53,881	1,490
Louisiana	62,519	5,963	67,274	4,955	61,216	4,955
Maine	14,076	1,528	16,035	530	24,227	530
Maryland	190,310	844,417	191,192	889,306	231,827	1,086,510
Massachusetts	316,215	1,182,785	395,390	1,376,366	352,288	1,245,381
Michigan	150,255	200,087	146,171	198,430	183,572	240,437
Minnesota	155,980	249,253	116,589	270,639	195,772	309,427
Mississippi	35,066	1,600	25,431	1,600	23,609	1,600
Missouri	97,413	6,922	104,648	6,247	86,501	2,994
Montana	14,702	415	16,154	447	15,313	319
Nebraska	22,892	2,900	28,917	3,000	24,190	2,900
Nevada	52,793	0	49,385	0	45,022	107
New Hampshire	14,303	4,474	11,865	494	12,176	244
New Jersey	547,740	NR	685,717	1,157,687	523,244	918,027
New Mexico	30,838	9,297	35,541	18,417	35,203	6,665
New York	1,586,021	3,015,442	1,730,895	4,352,345	1,701,170	4,465,884
North Carolina	120,309	73,466	116,176	74,948	108,102	73,575
North Dakota	11,922	2,900	13,680	3,150	13,729	3,152
Ohio	179,053	15,817	192,156	10,839	173,313	7,300
Oklahoma	35,102	5,750	42,784	6,083	38,604	5,750
Oregon	165,425	39,921	166,601	108,055	177,176	32,670
Pennsylvania	409,290	1,145,567	424,423	1,225,108	406,059	1,091,936
Rhode Island	49,321	47,338	28,083	53,538	27,473	53,073
South Carolina	38,523	6,400	43,764	6,000	39,667	6,000
South Dakota	14,456	770	11,417	770	14,562	770
Tennessee	74,495	41,537	79,788	35,927	77,207	44,499
Texas	487,289	28,741	642,570	28,741	687,160	30,341
Utah	161,499	0	264,753	0	289,747	0
Vermont	10,671	5,899	18,817	6,328	5,914	6,843
Virginia	197,361	228,966	117,945	189,478	192,256	239,203
Washington	289,569	39,752	365,506	57,212	345,601	52,776
West Virginia	27,875	3,023	23,382	2,833	18,859	2,786
Wisconsin	81,038	125,180	84,708	132,066	69,540	117,852
Wyoming	8,023	2,496	8,090	2,496	9,233	2,522
United States, total	9,104,100	11,140,442	10,063,053	13,630,074	10,214,424	14,233,797

KEY: NR = not reported.

SOURCE: American Association of State Highway and Transportation Officials, *Survey of State Funding for Public Transportation* 2014, as of July 2015.

Table 6-11: Average Motor Gasoline Prices Excluding Taxes, All Grades: 2008-2010
(Cents per gallon excluding taxes)

State	2008	2009	2010
Alabama	276.7	182.8	225.2
Alaska	339.1	260.9	311.7
Arizona	278.0	190.0	234.7
Arkansas	270.3	176.0	224.7
California	290.6	212.2	252.7
Colorado	276.6	185.2	224.6
Connecticut	280.4	194.4	241.5
Delaware	275.5	187.4	231.2
District of Columbia	280.8	NA	239.6
Florida	276.2	186.0	228.4
Georgia	279.3	185.0	227.4
Hawaii	317.1	235.0	290.1
Idaho	281.9	189.8	242.7
Illinois	279.2	191.4	234.7
Indiana	273.4	186.5	226.7
Iowa	272.3	187.9	228.5
Kansas	267.6	181.3	223.3
Kentucky	276.2	188.2	229.6
Louisiana	277.0	185.4	225.2
Maine	284.8	198.4	236.0
Maryland	280.8	188.3	231.5
Massachusetts	282.0	196.9	235.8
Michigan	273.8	187.9	228.2
Minnesota	270.0	187.7	231.6
Mississippi	272.6	184.0	226.0
Missouri	267.5	182.5	224.3
Montana	280.4	190.9	238.6
Nebraska	266.8	185.8	229.5
Nevada	282.9	200.0	240.3
New Hampshire	280.9	194.0	237.5
New Jersey	281.7	192.2	235.0
New Mexico	281.9	195.3	236.2
New York	282.8	191.7	234.4
North Carolina	274.3	181.9	223.7
North Dakota	278.2	197.1	242.2
Ohio	269.5	185.3	225.9
Oklahoma	268.5	182.1	224.8
Oregon	292.4	205.7	245.8
Pennsylvania	274.2	188.0	229.7
Rhode Island	272.9	189.6	232.9
South Carolina	276.2	181.7	223.3
South Dakota	274.1	191.3	234.6
Tennessee	273.6	181.1	223.8
Texas	271.3	182.5	223.4
Utah	277.8	190.4	241.5
Vermont	292.5	198.9	242.2
Virginia	275.4	186.6	229.1
Washington	285.6	201.2	241.6
West Virginia	282.5	192.7	235.4
Wisconsin	273.9	188.5	229.2
Wyoming	283.9	187.3	234.3
United States, average	277.2	189.3	231.6

KEY: NA = Not available.

NOTE: Data includes sales to end users through retail outlets as well as all direct sales to end users that were not made through company-operated retail outlets (e.g., sales to agricultural customers, commercial sales, and industrial sales).

SOURCE: U.S. Department of Energy, Energy Information Administration, *Gasoline Prices by Formulation*, Grade, Sales Type available at www.eia.gov/dnav/pet/pet_pri_allmg_a_epm0_pta_dpgal_a.htm as of June 2013.

Table 6-12: State Motor-Fuel Tax Rates: 2013
(Cents per gallon)

State	Gasoline	Diesel	Liquefied petroleum gas	Gasohol
Alabama	18.00	19.00	0.00	18.00
Alaska	8.00	8.00	0.00	8.00
Arizona	18.00	26.00	0.00	18.00
Arkansas	21.50	22.50	16.50	21.50
California	39.50	10.00	6.00	39.50
Colorado	22.00	20.50	20.50	22.00
Connecticut	25.00	51.20	0.00	25.00
Delaware	23.00	22.00	22.00	23.00
District of Columbia	23.50	23.50	20.00	23.50
Florida	16.90	16.90	14.50	16.90
Georgia	7.50	7.50	7.50	7.50
Hawaii	17.00	17.00	5.20	16.00
Idaho	25.00	25.00	18.10	25.00
Illinois	19.00	21.50	19.00	19.00
Indiana	18.00	16.00	0.00	18.00
Iowa	21.00	22.50	20.00	19.00
Kansas	24.00	26.00	23.00	24.00
Kentucky	30.90	27.90	30.90	30.90
Louisiana	20.00	20.00	16.00	20.00
Maine	30.00	31.20	0.00	23.00
Maryland	23.50	24.30	0.00	0.00
Massachusetts	24.00	24.00	13.50	24.00
Michigan	19.00	15.00	15.00	19.00
Minnesota	28.50	28.50	21.05	28.00
Mississippi	18.40	18.40	17.00	18.40
Missouri	17.00	17.00	17.00	17.00
Montana	27.75	28.50	0.00	23.75
Nebraska	26.30	26.30	26.30	26.20
Nevada	24.00	27.00	22.00	24.00
New Hampshire	19.63	19.63	0.00	18.00
New Jersey	10.50	13.50	5.25	10.50
New Mexico	18.88	22.88	12.00	18.88
New York	26.65	24.85	8.05	26.65
North Carolina	37.75	35.75	27.10	37.75
North Dakota	23.00	23.00	23.00	23.00
Ohio	28.00	28.00	28.00	28.00
Oklahoma	17.00	14.00	17.00	17.00
Oregon	30.00	30.00	23.10	30.00
Pennsylvania	31.20	38.10	22.80	31.20
Rhode Island	32.00	32.00	32.00	32.00
South Carolina	16.00	16.00	16.00	16.00
South Dakota	22.00	22.00	20.00	8.00
Tennessee	20.00	17.00	14.00	20.00
Texas	20.00	20.00	15.00	20.00
Utah	24.50	24.50	24.50	24.50
Vermont	19.20	31.00	0.00	0.00
Virginia	11.10	20.20	11.10	11.10
Washington	37.50	37.50	37.50	37.50
West Virginia	34.70	34.70	34.70	34.70
Wisconsin	30.90	30.90	22.60	30.90
Wyoming	24.00	24.00	24.00	24.00
Federal tax	18.4	24.4	13.6	18.40

NOTE: Tax rates in effect as of December 2013. Only taxes that are levied as a dollar amount per volume of motor fuel are included. Taxes that apply to all petroleum products without distinguishing motor fuel are omitted. Local option taxes are included only when they have been adopted uniformly Statewide.

SOURCE: U.S. Department of Transportation, Federal Highway Administration, *Highway Statistics*, MF-121T, available at www.fhwa.dot.gov/policyinformation/statistics.cfm as of June 2015.

Chapter 7

Energy and Environment

Table 7-1: Transportation Energy Consumption by Energy Source: 2013
(Trillion Btu)

State	Natural gas[1]	Petroleum Distillate fuel (diesel)	Jet fuel	Motor gasoline[2,4]	Residual fuel	Other[3]	Total petroleum	Ethanol[4]	Electricity	Net energy[4]	Electrical system energy losses[5]	Total[4]
Alabama	22.7	117.3	13.2	308.2	5.0	3.0	446.8	21.7	0.0	469.5	0.0	469.5
Alaska	0.9	32.0	107.3	31.3	0.0	1.2	171.9	1.7	0.0	172.8	0.0	172.8
Arizona	14.9	106.6	21.0	314.0	0.0	3.3	444.9	19.9	0.0	459.8	0.0	459.8
Arkansas	11.8	91.2	6.0	164.5	0.0	2.8	264.5	11.6	<0.05	276.3	<0.05	276.3
California	27.9	438.1	563.1	1,727.1	124.1	19.6	2,872.0	121.7	2.9	2,902.8	5.1	2,907.8
Colorado	10.2	80.4	53.5	254.5	0.0	2.8	391.3	14.8	0.2	401.7	0.5	402.2
Connecticut	4.5	38.3	10.8	171.0	0.0	1.6	221.6	12.1	0.6	226.8	1.2	228.0
Delaware	1.0	8.1	0.7	51.0	0.5	0.6	60.9	3.6	0.0	62.0	0.0	62.0
District of Columbia	2.5	2.0	0.0	11.5	0.0	0.2	13.7	0.8	1.1	17.3	2.4	19.8
Florida	12.8	225.2	180.2	981.8	57.4	7.7	1,452.3	64.5	0.3	1,465.4	0.6	1,466.0
Georgia	9.3	181.0	22.6	576.5	26.9	5.2	812.3	37.9	0.5	822.2	1.0	823.2
Hawaii	<0.05	17.7	64.2	53.3	5.5	0.4	141.2	3.0	0.0	141.2	0.0	141.2
Idaho	6.2	41.4	4.3	81.6	0.0	1.0	128.4	4.8	0.0	134.6	0.0	134.6
Illinois	27.8	219.2	137.6	548.9	0.1	10.6	916.3	38.7	2.0	946.1	4.3	950.4
Indiana	7.8	205.4	46.7	354.0	0.6	5.2	611.9	25.0	0.1	619.8	0.2	620.0
Iowa	11.8	95.8	6.1	182.6	0.0	3.4	288.0	11.9	0.0	299.7	0.0	299.7
Kansas	23.9	97.4	10.1	152.4	0.0	3.5	263.4	8.3	0.0	287.3	0.0	287.3
Kentucky	7.8	127.3	48.5	253.2	0.0	3.4	432.4	17.8	0.0	440.2	0.0	440.2
Louisiana	41.5	150.7	123.6	269.3	70.8	4.2	618.6	19.0	<0.05	660.1	0.1	660.2
Maine	0.9	28.4	6.3	87.5	4.1	0.8	127.1	5.8	0.0	128.0	0.0	128.0
Maryland	7.7	67.8	11.1	335.0	1.2	2.0	417.2	23.5	1.8	426.7	4.2	430.9
Massachusetts	5.5	80.5	35.7	326.7	1.2	2.8	447.0	23.0	1.2	453.8	2.4	456.2
Michigan	19.8	133.7	22.1	546.7	1.5	9.3	713.2	38.5	<0.05	733.1	<0.05	733.1
Minnesota	12.1	103.3	33.1	294.2	0.5	4.9	435.9	24.6	0.1	448.1	0.1	448.2
Mississippi	25.5	88.5	56.6	191.3	4.3	1.9	342.6	13.5	0.0	368.1	0.0	368.1
Missouri	5.8	145.7	18.6	365.4	0.0	6.6	536.3	21.2	0.1	542.2	0.2	542.3
Montana	7.0	44.8	5.0	60.1	0.0	1.2	111.1	3.5	0.0	118.1	0.0	118.1
Nebraska	7.2	79.6	6.1	99.9	0.0	2.3	187.9	5.4	0.0	195.1	0.0	195.1
Nevada	5.8	43.0	26.9	130.9	0.0	1.0	201.7	7.3	<0.05	207.6	<0.05	207.6
New Hampshire	0.1	12.9	1.9	83.9	<0.05	0.5	99.3	5.8	0.0	99.4	0.0	99.4
New Jersey	7.1	119.1	204.6	473.9	34.8	4.4	836.8	33.4	1.0	845.0	2.1	847.1
New Mexico	9.3	72.7	6.2	111.6	0.0	1.6	192.1	7.1	0.0	201.5	0.0	201.5
New York	27.3	152.4	154.8	635.1	39.6	6.2	988.1	43.5	9.8	1,025.1	17.6	1,042.8
North Carolina	4.2	142.8	57.4	511.0	0.0	5.0	716.3	33.6	<0.05	720.5	0.1	720.5
North Dakota	17.4	61.8	6.6	52.8	0.0	1.1	122.2	3.7	0.0	139.6	0.0	139.6
Ohio	11.1	236.5	75.2	588.2	0.0	9.0	908.7	41.5	0.2	920.0	0.3	920.3
Oklahoma	44.5	140.5	44.0	220.2	0.0	4.8	409.4	11.9	0.0	453.9	0.0	453.9
Oregon	4.3	89.9	25.9	173.4	3.8	3.7	296.8	9.7	0.1	301.2	0.1	301.3
Pennsylvania	43.0	215.9	41.5	592.8	6.3	8.0	864.7	40.0	2.8	910.4	5.6	916.0
Rhode Island	1.5	8.9	3.9	43.2	<0.05	0.4	56.5	3.0	0.1	58.1	0.1	58.3
South Carolina	2.6	107.4	11.6	319.5	9.7	2.0	450.3	21.0	0.0	452.9	0.0	452.9
South Dakota	7.1	31.5	3.8	51.8	0.0	1.2	88.3	3.6	0.0	95.4	0.0	95.4
Tennessee	8.2	144.3	63.6	375.0	0.3	4.8	588.0	26.4	<0.05	596.2	<0.05	596.2
Texas	304.9	749.2	386.7	1,498.4	118.3	15.4	2,767.9	93.6	0.2	3,073.1	0.4	3,073.5
Utah	14.5	68.1	36.3	129.0	0.0	1.4	234.9	7.5	0.2	249.6	0.4	250.0
Vermont	0.1	9.8	1.3	37.7	0.0	0.3	49.1	2.5	0.0	49.2	0.0	49.2
Virginia	9.1	148.6	100.1	465.9	4.1	3.4	722.2	31.9	0.7	732.0	1.4	733.4
Washington	11.1	106.6	89.7	321.0	60.2	4.4	581.8	17.9	<0.05	592.9	<0.05	593.0
West Virginia	31.9	41.3	1.2	94.3	0.0	1.5	138.3	6.2	<0.05	170.1	<0.05	170.2
Wisconsin	3.0	105.4	8.9	290.5	0.0	4.5	409.2	20.3	0.0	412.2	0.0	412.2
Wyoming	16.0	53.8	2.3	41.0	0.0	0.8	98.0	2.4	0.0	114.0	0.0	114.0
United States, total	921.3	5,909.6	2,968.6	16,034.9	581.2	197.3	25,691.4	1,071.6	26.0	26,638.7	50.7	26,689.4

[1]Transportation use of natural gas is gas consumed in the operation of pipelines, primarily in compressors, and gas consumed as vehicle fuel.
[2]Includes ethanol blended into motor gasoline.
[3]"Other" is the sum of aviation gasoline, liquefied petroleum gas (LPG), and lubricants.
[4]Ethanol blended into motor gasoline is included in motor gasoline, but is also shown separately to display the use of renewable energy by the transportation sector. It is counted only once in the total.
[5]Incurred in the generation, transmission, and distribution of electricity plus plant use and unaccounted for electrical system energy losses.

KEY: Btu = British thermal unit

NOTE: Totals may not equal sum of components due to independent rounding.

SOURCE: U.S. Department of Energy, Energy Information Administration, *State Energy Data System*, Consumption Estimates, available at www.eia.gov/state/seds as of July 2015.

Table 7-2: Energy Consumption by End-Use Sector: 2013
(Trillion Btu)

State	Total energy consumed[1]	Transportation Trillion Btu	Transportation Percent	Residential Trillion Btu	Residential Percent	Commercial Trillion Btu	Commercial Percent	Industrial Trillion Btu	Industrial Percent
Alabama	1,931.4	469.5	24.3	358.5	18.6	256.8	13.3	846.5	43.8
Alaska	609.0	172.8	28.4	48.9	8.0	63.0	10.3	324.3	53.3
Arizona	1,414.8	459.8	32.5	398.1	28.1	346.2	24.5	210.7	14.9
Arkansas	1,093.0	276.3	25.3	241.3	22.1	176.6	16.2	398.8	36.5
California	7,684.1	2,907.8	37.8	1,480.0	19.3	1,483.8	19.3	1,812.4	23.6
Colorado	1,471.8	402.2	27.3	367.1	24.9	285.6	19.4	417.0	28.3
Connecticut	748.1	228.0	30.5	249.1	33.3	189.2	25.3	81.9	10.9
Delaware	274.5	62.0	22.6	65.4	23.8	56.6	20.6	90.5	33.0
District of Columbia	170.9	19.8	11.6	37.0	21.7	111.3	65.1	2.9	1.7
Florida	4,077.9	1,466.0	35.9	1,168.3	28.6	968.2	23.7	475.4	11.7
Georgia	2,795.4	823.2	29.4	688.1	24.6	530.8	19.0	753.3	26.9
Hawaii	277.1	141.2	51.0	35.7	12.9	39.0	14.1	61.2	22.1
Idaho	529.5	134.6	25.4	127.3	24.0	88.1	16.6	179.6	33.9
Illinois	4,011.5	950.4	23.7	1,011.9	25.2	804.4	20.1	1,244.7	31.0
Indiana	2,900.0	620.0	21.4	569.6	19.6	385.0	13.3	1,325.5	45.7
Iowa	1,516.5	299.7	19.8	253.7	16.7	215.7	14.2	747.3	49.3
Kansas	1,163.1	287.3	24.7	236.1	20.3	210.1	18.1	429.5	36.9
Kentucky	1,822.7	440.2	24.2	385.2	21.1	284.4	15.6	712.9	39.1
Louisiana	3,835.0	660.2	17.2	343.6	9.0	269.1	7.0	2,562.0	66.8
Maine	407.1	128.0	31.4	85.6	21.0	58.9	14.5	134.6	33.1
Maryland	1,403.8	430.9	30.7	431.5	30.7	424.6	30.2	116.8	8.3
Massachusetts	1,442.6	456.2	31.6	452.6	31.4	290.9	20.2	242.8	16.8
Michigan	2,843.2	733.1	25.8	773.6	27.2	600.7	21.1	735.8	25.9
Minnesota	1,859.8	448.2	24.1	417.3	22.4	358.0	19.2	636.3	34.2
Mississippi	1,141.8	368.1	32.2	211.2	18.5	160.3	14.0	402.2	35.2
Missouri	1,857.0	542.3	29.2	538.3	29.0	411.2	22.1	365.2	19.7
Montana	401.2	118.1	29.4	85.2	21.2	76.9	19.2	121.0	30.2
Nebraska	871.8	195.1	22.4	163.8	18.8	140.4	16.1	372.5	42.7
Nevada	657.1	207.6	31.6	162.1	24.7	121.3	18.5	166.1	25.3
New Hampshire	302.8	99.4	32.8	92.8	30.6	70.4	23.2	40.1	13.2
New Jersey	2,314.5	847.1	36.6	599.4	25.9	600.7	26.0	267.3	11.5
New Mexico	688.5	201.5	29.3	123.9	18.0	125.8	18.3	237.4	34.5
New York	3,625.3	1,042.8	28.8	1,072.1	29.6	1,134.2	31.3	376.3	10.4
North Carolina	2,524.1	720.5	28.5	692.1	27.4	555.8	22.0	555.7	22.0
North Dakota	588.6	139.6	23.7	73.4	12.5	85.4	14.5	290.1	49.3
Ohio	3,745.4	920.3	24.6	914.3	24.4	694.9	18.6	1,216.0	32.5
Oklahoma	1,622.8	453.9	28.0	323.0	19.9	258.1	15.9	587.8	36.2
Oregon	996.7	301.3	30.2	258.1	25.9	190.9	19.2	246.4	24.7
Pennsylvania	3,795.0	916.0	24.1	930.0	24.5	630.8	16.6	1,318.2	34.7
Rhode Island	193.6	58.3	30.1	66.2	34.2	49.0	25.3	20.0	10.3
South Carolina	1,591.4	452.9	28.5	351.6	22.1	259.5	16.3	527.4	33.1
South Dakota	390.4	95.4	24.4	73.5	18.8	65.2	16.7	156.3	40.0
Tennessee	2,135.9	596.2	27.9	531.9	24.9	428.0	20.0	579.8	27.1
Texas	12,944.1	3,073.5	23.7	1,685.9	13.0	1,609.9	12.4	6,574.8	50.8
Utah	830.6	250.0	30.1	175.3	21.1	163.5	19.7	241.8	29.1
Vermont	133.6	49.2	36.8	42.7	32.0	26.0	19.5	15.8	11.8
Virginia	2,410.7	733.4	30.4	626.6	26.0	612.1	25.4	438.6	18.2
Washington	2,039.3	593.0	29.1	494.9	24.3	382.8	18.8	568.6	27.9
West Virginia	737.8	170.2	23.1	174.1	23.6	112.3	15.2	281.2	38.1
Wisconsin	1,804.0	412.2	22.8	445.1	24.7	369.1	20.5	577.6	32.0
Wyoming	535.5	114.0	21.3	49.2	9.2	63.1	11.8	309.2	57.7
United States, total	97,144.7	26,689.4	27.5	21,182.0	21.8	17,894.3	18.4	31,378.9	32.3

[1] U.S. total energy and U.S. industrial sector include 4.0 trillion Btu of net imports of coal coke that is not allocated to the States.
[2] End-use sector data include electricity sales and associated electrical system energy losses.

KEY: Btu = British thermal unit.

NOTE: Totals may not equal sum of components due to rounding.

SOURCE: U.S. Department of Energy, Energy Information Administration, *State Energy Data System*, Consumption Estimates, available at www.eia.gov/state/seds as of July 2015.

Table 7-3: Transportation Energy Consumption per Capita: 2013

State	Population (thousands)	Petroleum Total (trillion Btu)	Petroleum Per capita (million Btu)	All energy sources Total (trillion Btu)	All energy sources Per capita (million Btu)
Alabama	4,834.0	446.8	92.4	97.1	98.2
Alaska	737.3	171.9	233.2	234.4	243.3
Arizona	6,635.0	444.9	67.1	69.3	71.9
Arkansas	2,958.8	264.5	89.4	93.4	94.8
California	38,431.4	2,872.0	74.7	75.7	78.1
Colorado	5,272.1	391.3	74.2	76.3	80.0
Connecticut	3,599.3	221.6	61.6	63.3	63.8
Delaware	925.2	60.9	65.8	67.0	69.0
District of Columbia	649.1	13.7	21.1	30.5	32.9
Florida	19,600.3	1,452.3	74.1	74.8	78.0
Georgia	9,994.8	812.3	81.3	82.4	85.0
Hawaii	1,409.0	141.2	100.2	100.2	103.8
Idaho	1,612.8	128.4	79.6	83.5	85.9
Illinois	12,890.6	916.3	71.1	73.7	74.1
Indiana	6,570.7	611.9	93.1	94.4	95.6
Iowa	3,092.3	288.0	93.1	96.9	98.4
Kansas	2,895.8	263.4	91.0	99.2	100.7
Kentucky	4,399.6	432.4	98.3	100.1	101.4
Louisiana	4,629.3	618.6	133.6	142.6	145.6
Maine	1,328.7	127.1	95.7	96.3	96.4
Maryland	5,938.7	417.2	70.3	72.6	74.6
Massachusetts	6,708.9	447.0	66.6	68.0	69.7
Michigan	9,898.2	713.2	72.1	74.1	74.2
Minnesota	5,422.1	435.9	80.4	82.7	84.5
Mississippi	2,992.2	342.6	114.5	123.0	124.1
Missouri	6,044.9	536.3	88.7	89.7	90.6
Montana	1,014.9	111.1	109.5	116.4	119.4
Nebraska	1,869.0	187.9	100.5	104.4	106.8
Nevada	2,791.5	201.7	72.3	74.4	76.9
New Hampshire	1,322.6	99.3	75.1	75.2	75.5
New Jersey	8,911.5	836.8	93.9	95.1	96.4
New Mexico	2,086.9	192.1	92.1	96.6	97.9
New York	19,695.7	988.1	50.2	52.9	53.8
North Carolina	9,848.9	716.3	72.7	73.2	75.6
North Dakota	723.9	122.2	168.8	192.9	207.6
Ohio	11,572.0	908.7	78.5	79.5	79.8
Oklahoma	3,853.1	409.4	106.3	117.8	121.0
Oregon	3,928.1	296.8	75.6	76.7	78.6
Pennsylvania	12,781.3	864.7	67.7	71.7	72.1
Rhode Island	1,053.4	56.5	53.6	55.3	55.4
South Carolina	4,771.9	450.3	94.4	94.9	97.9
South Dakota	845.5	88.3	104.4	112.8	117.2
Tennessee	6,497.3	588.0	90.5	91.8	93.9
Texas	26,505.6	2,767.9	104.4	116.0	122.2
Utah	2,902.8	234.9	80.9	86.1	90.5
Vermont	626.9	49.1	78.3	78.5	78.6
Virginia	8,270.3	722.2	87.3	88.7	91.7
Washington	6,973.7	581.8	83.4	85.0	88.2
West Virginia	1,853.6	138.3	74.6	91.8	91.9
Wisconsin	5,743.0	409.2	71.3	71.8	72.5
Wyoming	583.2	98.0	168.0	195.5	202.3
United States	316,497.5	25,691.4	81.2	84.3	86.4

KEY: Btu = British thermal unit

NOTE: Totals may not equal sum of components due to rounding.

SOURCE: Population: U.S. Department of Commerce, U.S. Census Bureau, Population Estimates, available at www.census.gov/popest as of July 2015. Consumption: U.S. Department of Energy, Energy Information Administration, *State Energy Data System*, Consumption Estimates, available at www.eia.gov/state/seds as of July 2015.

Table 7-4: Motor-Fuel Use: 2013
(Millions of gallons)

State	Gasoline Highway use Private and commercial	Gasoline Highway use Public use	Gasoline Nonhighway use Private and commercial	Gasoline Nonhighway use Public use	Special fuel (mainly diesel) Private and commercial	Total use Private and commercial	Total use Public use	Total use Combined total	Total Gallons Per Capita
Alabama	2,481	39	49	2	737	3,267	41	3,308	684
Alaska	244	8	27	<0.5	133	404	8	412	559
Arizona	2,539	39	66	2	717	3,322	41	3,363	507
Arkansas	1,315	27	53	1	598	1,966	28	1,995	674
California	13,977	225	340	11	2,859	17,176	236	17,413	453
Colorado	2,058	38	46	2	566	2,669	39	2,709	514
Connecticut	1,377	21	38	1	270	1,685	22	1,707	474
Delaware	401	7	22	<0.5	61	485	7	492	532
District of Columbia	88	6	2	<0.5	16	107	7	113	175
Florida	7,851	104	286	5	1,416	9,553	109	9,661	493
Georgia	4,674	63	87	3	1,249	6,010	66	6,076	608
Hawaii	427	11	9	1	53	490	11	501	356
Idaho	653	14	36	1	263	952	15	967	599
Illinois	4,410	94	119	5	1,490	6,019	99	6,118	475
Indiana	2,854	52	100	3	1,240	4,194	54	4,248	647
Iowa	1,464	31	146	2	665	2,275	33	2,308	746
Kansas	1,225	29	29	1	488	1,742	31	1,773	612
Kentucky	2,037	37	47	2	742	2,826	39	2,865	651
Louisiana	2,154	37	86	2	680	2,920	39	2,959	639
Maine	705	10	20	1	201	927	11	938	706
Maryland	2,714	31	56	1	488	3,258	32	3,290	554
Massachusetts	2,644	38	58	2	504	3,206	40	3,246	484
Michigan	4,386	70	122	3	911	5,419	73	5,492	555
Minnesota	2,343	47	128	2	662	3,133	49	3,182	587
Mississippi	1,537	28	45	1	551	2,133	29	2,162	723
Missouri	2,943	50	52	2	960	3,956	52	4,008	663
Montana	481	11	19	1	265	765	11	776	765
Nebraska	801	19	31	1	430	1,262	20	1,282	686
Nevada	1,060	15	20	1	318	1,398	16	1,414	507
New Hampshire	675	10	19	<0.5	92	786	11	796	602
New Jersey	3,829	54	80	3	790	4,699	57	4,756	534
New Mexico	901	18	21	1	507	1,429	19	1,448	694
New York	5,079	109	155	5	1,351	6,586	115	6,701	340
North Carolina	4,117	61	128	3	983	5,228	64	5,292	537
North Dakota	424	9	17	<0.5	395	836	9	845	1,167
Ohio	4,730	86	115	4	1,504	6,348	90	6,438	556
Oklahoma	1,763	35	71	2	871	2,705	37	2,742	712
Oregon	1,392	28	54	1	523	1,968	29	1,998	509
Pennsylvania	4,789	79	122	4	1,548	6,459	83	6,542	512
Rhode Island	344	8	10	<0.5	60	413	9	422	401
South Carolina	2,570	27	66	1	769	3,405	29	3,434	720
South Dakota	415	10	18	1	218	651	11	661	782
Tennessee	3,026	48	64	2	886	3,976	51	4,026	620
Texas	12,151	172	343	8	4,741	17,236	180	17,416	657
Utah	1,036	22	27	1	479	1,541	23	1,564	539
Vermont	303	6	7	<0.5	60	371	6	377	601
Virginia	3,765	56	73	3	1,005	4,843	59	4,902	593
Washington	2,584	41	87	2	656	3,326	43	3,369	483
West Virginia	757	17	14	1	287	1,058	18	1,076	581
Wisconsin	2,323	47	75	2	728	3,126	49	3,175	553
Wyoming	327	7	30	<0.5	369	726	7	733	1,257
United States	126,665	2,153	3,736	106	38,352	168,753	2,260	173,493	548

NOTES: Consumption based on reports from state motor fuel tax agencies. Gasohol is included with gasoline. Public use and nonhighway use were estimated by the Federal Highway Administration. Estimates may not be comparable to data for prior years due to revised estimation procedures.The term motor fuel applies to gasoline and all other fuels, including special fuels, coming under the purview of the state motor-fuel tax laws. Special fuels include diesel fuel and, to the extent they can be quantified, liquefied petroleum gases such as propane. Gasohol, a blend of gasoline and fuel alcohol, is included with gasoline.

SOURCE: Motor-fuel use: U.S. Department of Transportation, Federal Highway Administration, Highway Statistics, MF-21, available at www. fhwa.dot.gov/policyinformation/statistics.cfm as of July 2015. Population: U.S. Department of Commerce, U.S. Census Bureau, Population Estimates,available at www.census.gov/popest as of July 2015.

Table 7-5: Alternative Fuel Vehicle Fleet by Fuel Type: 2013
(Number of vehicles)

State	Compressed Natural Gas	Electricity[1]	Ethanol (E85)[2]	Hydrogen	Liquified Natural Gas	Liquified Petroleum Gas	Total
Alabama	345	76	4,573	0	0	169	5,163
Alaska	35	18	1,148	0	0	9	1,210
Arizona	710	451	8,902	0	0	349	10,412
Arkansas	85	18	1,447	0	0	65	1,615
California	8,922	3,078	27,766	26	428	1,455	41,675
Colorado	224	52	7,103	0	0	206	7,585
Connecticut	36	22	2,417	0	2	36	2,513
Delaware	3	4	1,868	0	0	7	1,882
District of Columbia	696	88	4,810	0	0	0	5,594
Florida	205	350	13,904	0	0	260	14,719
Georgia	765	372	10,982	0	0	390	12,509
Hawaii	0	179	2,557	3	1	17	2,757
Idaho	58	18	2,738	0	0	17	2,831
Illinois	258	41	13,630	0	0	131	14,060
Indiana	38	44	4,156	0	0	214	4,452
Iowa	0	12	3,809	0	0	32	3,853
Kansas	37	78	2,843	0	0	47	3,005
Kentucky	6	53	5,235	0	1	52	5,347
Louisiana	54	147	5,426	0	0	42	5,669
Maine	2	23	1,058	0	0	44	1,127
Maryland	256	163	8,955	0	0	20	9,394
Massachusetts	793	82	2,576	0	0	31	3,482
Michigan	139	144	10,373	0	0	220	10,876
Minnesota	23	36	7,743	0	4	78	7,884
Mississippi	16	73	3,625	0	2	248	3,964
Missouri	47	90	8,389	0	0	275	8,801
Montana	4	10	1,760	0	0	40	1,814
Nebraska	174	0	2,585	0	0	28	2,787
Nevada	286	50	3,043	0	0	84	3,463
New Hampshire	39	13	572	0	0	50	674
New Jersey	630	6	8,786	0	2	60	9,484
New Mexico	144	9	5,801	0	0	99	6,053
New York	3,385	632	8,639	0	0	98	12,754
North Carolina	278	208	12,766	0	1	373	13,626
North Dakota	1	1	1,677	0	0	8	1,687
Ohio	353	71	9,528	0	0	133	10,085
Oklahoma	859	26	3,228	0	0	221	4,334
Oregon	302	107	4,803	0	0	19	5,231
Pennsylvania	319	67	8,361	0	0	70	8,817
Rhode Island	230	28	1,023	0	0	0	1,281
South Carolina	49	85	8,781	1	0	148	9,064
South Dakota	1	4	3,030	0	0	53	3,088
Tennessee	128	97	8,893	0	0	89	9,207
Texas	1,497	278	29,312	0	58	1,034	32,179
Utah	490	12	3,639	0	0	48	4,189
Vermont	15	12	889	0	0	6	922
Virginia	237	299	11,188	0	0	103	11,827
Washington	271	235	7,278	0	0	58	7,842
West Virginia	24	26	808	0	0	10	868
Wisconsin	23	29	4,864	0	0	141	5,057
Wyoming	67	1	1,328	0	0	14	1,410
United States, total	23,559	8,018	320,615	30	499	7,401	360,122

[1]Excludes gasoline-electric hybrids.

[2]Includes only those E85 vehicles believed to be used as alternative-fuels vehicles (AFVs), primarily fleet-operated vehicles; excludes other vehicles with E85-fueling capability.

NOTE: The aternative fuel vehicle (AFV) fleet includes vehicles in use by four user groups: federal government, state government, transit agencies, and fuel providers.

SOURCE: U.S. Department of Energy, Energy Information Administration, Renewable & Alternative Fuels, Alternative Vehicle Fuel Data, available at www.eia.gov/renewable/afv as of October 2015.

Table 7-6: Alternative Fuel Stations by Fuel Type: 2013

State	Compressed natural gas	85% Ethanol	Liquefied petroleum gas	Electric[1]	Biodiesel	Hydrogen	Liquefied natural gas	Total[2]
Alabama	21	29	113	50	10	0	2	225
Alaska	1	0	7	0	2	0	0	10
Arizona	32	31	62	710	79	1	6	921
Arkansas	8	30	39	38	5	0	0	120
California	258	88	233	5,176	84	21	43	5,903
Colorado	36	85	52	256	19	1	0	449
Connecticut	16	1	15	217	2	2	1	254
Delaware	1	1	4	20	1	0	0	27
District of Columbia	2	3	0	62	7	0	0	74
Florida	33	54	65	996	17	0	0	1,165
Georgia	25	61	57	370	25	0	1	539
Hawaii	1	3	3	351	9	3	0	370
Idaho	8	9	25	13	6	0	5	66
Illinois	40	218	102	527	11	1	0	899
Indiana	20	169	174	183	7	0	1	554
Iowa	4	186	21	87	7	0	0	305
Kansas	6	28	36	109	7	0	0	186
Kentucky	4	55	47	45	4	0	0	155
Louisiana	20	4	34	53	2	0	1	114
Maine	1	1	12	24	3	0	0	41
Maryland	9	25	17	553	9	0	0	613
Massachusetts	23	8	17	546	12	1	0	607
Michigan	19	163	73	721	19	4	0	999
Minnesota	11	336	33	235	11	0	0	626
Mississippi	5	1	125	37	4	0	0	172
Missouri	12	106	64	146	4	1	0	333
Montana	2	4	45	2	6	0	0	59
Nebraska	9	75	22	28	3	0	0	137
Nevada	7	20	39	107	6	1	2	182
New Hampshire	3	0	10	40	5	0	0	58
New Jersey	29	5	10	219	5	0	0	268
New Mexico	11	13	45	33	8	0	0	110
New York	111	81	63	693	38	9	0	995
North Carolina	36	22	97	524	135	0	0	814
North Dakota	1	58	18	4	3	0	0	84
Ohio	25	97	66	175	19	1	2	385
Oklahoma	94	27	149	32	5	0	0	307
Oregon	14	8	34	915	24	0	0	995
Pennsylvania	51	33	73	263	7	2	0	429
Rhode Island	6	1	6	143	7	0	0	163
South Carolina	10	82	44	218	60	2	1	417
South Dakota	0	87	17	13	2	0	0	119
Tennessee	9	52	102	866	44	0	0	1,073
Texas	62	81	458	1,599	20	1	10	2,231
Utah	88	3	27	72	3	0	7	200
Vermont	3	1	3	51	2	0	0	60
Virginia	20	19	58	370	12	1	0	480
Washington	24	24	68	1,325	33	1	1	1,476
West Virginia	3	4	12	42	2	0	0	63
Wisconsin	45	115	54	211	4	0	1	430
Wyoming	11	9	17	2	13	0	0	52
United States, total	1,290	2,616	2,967	19,472	832	53	84	27,314

[1]Does not include residential electric charging infrastructure.
[2]Total number of fuel types available at stations. Stations are counted once for each type of fuel available.

NOTE: Counts as of December 2013.

SOURCE: U.S. Department of Energy, Office of Energy Efficiency and Renewable Energy, Alternative Fuels Data Center, Alternative Fueling Stations, available at http://www.afdc.energy.gov/ as of July 2015.

Table 7-7: Air Pollution in the 50 Largest Metropolitan Areas: 2009–2014
(Number of days with AQI value greater than 100)

Metropolitan area	AQI days > 100					
	2009	2010	2011	2012	2013	2014
Atlanta-Sandy Springs-Marietta, GA	18	29	46	19	3	10
Austin-Round Rock, TX	5	3	7	4	1	0
Baltimore-Towson, MD	15	36	25	20	5	4
Birmingham-Hoover, AL	5	15	23	10	1	3
Boston-Cambridge-Quincy, MA-NH	5	5	3	6	5	0
Buffalo-Niagara Falls, NY	2	3	2	8	1	0
Charlotte-Concord-Gastonia, NC-SC	4	15	18	11	0	0
Chicago-Naperville-Joliet, IL-IN-WI	34	38	27	47	12	16
Cincinnati-Middletown, OH-KY-IN	11	30	47	43	11	10
Cleveland-Elyria-Mentor, OH	63	74	75	59	13	15
Columbus, OH	1	8	11	14	2	1
Dallas-Fort Worth-Arlington, TX	34	18	40	36	33	14
Denver-Aurora, CO	8	17	21	26	23	11
Detroit-Warren-Livonia, MI	12	27	20	38	7	12
Hartford-West Hartford-East Hartford, CT	3	9	8	16	11	8
Houston-Sugar Land-Baytown, TX	31	35	38	34	19	7
Indianapolis-Carmel, IN	20	20	31	29	11	30
Jacksonville, FL	4	18	19	5	2	3
Kansas City, MO-KS	46	25	53	72	42	53
Las Vegas-Paradise, NV	8	11	25	29	16	7
Los Angeles-Long Beach-Anaheim, CA	112	85	105	106	80	90
Louisville/Jefferson County, KY-IN	35	55	36	45	18	31
Memphis, TN-MS-AR	4	14	22	20	2	2
Miami-Fort Lauderdale-Pompano Beach, FL	2	4	9	2	3	3
Milwaukee-Waukesha-West Allis, WI	7	9	5	26	0	3
Minneapolis-St. Paul-Bloomington, MN-WI	8	9	2	5	2	1
Nashville-Davidson--Murfreesboro--Franklin, TN	1	10	13	23	1	2
New Orleans-Metairie-Kenner, LA	95	68	89	44	25	11
New York-Northern New Jersey-Long Island, NY-NJ-PA	26	41	29	22	15	11
Oklahoma City, OK	5	3	27	23	3	0
Orlando-Kissimmee, FL	1	2	8	1	0	1
Philadelphia-Camden-Wilmington, PA-NJ-DE-MD	15	38	20	27	11	15
Phoenix-Mesa-Scottsdale, AZ	67	44	121	94	87	107
Pittsburgh, PA	69	82	54	59	18	18
Portland-Vancouver-Beaverton, OR-WA	15	2	17	2	16	1
Providence-New Bedford-Fall River, RI-MA	2	16	11	14	9	1
Raleigh-Cary, NC	0	3	7	5	0	0
Richmond, VA	1	11	12	12	1	1
Riverside-San Bernardino-Ontario, CA	145	139	151	153	130	140
Sacramento--Roseville--Arden-Arcade, CA	46	24	60	51	35	35
Salt Lake City, UT	30	21	22	11	45	17
San Antonio-New Braunfels, TX	3	4	12	8	10	3
San Diego-Carlsbad-San Marcos, CA	30	19	13	22	19	18
San Francisco-Oakland-Hayward, CA	14	10	8	5	7	7
San Jose-Sunnyvale-Santa Clara, CA	9	10	4	4	8	5
Seattle-Tacoma-Bellevue, WA	21	1	13	9	8	6
St. Louis, MO-IL	93	87	78	97	35	9
Tampa-St. Petersburg-Clearwater, FL	18	12	14	13	3	1
Virginia Beach-Norfolk-Newport News, VA-NC	0	8	11	4	0	0
Washington-Arlington-Alexandria, DC-VA-MD-WV	7	34	21	24	5	4

KEY: AQI = Air Quality Index

NOTES: Historical data are reviesd. Air Quality Index (AQI) is an indicator of overall air quality and takes into account all of the criteria air pollutants measured within a geographic area. Although AQI includes all available pollutant measurements, areas may have monitoring stations for some, but not all, pollutants. An AQI value greater than 100 is considered unhealthy. Metropolitan area rank is based on 2010 U.S. Census population.

SOURCE: U.S. Environmental Protection Agency, AirData, available at www.epa.gov/airquality/airdata as of July 2015.

Appendices

A   Information on Data Sources
B   Data Sources and Availability
C   State DOT Contact Information
D   Glossary

Appendix A: Information on Data Sources

Airline freight and passenger data

The U.S. Department of Transportation's (USDOT), Bureau of Transportation Statistics (BTS) collects and compiles data on the volume of revenue passengers, freight, and mail traffic handled and reported by the nation's large certificated air carriers. These carriers hold Certificates of Public Convenience and Necessity (CPCN) issued by the USDOT authorizing the performance of air transportation. Large certificated air carriers operate aircraft with seating capacity of more than 60 seats or a maximum payload capacity of more than 18,000 pounds or conduct international operations. Data for commuters, intrastate, nonscheduled air taxi operators, and foreign flag air carriers are not included.

Additional information:

Contact: USDOT, Bureau of Transportation Statistics, Office of Airline Information

Internet: www.bts.gov

Border-crossing/entry data

U.S. Customs and Border Protection personnel collect passenger and vehicle border-crossing/entry data at land ports of entry and provide BTS with aggregate monthly information. These numbers reflect all entries, and it is not possible to divide these data into separate entries for same-day and overnight travel or by country of residence for the traveler. Additionally, for border-crossing figures, the total number of people is not the number of unique individuals, but rather indicates the number of border crossings. Multiple crossings by the same individual count as multiple border crossings.

Additional information:

Contact: USDOT, Bureau of Transportation Statistics

Internet: www.bts.gov

Commodity Flow Survey

The Commodity Flow Survey (CFS) provides data on the movement of freight by type of commodity shipped and by mode of transport. In 2012, approximately 102,000 domestic establishments were randomly selected from a universe of approximately 716,000 engaged in mining, manufacturing, wholesale trade, warehouses and managing offices of multi-establishment companies, and some selected activities in retail and services based on the 2007 NAICS classification system. The survey excluded establishments classified as farms, forestry, fisheries, governments, construction, transportation, foreign establishments, and most services and retail trade establishments. The sample for the 2012 CFS was selected using a stratified three-stage design in which the first-stage sampling units were establishments, the second-stage sampling units were groups of four 1-week periods (reporting weeks) within the survey year, and the third-stage sampling units were shipments. This produced a total sample of approximately 4.5 million shipments. Due to industrywide reporting problems, shipments by oil and gas extraction establishments were excluded from data tabulations.

For each sampled 2012 CFS shipment, zip code of origin and destination, 5-digit Standard Classification of Transported Goods (SCTG) code, weight, value, and modes of transport were provided. Information on whether the shipment was a hazardous material or an export was also obtained. The miles traveled by each shipment was determined using the shipment information reported by the respondents, and a software tool, called GeoMiler, that has been developed by the Bureau of Transportation Statistics (BTS) for estimating freight travel. Distance was used to compute ton-mileage by mode of transport. The 2012 CFS also provides nationwide geographic coverage and in-state and selected substate areas.

Additional information:

Contact: USDOT, Bureau of Transportation Statistics

Print source: USDOT, Bureau of Transportation Statistics and U.S. Department of Commerce (USDOC), U.S.

Census Bureau, 2012 Commodity Flow Survey (Washington, DC: 2015).

Internet: www.bts.gov and www.census.gov/

Commuting data

Commuting data are from the American Community Survey (ACS), a nationwide Census Bureau survey designed to replace the long form in the decennial census. Instead of collecting data every ten years, the data collection occurs continuously. The ACS uses a series of monthly samples to produce annually updated data. This survey has an annual sample of three million housing units and will provide estimates of demographic, housing, social, and economic characteristics every year for states, cities, counties, metropolitan areas, and other geographic areas. Data products based on twelve-month periods are already available for geographic areas of 65,000 and greater population. Data products based on thirty-six-month periods are available starting in 2005–2007 for geographic areas of 20,000 and greater population. Data products based on sixty-month periods are available as of 2005–2009 for all geographic areas. Once the data products based on sample periods of more than twelve months are released for the first time, they will be released annually thereafter.

Additional information:

Contact: USDOC, U.S. Census Bureau

Internet: www.census.gov/

Gas and hazardous liquid pipeline data

Fatality and injury data for natural gas pipelines and hazardous liquid pipelines are based on reports filed with the USDOT, Pipeline and Hazardous Materials Safety Administration, Office of Pipeline Safety under 49 CFR 191 and 49 CFR 195. Accidents must be reported as soon as possible, but no later than 30 days after discovery. Undetected releases are a possible source of error; even if subsequently detected and reported, it may not be possible to accurately reconstruct the accident. Property damage figures are estimates.

Gas pipeline incidents involve: 1) releases of gas from a pipeline or liquefied natural gas (LNG) or gas from an LNG facility that results in a) death or personal injury necessitating in-patient hospitalization, or b) estimated property damage, including cost of gas lost, of the operator or others, or both, of $50,000 or more; 2) an event that results in an emergency shutdown of an LNG facility; or 3) an event that is significant, in the judgment of the operator, even though it did not meet the criteria of 1) or 2).

For hazardous liquid pipelines, an accident report is required for each failure in a pipeline system in which there is a release of the hazardous liquid or carbon dioxide transported resulting in any of the following: 1) explosion or fire not intentionally set by the operator; 2) loss of 50 or more gallons of hazardous liquid or carbon dioxide; 3) release to the atmosphere of more than 5 barrels (0.8 cubic meters) per day of highly volatile liquids; 4) death of any person; 5) bodily harm to any person resulting in one or more of the following: a) loss of consciousness, b) an individual being carried from the scene, c) medical treatment, or d) disability that prevents the discharge of normal duties or the pursuit of normal activities beyond the day of the accident; or 6) estimated property damage, including cost of cleanup and recovery, value of lost product, and damage to the property of the operator or others, or both, exceeding $50,000.

Additional information:

Contact: USDOT, Pipeline and Hazardous Materials Safety Administration, Office of Pipeline Safety

Internet: http://phmsa.dot.gov/pipeline

Government transportation revenue and expenditure data

The U.S. Department of Commerce, U.S. Census Bureau conducts an Annual Survey of Government Finances. Alternatively, every five years, in years ending in a '2'or '7', a Census of Governments, including a finance portion, is conducted. The survey coverage includes all state and local governments in the United States. For both the census and annual survey, the finance detail data encompass revenue, expenditure, debt, and assets. These data are the primary source of state and local government data used by BTS to produce Government Transportation Financial Statistics.

The data collection for the annual survey by the U.S. Census Bureau uses two methods: mail canvas and central collection from state sources. Data for local governments include counties, municipal, townships, special districts, and school districts. Data for state governments are compiled from state government audits, budgets, and other financial reports into the classification categories used for reporting by the Census Bureau.

Reporting of government finances by the Census Bureau involves presentation of data in uniform categories. While often similar to, or identical to, the classification used by the state or local government, there could be instances in which a significant difference exists between the name used by a state for a financial item and the final category to which it is assigned by the Census Bureau.

Like financial transactions are combined. The financial categories for revenue involve grouping of items by source. Revenue items of the same kind are merged. Financial transactions for expenditures are classified both by function and by object category. Debt items are classified by term (short and long term), as well as by type of debt and, to a limited extent, by purpose. Assets also are put into uniform categories, grouped by type of holding, with holdings for insurance trust systems grouped separately from general government.

The share of government sector financial totals contributed by a state government or by local governments differs materially from one state to another. Users can review the Government Finance and Employment Classification Manual for additional information regarding the financial categories. The financial amounts in the tables and files are statistical in nature and do not represent accounting statements or conditions.

The local government statistics are developed from a sample survey. Therefore, the local totals, as well as state and local aggregates, are considered estimated amounts subject to sampling error. State government finance data are not subject to sampling. Consequently, state-local aggregates for individual states are more reliable (on a relative standard error basis) than the local government estimates they include.

Additional information:

Contact: USDOC, U.S. Census Bureau, Finance Branch; or USDOT, Bureau of Transportation Statistics.

Internet: http://www.census.gov and www.bts.gov

Hazardous materials incidents data

Incidents resulting in certain unintentional releases of hazardous materials must be reported under 49 CFR 171.16. Each carrier must submit a report to the USDOT, Pipeline and Hazardous Materials Safety Administration (PHMSA) within 30 days of the incident, including information on the mode of transportation involved, results of the incident, and a narrative description of the accident. These reports are generally made available on PHMSA's incident database within 90 days of receipt.

Fatalities and injuries are counted only if directly caused by a hazardous material. For example, a truck operator killed by impact forces during a motor vehicle crash would not be counted as a hazardous-material fatality. PHMSA contacts the submitting carrier by telephone to verify all reported fatalities.

Although PHMSA acknowledges there is some level of underreporting, it believes the underreporting is mostly limited to small, nonserious incidents. The reporting requirements were extended to intrastate highway carriers on Oct. 1, 1998. Property damage figures are estimates determined by the carrier prior to the 30-day reporting deadline and are generally not subsequently updated. Property damage figures, therefore, may underestimate actual damages.

Additional information:

Contact: USDOT, Pipeline and Hazardous Materials Safety Administration, Office of Hazardous Materials Planning and Analysis

Internet: http://phmsa.dot.gov/hazmat

Highway mileage, condition, usage, driver license, and highway vehicle registration data

Data on roadway mileage, condition, and use are extracted from the Highway Performance Monitoring System (HPMS), which uses a stratified simple random sample of highway links (small sections of roadway) selected from state inventory files. The HPMS sample was designed as a fixed sample to minimize data-collection costs, but adjustments to maintain adequate representation are carried out periodically. The HPMS also consists of universe reporting (a complete census) for the Interstate and the National Highway System, and tabular summary reporting of limited information.

Data are collected independently by the states, metropolitan planning organizations (MPOs), and other local jurisdictions. Many of the geometric data items (e.g., number of lanes) change slowly, while other data items (e.g., traffic volumes) are more dynamic over time. The U.S. Department of Transportation, Federal Highway Administration (FHWA) provides guidelines for data collection in the HPMS Field Manual, which the states follow to varying extents, depending on factors such as staff, resources, state perspective, uses of the data, and state/MPO/ local needs for the data. State Departments of Transportation (DOTs) report HPMS data annually to FHWA.

HPMS data are subject to sampling and nonsampling error. Nonsampling error is the major concern with these data. For some of the most variable and important data items, such as traffic, guidelines for measurement and data collection have been produced. States have the option of using the guidelines or using their own procedures. Many data items are difficult and costly to collect and are reported as estimates not based on direct measurement. The data are collected and reported by many entities within the responsible organizations.

States provide vehicle registration data to FHWA. Vehicle registration data are shown on a calendar year basis. Efforts are made to exclude transfers, re-registrations, and any other factors that could result in duplication in the vehicle counts. Registration practices for commercial vehicles differ greatly among the states. Some states register a tractor-semitrailer combination as a single unit; others register the tractor and the semitrailer separately. Some states register buses with trucks or automobiles, while many states do not report house and light utility trailers separately from commercial trailers or semitrailers. Some states do not require registration of car or light utility trailers. In some instances, FHWA has supplemented the data supplied by the states with information obtained from other sources.

States also provide driver licensing data to FHWA. Although efforts are made to minimize license duplication, drivers who move from one state to another are sometimes counted in both states until the license from the previous state of residence expires. Problems with the data also arise because: 1) some individuals obtain their drivers licenses in states other than those of legal residence; 2) some individuals fraudulently obtain multiple licenses; 3) not all individuals who drive are licensed; and 4) the purging of expired licenses or licenses from deceased individuals is not performed on a continual basis.

Additional information:

Contact: USDOT, Federal Highway Administration, Office of Highway Policy Information

Print source: USDOT, Federal Highway Administration, Highway Statistics (Washington, DC: Annual Issues).

Internet: http://www.fhwa.dot.gov/policyinformation/statistics.cfm

Highway safety data

Fatalities: Highway fatality data are extracted from the Fatality Analysis Reporting System (FARS), which is compiled by USDOT National Highway Traffic Safety Administration (NHTSA). Data are gathered from a census of police accident reports (PARs), state vehicle registration files, state drivers licensing files, state highway department data, vital statistics, death certificates, coroner/medical examiner reports, hospital medical reports, and emergency medical service reports. A separate form is completed for each fatal crash. Blood alcohol concentration (BAC) is estimated when not known. Statistical procedures used for unknown data in the FARS can be found in the NHTSA report, A Method for Estimating Posterior BAC Distributions for Persons Involved in Fatal Traffic Accidents, DOT HS 807 094 (Washington, DC: July 1986).

Data are collected from relevant state agencies and electronically submitted for inclusion in the FARs database on a continuous basis. Cross-verification of PARs with death certificates helps prevent undercounting. Moreover, when data are entered, they are checked automatically for acceptable range values and consistency, enabling quick corrections when necessary. Several programs continually monitor the data for completeness and accuracy. Periodically, sample cases are analyzed for accuracy and consistency.

FARS data do not include motor vehicle fatalities on nonpublic roads. These are thought to account for about 2 percent or fewer of the total motor vehicle fatalities per year.

Injuries and crashes: NHTSA's General Estimates System (GES) data are a nationally representative sample of police-reported crashes that contributed to an injury or fatality or resulted in property damage and involved at least one motor vehicle traveling on a traffic way. GES data collectors randomly sample PARs and forward copies to a central contractor for coding into a standard GES system format. Documents such as police diagrams or supporting text provided by the officers might be further reviewed to complete a data entry.

Additional information:

Contact: USDOT, National Highway Traffic Safety Administration, National Center for Statistics and Analysis

Print source: USDOT, National Highway Traffic Safety Administration, Traffic Safety Facts (Washington, DC: Annual Issues).

Internet: http://www.nhtsa.gov

International visitors data

Data on international visitors to the United States are based on international arrivals by air to the United States (excluding those from Canada and Mexico). Information is derived from the U.S. Department of Homeland Security Customs and Border Protection's Visitor Arrivals Program (I-94) and the U.S. Department of Commerce, Tourism Industries Office's Survey of International Air Travelers. The survey obtains data on overseas travel patterns, characteristics, and spending patterns of international travelers to and from the United States. Between 69,000 and 95,000 travelers are surveyed each year. The survey results are weighted so that they represent the international travel populations of U.S. residents and nonresidents based on U.S. Customs and Border Protection's data.

Additional information:

Contact: U.S. Department of Commerce (USDOC), International Trade Administration, Tourism Industries Office

Print source: USDOC, International Trade Administration, Office of Travel and Tourism Industries, Overseas Visitors to Select U.S. States and Territories (Washington, DC: Annual Issues); and USDOC, International Trade Administration, Office of Travel and Tourism Industries, Overseas Visitors to Select U.S. Cities/Hawaiian Islands (Washington, DC: Annual Issues).

Internet: http://tinet.ita.doc.gov

Railroad industry and shipments data

The Association of American Railroads (AAR) database aggregates data from several sources and covers the freight railroad industry and movement of freight, both nationally and statewide. The state-level data include commerce, employment, and financial contributions.

The primary source of data for Class I railroads is Schedule 702 of the R-1 Annual Report to the Surface Transportation Board (STB) by individual carriers (100 percent reporting) and the Carload Waybill Sample. The primary source of data for non-Class I railroads is AAR's Profiles of U.S. Railroads from statistics supplied annually by nearly all operating U.S. freight railroads. Some of the data are estimated based on more aggregated, national figures.

The STB defines Class I railroads as having operating revenues at or above a threshold indexed to a base of $250 million (1991) and adjusted annually in concert with changes in the Railroad Freight Rate Index published by the Bureau of Labor Statistics. In 2013, the STB Class I threshold was annual operating revenue of $467.0 million. Declassification from Class I status occurs when a railroad falls below the applicable threshold for three consecutive years. Although few in number, Class I railroads account for over 90 percent of the industry's revenue.

AAR determines the number of non-Class I railroads through an annual survey sent to each U.S. freight railroad.

Historical reliability may vary due to changes in the railroad industry, including bankruptcies, mergers, and declassification by STB. Small data errors may also have occurred because of independent rounding in this series by AAR.

Additional information:

Contact: AAR, Policy and Economics Department

Internet: http://www.aar.org

Railroad safety data

Railroads are required to file a report for each accident or incident to the Federal Railroad Administration (FRA). These include: 1) train accidents, reported on Form F 6180.54, comprised of collisions, derailments, and other events involving the operation of on-track equipment and causing reportable damage above an established threshold ($9,900 for 2013); 2) highway-rail grade crossing incidents, reported on Form F 6180.57, involving an impact between railroad on-track equipment and highway users at crossings; and 3) other incidents, reported on Form F 6180.55a, involving all other reportable incidents or exposures that cause a fatality or injury to any person or an occupational illness to a railroad employee.

Railroads are required by FRA regulations to use the current FRA Guide for Preparing Accident/Incident Reports when preparing reports.

The Systems Support Division of FRA maintains the Railroad Accident/Incident Reporting System (RAIRS), consisting of four databases: rail equipment, injury/illness, grade-crossing accidents, and railroad summary (freight and passenger). These databases include information on all railroad accidents, grade-crossing accidents, railroad employee casualties, and any other injuries on railroad property, and provide the basis for accident analyses and assessment as well as annual reports. The databases are updated monthly from information submitted by the railroads.

Additional information:

Contact: USDOT, Federal Railroad Administration, Office of Safety

Print publication: USDOT, Federal Railroad Administration, Railroad Safety Statistics (Washington, DC: Annual Issues).

Internet: http://www.fra.dot.gov

Recreational boating safety and registration data

The U.S. Coast Guard, of the U.S. Department of Homeland Security, collects data on recreational boating accidents from two sources: 1) Boating Accident Report (BAR) data forwarded to the Coast Guard by jurisdictions with an approved boat numbering and casualty reporting system, and 2) reports of Coast Guard investigations of fatal boating accidents that occurred on waters under federal jurisdiction. Recreational Boating Accident Investigation data are used if submitted to the Coast Guard and are relied on as much as possible to provide accident statistics. In the absence of investigations, information is collected from reports filed by boat operators.

Boat operators are required to file a BAR if an accident results in 1) loss of life, 2) personal injury that requires medical treatment beyond first aid, 3) damage to the vessel and other property exceeding $2,000, or complete loss of the vessel, or 4) disappearance of a person from the vessel under circumstances that indicate death or injury.

Boat operators are required to report their accidents to authorities in the state where the accident occurred. States with approved boat numbering systems furnish the Coast Guard with BAR data. The minimum reporting requirements are set by federal regulation, but states are allowed to have stricter requirements. The Coast Guard reports recreational boating safety data in their report Boating Statistics, which covers accidents meeting the federal minimum reporting requirements.

The data in Boating Statistics cover boating accidents reported on waters of joint federal and state jurisdiction and exclusive state jurisdiction.

The Coast Guard believes nearly all fatal accidents and most boating accidents that result in serious injury (i.e., hospital admission) are included in Boating Statistics. A smaller percentage of nonfatal accidents are reported because of reporting thresholds, ignorance of the law, and difficulties enforcing the law. Federal law does not require the reporting of accidents on private waters where states have no jurisdiction. Reports of accidents on such waters are included when received by the Coast Guard if they satisfy the other requirements of inclusion. Accidents excluded are those in which the boat was used as a platform for other activities (e.g., swimming), and those in which a person dies of natural causes aboard a boat. However, the data do include accidents involving people in the water who are struck by their boat or another boat.

Additional information:

Contact: U.S. Department of Homeland Security (USDHS), U.S. Coast Guard, Office of Boating Safety

Print source: USDHS, U.S. Coast Guard, Office of Boating Safety, Boating Statistics (Washington, DC: Annual Issues).

Internet: http://www.uscgboating.org

Transborder freight data

The TransBorder Freight Data is extracted from the Census Bureau's Foreign Trade Statistics Program and made available by the Bureau of Transportation Statistics. Import and export data are extracted from administrative records required by the Departments of Commerce and Treasury. This dataset incorporates all shipments entering or exiting the United States by modes of transport to and from Canada or Mexico. Prior to January 1997, this dataset also included transhipments in its detailed tables (i.e., shipments entering or exiting the United States by way of U.S. Customs ports on the northern or southern borders, even when the actual origin or final destination of the goods was other than Canada or Mexico).

Users should be aware that the trade data fields (e.g., value and commodity classification) are typically more rigorously reviewed than transportation data fields (i.e., mode of transportation and port of entry/exit). Also, although this dataset provides information for individual Customs districts and ports on the northern and southern borders, filing procedures for trade documents do not always correspond to the port where goods physically crossed the border. This is because the filer of information may choose to file trade documents at one port, while shipments actually enter or exit at another port.

Import data are generally more accurate than export data primarily because Customs uses import documents for enforcement purposes, while it performs no similar function for exports.

Additional information:

Contact: USDOT, Bureau of Transportation Statistics

Internet: http://www.bts.gov

Transit operating, financial, and safety data

Transit data are from the National Transit Database (NTD) produced by the USDOT, Federal Transit Administration (FTA). Data are collected from transit agencies that receive Urbanized Area Formula Program funds. Transit operators that do not report to FTA are those that do not receive federal funding, typically private, small, and rural operators. FTA reviews and validates information submitted by individual transit agencies. Reliability may vary because some transit agencies cannot obtain accurate information or may interpret certain data definitions differently than intended.

In 2013, 849 agencies submitted data to the NTD. Of that, 536 agencies submitted full reports, 282 agencies submitted small systems waivers for agencies that operate 30 or fewer vehicles across all modes and types of service, 5 agencies submitted reporting separately, and 26 received a waiver from detailed reporting. In total, 786 agencies are included in the NTD database. Data are collected on a range of variables including capital and operating funding, transit service supplied and consumed, and transit safety and security. Transit operators must report fatalities, injuries, accidents, incidents, and property damage in excess of $25,000.

Additional information:

Contact: USDOT, Federal Transit Administration

Print source: USDOT, Federal Transit Administration, Data Tables (Washington, DC: Annual Issues); and USDOT, Federal Transit Administration, National Transit Database Reporting Manual (Washington, DC: Annual Issues).

Internet: http://www.ntdprogram.gov/ntdprogram/

Transportation establishment, employees, and payroll data

Data on employees, establishments, and payroll are taken from County Business Patterns, a database of employment in the United States using the North American Industry Classification System (NAICS). Data are collected annually. Data are extracted from the Business Register, the Census Bureau's file of all known single and multi-establishment companies. The Annual Company Organization Survey and quinquennial Economic Censuses provide individual establishment data for multi-location firms. Data for single-location firms are obtained from various programs conducted by the Census Bureau, such as the Economic Censuses, the Annual Survey of Manufacturer, and Current Business Surveys. They are also obtained from administrative records of the Internal Revenue Service, the Social Security Administration, and the Bureau of Labor Statistics.

Additional information:

Contact: USDOC, U.S. Census Bureau, Economic Planning and Coordination Division

Internet: http://www.census.gov/econ/cbp/index.html

Waterborne shipments data

The U.S. Army Corps of Engineers' (Corps) Navigation Data Center (NDC) collects data on waterborne commodity and vessel movements, domestic commercial vessel characteristics, port and waterway facilities, and navigation dredging projects.

The NDC's databases contain information on physical characteristics, infrastructure, and commodities for principal facilities on the U.S. coast, Great Lakes, and inland ports. The data consist of listings of port area's waterfront facilities, including information on berthing, cranes, transit sheds, grain elevators, marine repair plants, fleeting areas, and docking and storage facilities.

All vessel operators of record report their domestic waterborne traffic movements to the Corps via ENG Forms 3925 and 3925b. Cargo movements are reported according to points of loading and unloading. Excluded cargo movements are: 1) cargo carried on general ferries, 2) coal and petroleum products loaded from shore facilities directly into vessels for fuel use, 3) military cargo moved in U.S. Department of Defense vessels, and 4) cargo weighing less than 100 tons moved on government equipment. The Corps calculates ton-miles by multiplying the cargo's tonnage by the distance between points of loading and unloading.

An annual survey of companies that operate inland waterway vessels is the principal source of data for inland nonself-propelled, self-propelled, flag passenger, and cargo vessels. More than 3,000 surveys are sent to these companies, and response rates are typically above 90 percent.

Additional information:

Contact: U.S. Army Corps of Engineers, Waterborne Commerce Statistics Center

Print source: U.S. Army Corps of Engineers, Waterborne Commerce of the United States (New Orleans, LA: Annual Issues).

Internet: http://www.navigationdatacenter.us/data/datawcus.htm

Appendix B: Data Sources and Availability

Publication/database	Source	Website	Tables	Update available (approx.)
Air Carrier Activity Information System (ACAIS)	U.S. DOT, Federal Aviation Administration, Office of Airports	http://www.faa.gov/airports/planning_capacity/passenger_allcargo_stats/passenger/	3-9	4th quarter
Air Carrier Statistics	U.S. DOT, Bureau of Transportation Statistics, Office of Airline Information	http://www.transtats.bts.gov/	1-11, 1-12, 3-8, 4-6, 4-7	3rd quarter
AirData	U.S. EPA	http://www.epa.gov/airdata/	7-7	4th quarter
Airport Facilities Data	U.S. DOT, Federal Aviation Administration, Office of Aeronautical Information Services	http://www.faa.gov/airports/airport_safety/	1-10	Bimonthly
Alcohol-Impaired Driving	U.S. DOT, National Highway Traffic Safety Administration	http://www-nrd.nhtsa.dot.gov/CMSWeb/index.aspx	2-8	4th quarter
Alternative Fueling Stations	U.S. DOE, Office of Energy Efficiency and Renewable Energy, Alternative Fuels and Advanced Vehicles Data Center	http://www.afdc.energy.gov/	7-6	Monthly
Alternatives to Traditional Transportation Fuels	U.S. DOE, Energy Information Administration, Office of Energy Consumption and Efficiency Statistics	http://www.eia.gov/renewable/	7-5	4th quarter
American Community Survey	U.S. Census Bureau	http://www.census.gov/programs-surveys/acs/	4-1	4th quarter
Boating Registration	U.S. Coast Guard, Office of Auxiliary and Boating Safety	http://www.uscgboating.org/	5-6	2nd quarter
Boating Statistics	U.S. Coast Guard, Office of Auxiliary and Boating Safety	http://www.uscgboating.org	2-17, 2-18	2nd quarter
Border Crossing/Entry Data	U.S. DOT, Bureau of Transportation Statistics	http://www.bts.gov/programs/international	3-12, 3-13, 3-14, 3-15, 3-16, 3-17, 3-18, 3-19, 3-20, 3-21, 3-22, 3-23, 4-9, 4-10, 4-11, 4-12, 4-13, 4-14, 4-15, 4-16, 4-17, 4-18, 4-19, 4-20	2nd quarter
Commodity Flow Survey	U.S. DOT, Bureau of Transportation Statistics	http://www.bts.gov/publications/commodity_flow_survey/	3-1, 3-2, 3-3	2012 (quinquennial)
County Business Patterns	U.S. Census Bureau	http://www.census.gov/econ/cbp/index.html	6-1, 6-2, 6-3, 6-4, 6-5, 6-6	2nd quarter
Cruise Passenger Statistics	U.S. DOT, Maritime Administration	http://www.marad.dot.gov/resources/data-statistics/	4-8	2nd quarter
Fatality Analysis Reporting System Encyclopedia	U.S. DOT, National Highway Traffic Safety Administration	http://www-fars.nhtsa.dot.gov/Main/index.aspx	2-1, 2-2, 2-3, 2-7, 2-25, 2-26	4th quarter
Gasoline Prices by Formulation, Grade, Sales Type	U.S. DOE, Energy Information Administration	http://www.eia.gov/dnav/pet/pet_pri_allmg_a_epm0_pta_dpgal_a.htm	6-11	4th quarter
General Aviation and Part 135 Activity Surveys	U.S. DOT, Federal Aviation Administration	http://www.faa.gov/data_research/aviation_data_statistics/general_aviation/	5-7	1st quarter
Hazmat Summary by State	U.S. DOT, PHMSA, Office of Hazardous Material Safety	http://www.phmsa.dot.gov/hazmat/library/data-stats/incidents	2-19, 2-20	Monthly
Highway Statistics	U.S. DOT, Federal Highway Administration	http://www.fhwa.dot.gov/policyinformation/statistics.cfm	1-1, 1-2, 1-4, 2-1, 4-2, 5-1, 5-2, 5-3, 5-4, 6-12, 7-4	1st quarter
Maritime Statistics	U.S. DOT, Maritime Administration	http://www.marad.dot.gov/resources/data-statistics/	3-6, 3-7	3rd quarter
Maximum Posted Speed Limits for Passenger Vehicles	Insurance Institute for Highway Safety, Highway Loss Data Institute	http://www.iihs.org/iihs/topics/laws/speedlimits?topicName=speed	2-9	Monthly
Motorcycle and Bicycle Helmet Laws	Insurance Institute for Highway Safety, Highway Loss Data Institute	http://www.iihs.org/iihs/topics#statelaws	2-5	Monthly
National Bridge Inventory	U.S. DOT, Federal Highway Administration, Office of Bridge Technology	http://www.fhwa.dot.gov/bridge/nbi.cfm	1-5, 1-6, 1-7	4th quarter
National Transit Database	U.S. DOT, Federal Transit Administration	http://www.ntdprogram.gov	1-8, 1-9, 2-16, 4-3, 4-4	3rd quarter
Overseas Visitors to Selected U.S. States and Territories and Overseas Visitors to Select U.S. Cities/Hawaiian Islands	U.S. Dept. of Commerce, International Trade Administration, Office of Travel & Tourism Industries	http://travel.trade.gov/	4-21, 4-22	2nd quarter
Pipeline Statistics	U.S. DOT, PHMSA, Office of Pipeline Safety	http://www.phmsa.dot.gov/pipeline	2-21, 2-22, 2-23	2nd quarter
Population Estimates	U.S. Department of Commerce, U.S. Census Bureau	http://www.census.gov/popest/index.html	2-1, 2-7, 2-26, 5-3, 7-3, 7-4	2nd quarter
Office of Safety Analysis	U.S. DOT, Federal Railroad Administration, Office of Safety Analysis	http://safetydata.fra.dot.gov/OfficeofSafety	2-10, 2-11, 2-12, 2-13, 2-14, 2-15	4th quarter
Railroads and States	Association of American Railroads	http://www.aar.org	1-13, 1-14, 3-4, 6-7	2nd quarter
Safety Belt Use	U.S. DOT, National Highway Traffic Safety Administration	http://www-nrd.nhtsa.dot.gov/CMSWeb/index.aspx	2-6	3rd quarter
Safety Belt Use Laws	Insurance Institute for Highway Safety, Highway Loss Data Institute	http://www.iihs.org/iihs/topics/laws/safetybeltuse	2-4	Monthly

Appendix B: Data Sources and Availability (continued)

Publication/database	Source	Website	Tables	Update available (approx.)
State and Local Government Finances	U.S. Department of Commerce, U.S. Census Bureau	https://www.census.gov/govs/local/	6-8, 6-9	3rd quarter
State Energy Data System	U.S. Dept. of Energy, Energy Information Administration	http://www.eia.gov/state/seds/seds-data-complete.cfm#consumption	7-1, 7-2, 7-3	2nd quarter
State Fact Sheets	National Passenger Railroad Corporation (Amtrak), News & Media	http://www.amtrak.com/servlet/ContentServer?c=Page&pagename=am%2FLayout&cid=1246041980432	4-5	Annual
State Laws	U.S. DOT, National Highway Traffic Safety Administration	http://www.distraction.gov/	2-24	Regular
Survey of State Funding for Pub	American Association of State Highway and Transportation Officials	http://scopt.transportation.org/Pages/MTAPPublications.aspx	6-10	2nd quarter
Toll Facilities in the United States: Bridges-Roads-Tunnels-Ferries	U.S. DOT, Federal Highway Administration	http://www.fhwa.dot.gov/ohim/tollpage.htm	1-3	no historical information
Transborder Surface Freight Data	U.S. DOT, Bureau of Transportation Statistics	http://www.bts.gov/programs/international/transborder/	3-10, 3-11, 3-24	1st quarter
U.S. Civil Airmen Statistics	U.S. DOT, Federal Aviation Administration	http://www.faa.gov/data_research/aviation_data_statistics/civil_airmen_statistics/	5-8	3rd quarter
Urban Mobility Report	Texas Transportation Institute	http://mobility.tamu.edu/ums/	5-5	3rd quarter
USA Trade Online	U.S. Department of Commerce, U.S. Census Bureau	https://usatrade.census.gov/	3-24	Regular
Waterborne Commerce in the United States	U.S. Army Corps of Engineers, Navigation Data Center	http://www.navigationdatacenter.us/	1-15, 1-16, 3-5, 3-24	4th quarter

KEY: PHMSA = Pipeline and Hazardous Materials Safety Administration; MARAD = Maritime Administration; U.S. DOE = U.S. Department of Energy; U.S. DOT = U.S. Department of Transportation; U.S. EPA = U.S. Environmental Protection Agency.

Appendix C: State Departments of Transportation

State	Agency	Website address
Alabama	Alabama Department of Transportation	www.dot.state.al.us
Alaska	Alaska Department of Transportation and Public Facilities	www.dot.state.ak.us
Arizona	Arizona Department of Transportation	www.azdot.gov
Arkansas	Arkansas State Highway and Transportation Department	www.arkansashighways.com
California	California Department of Transportation	www.dot.ca.gov
Colorado	Colorado Department of Transportation	www.codot.gov
Connecticut	Connecticut Department of Transportation	www.ct.gov/dot
Delaware	Delaware Department of Transportation	www.deldot.gov
District of Columbia	District Department of Transportation	www.ddot.dc.gov
Florida	Florida Department of Transportation	www.dot.state.fl.us
Georgia	Georgia Department of Transportation	www.dot.ga.gov
Hawaii	State of Hawaii Department of Transportation	hidot.hawaii.gov
Idaho	Idaho Transportation Department	www.itd.idaho.gov
Illinois	Illinois Department of Transportation	www.idot.illinois.gov
Indiana	Indiana Department of Transportation	www.in.gov/indot
Iowa	Iowa Department of Transportation	www.iowadot.gov
Kansas	Kansas Department of Transportation	www.ksdot.org
Kentucky	Kentucky Transportation Cabinet	www.transportation.ky.gov
Louisiana	Louisiana Department of Transportation and Development	wwwsp.dotd.la.gov
Maine	Maine Department of Transportation	www.maine.gov/mdot
Maryland	Maryland Department of Transportation	www.mdot.maryland.gov
Massachusetts	Massachusetts Department of Transportation	www.massdot.state.ma.us
Michigan	Michigan Department of Transportation	www.michigan.gov/mdot
Minnesota	Minnesota Department of Transportation	www.dot.state.mn.us
Mississippi	Mississippi Department of Transportation	mdot.ms.gov
Missouri	Missouri Department of Transportation	www.modot.org
Montana	Montana Department of Transportation	www.mdt.mt.gov
Nebraska	Nebraska Department of Roads	roads.nebraska.gov
Nevada	Nevada Department of Transportation	www.nevadadot.com
New Hampshire	New Hampshire Department of Transportation	www.nh.gov/dot
New Jersey	New Jersey Department of Transportation	www.state.nj.us/transportation
New Mexico	New Mexico Department of Transportation	www.dot.state.nm.us
New York	New York State Department of Transportation	www.dot.ny.gov
North Carolina	North Carolina Department of Transportation	www.ncdot.org
North Dakota	North Dakota Department of Transportation	www.dot.nd.gov
Ohio	Ohio Department of Transportation	www.dot.state.oh.us
Oklahoma	Oklahoma Department of Transportation	www.okladot.state.ok.us
Oregon	Oregon Department of Transportation	www.oregon.gov/odot
Pennsylvania	Pennsylvania Department of Transportation	www.dot.state.pa.us
Rhode Island	Rhode Island Department of Transportation	www.dot.ri.gov
South Carolina	South Carolina Department of Transportation	www.dot.state.sc.us
South Dakota	South Dakota Department of Transportation	www.sddot.com
Tennessee	Tennessee Department of Transportation	www.tn.gov/tdot
Texas	Texas Department of Transportation	www.txdot.gov
Utah	Utah Department of Transportation	www.udot.utah.gov
Vermont	Vermont Agency of Transportation	vtrans.vermont.gov
Virginia	Virginia Department of Transportation	www.virginiadot.org
Washington	Washington State Department of Transporation	www.wsdot.wa.gov
West Virginia	West Virginia Department of Tranportation	www.transportation.wv.gov
Wisconsin	Wisconsin Department of Transportation	wisconsindot.gov
Wyoming	Wyoming Department of Transportation	www.dot.state.wy.us
United States	U.S. Department of Transportation	www.transportation.gov

Appendix D: Glossary

Air taxi: For-hire passenger or cargo aircraft operations in accordance with Federal Aviation Regulations (FAR) Part 135. An air taxi operates on an on-demand basis and does not meet the flight schedule qualifications of a commuter air carrier.

British thermal unit (Btu): The amount of energy required to raise the temperature of 1 pound of water 1 degree Fahrenheit (F) at or near 39.2 degrees F and 1 atmosphere of pressure.

Bus rapid transit: Fixed-route bus systems that either operate their routes predominantly on fixed-guideways (other than on highway high occupancy vehicle or shoulder lanes, such as for commuter bus service) or that operate routes of high-frequency service with the following elements: Substantial transit stations, traffic signal priority or pre-emption, low-floor vehicles or level-platform boarding, and separate branding of the service. High-frequency service is defined as 10-minute peak and 15-minute off-peak headways for at least 14 hours of service operations per day. This mode may include portions of service that are fixed-guideway and non-fixed guideway.

Certificated airport: An airport holding an operating certificate issued by the Federal Aviation Administration in accordance with Code of Federal Regulations (CFR) Title 14, Chapter 1, Part 139 allowing it to serve scheduled or nonscheduled air carrier aircraft designed for more than 30 passengers.

Class I (rail): As defined by the Surface Transportation Board in 2013, a Class I Railroad is a railroad with operating revenues of at least $467.0 million.

Commuter bus: Fixed-route bus systems that are primarily connecting outlying areas with a central city through bus service that operates with at least five miles of continuous closed-door service. This service typically operates using motorcoaches and usually features peak scheduling, multiple-trip tickets, and multiple stops in outlying areas with limited stops in the central city.

Commuter rail: A transit mode that is an electric or diesel propelled railway for urban passenger train service consisting of local short distance travel operating between a central city and adjacent suburbs. Service must be operated on a regular basis by or under contract with a transit operator for the purpose of transporting passengers within urbanized areas (UZAs), or between urbanized areas and outlying areas. Such rail service, using either locomotive hauled or self-propelled railroad passenger cars, is generally characterized by multi-trip tickets, specific station to station fares, railroad employment practices, and usually only one or two stations in the central business district. It does not include: heavy rail rapid transit or light rail / streetcar transit service. Intercity rail service is excluded, except for that portion of such service that is operated by or under contract with a public transit agency for predominantly commuter services.

Container: A box-like device used to store, protect, and handle a number of packages or items as a unit of transit that can be interchanged between trucks, trains, and ships without rehandling the contents. State Transportation

Controlled right-of-way: Lanes restricted for at least a portion of the day for use by transit vehicles and other high occupancy vehicles (HOVs).

Demand response: A transit mode comprised of passenger cars, vans or small buses operating in response to calls from passengers or their agents to the transit operator, who then dispatches a vehicle to pick up the passengers and transport them to their destinations. Service is usually provided using cars, vans, or buses with fewer than 25 seats.

Directional route-miles: The mileage in each direction over which public transportation vehicles travel while in revenue service. Directional route-miles are a measure of the facility or roadway, not the service carried on the facility such as the number of routes or vehicle-miles. Directional route-miles are computed with regard to direction of service, but without regard to the number of traffic lanes or rail tracks existing in the right-of-way.

Dry-bulk carrier (water): A ship with specialized holds for carrying dry cargo such as coal, grain, and iron ore in unpackaged bulk form.

Enplanements: The total number of revenue passengers boarding aircraft.

Exclusive right-of-way: Lanes reserved at all times for transit use and other high occupancy vehicles (HOVs).

Ferryboat (transit): Vessels for carrying passengers and / or vehicles over a body of water. The vessels are generally diesel powered conventional ferry vessels. They may also be hovercraft, hydrofoil and other high-speed vessels. The vessel is limited in its use to the carriage of deck passengers or vehicles or both, operates on a short run on a frequent schedule between two points over the most direct water routes other than in ocean or coastwise service, and is offered as a public service of a type normally attributed to a bridge or tunnel.

Full containership: Ships equipped with permanent container cells, with little or no space for other types of cargo.

General aviation: Civil aviation activity except that of air carriers operated in accordance with Federal Aviation Regulation (FAR) Parts 121, 123, 127, and 135. The types of aircraft used in general aviation range from corporate multi-engine jet aircraft piloted by professional crews to amateur-built single engine piston acrobatic planes, balloons, and dirigibles.

Heavy rail: A transit mode that is an electric railway with the capacity for a heavy volume of traffic. It is characterized by high speed and rapid acceleration passenger rail cars operating singly or in multi-car trains on fixed rails, separate rights-of-way from which all other vehicular and foot traffic are excluded, sophisticated signaling, and high platform loading. Also known as "subway", "elevated (railway)", or "metropolitan railway (metro)".

Hybrid rail: Rail System Primarily operating routes on the National system of railroads, but not operating with the characteristics of commuter rail. This service typically operates light rail-type vehicles as diesel multiple-unit trains. These trains do not meet Federal Railroad Administration standards, and so must operate with temporal separation from freight rail traffic.

Light rail: A transit mode that typically is an electric railway with a light volume traffic capacity compared to heavy rail. It is characterized by passenger rail cars operating singly (or in short, usually two car, trains) on fixed rails in shared or exclusive right-of-way, low or high platform loading, and vehicle power drawn from an overhead electric line via a trolley or a pantograph.

Local railroad: A railroad which is neither a Class I nor a Regional Railroad, and is engaged primarily in line-haul services.

Major arterial highway: A major highway used primarily for through traffic.

Metric ton: 2,205 pounds (2,000 pounds divided by 0.907).

Minor arterial: In rural areas, roads linking cities and larger towns. In urban areas, roads distributing trips to small geographic areas but not penetrating identifiable neighborhoods.

Minor collector highway: In rural areas, routes that serve intracounty rather than statewide travel. In urban areas, streets that provide direct access to neighborhoods and arterials.

Mixed right-of-way: Lanes used for general automobile traffic.

Motorbus: A transit mode comprised of rubber-tired passenger vehicles operating on fixed routes and schedules over roadways. Vehicles are powered by diesel, gasoline, battery, or alternative fuel engines contained within the vehicle.

Natural gas distribution pipeline: Smaller than transmission pipelines and maintained by companies that distribute natural gas locally (intrastate). Distribution pipeline systems are analogous to networks of lesser roads and residential streets that people travel after getting off the freeway.

Natural gas transmission pipeline: Analogous to a major freeway, it is the main interstate transportation route for moving large amounts of natural gas from the source of production to points of distribution. Transmission pipelines are designed to move large amounts of natural gas from areas where the gas is extracted and stored to the local distribution companies that provide natural gas to homes and businesses.

Principal arterial highway: Major streets or highways, many of multilane or freeway design, serving high-volume traffic corridor movements that connect major generators of travel.

Regional railroad: A non-Class I, line-haul railroad operating 350 or more miles of road or with revenues of at least $40 million or both.

Short ton: 2,000 pounds.

Streetcar rail: This mode is for rail transit systems operating entire routes predominantly on streets in mixed-traffic. This service typically operates with single-car trains powered by overhead catenaries and with frequent stops.

Switching and terminal railroad: A non-Class I Railroad engaged primarily in switching and/or terminal services for other railroads

Tanker: An oceangoing ship designed to haul liquid bulk cargo in world trade.

Ton-mile: The movement of one ton of cargo the distance of one statute mile.

Trackage rights: The authority of one railroad to use the tracks of another railroad for a fee.

Trolley bus: A transit mode comprised of electric rubber-tired passenger vehicles, manually steered and operating singly on city streets. Vehicles are propelled by a motor drawing current through overhead wires via trolleys, from a central power source not onboard the vehicle.

Unlinked passenger trips: The number of passengers boarding public transportation vehicles. A passenger is counted each time he or she boards a vehicle even if the boarding is part of the same journey from origin to destination.

Vanpool: A transit mode comprised of vans, small buses and other vehicles operating as a ride sharing arrangement, providing transportation to a group of individuals traveling directly between their homes and a regular destination within the same geographical area. The vehicles shall have a minimum seating capacity of seven persons, including the driver.

Vehicle-miles traveled (highway): Miles of travel by all types of motor vehicles as determined by the states on the basis of actual traffic counts and established estimating procedures.

Wigwag (railroad): An early 20th century railroad grade crossing signal that uses a pendulum like motion to signal the approach of a train.

www.ingramcontent.com/pod-product-compliance
Lightning Source LLC
Chambersburg PA
CBHW080451240526
45468CB00027BA/2707